P9-CSB-033

Globalization and Human Welfare

Other texts by Vic George and Paul Wilding:

Motherless Families

Ideology and Social Welfare

The Impact of Social Policy

Welfare and Ideology

*British Society and Social Welfare**

* Also published by Palgrave

Globalization and Human Welfare

Vic George and Paul Wilding

palgrave

© Vic George and Paul Wilding 2002

All rights reserved. No reproduction, copy or transmission of this publication may be made without written permission.

No paragraph of this publication may be reproduced, copied or transmitted save with written permission or in accordance with the provisions of the Copyright, Designs and Patents Act 1988, or under the terms of any licence permitting limited copying issued by the Copyright Licensing Agency, 90 Tottenham Court Road, London W1T 4LP.

Any person who does any unauthorised act in relation to this publication may be liable to criminal prosecution and civil claims for damages.

The authors have asserted their rights to be identified as the authors of this work in accordance with the Copyright, Designs and Patents Act 1988.

First published 2002 by
PALGRAVE
Houndmills, Basingstoke, Hampshire RG21 6XS and
175 Fifth Avenue, New York, N.Y. 10010
Companies and representatives throughout the world

PALGRAVE is the new global academic imprint of
St. Martin's Press LLC Scholarly and Reference Division and
Palgrave Publishers Ltd (formerly Macmillan Press Ltd).

ISBN 0–333–91566–6 hardcover
ISBN 0–333–91567–4 paperback

This book is printed on paper suitable for recycling and made from fully managed and sustained forest sources.

A catalogue record for this book is available from the British Library.

Library of Congress Cataloging-in-Publication Data

George, Victor.
  Globalization and human welfare / by Vic George and Paul Wilding.
     p.   cm.
  Includes bibliographical references and index.
  ISBN 0–333–91566–6—ISBN 0–333–91567–4 (alk.)
  1. Human services.   2. Social policy.   3. Globalization.
  I. Wilding, Paul.   II. Title.

HV40 .G455 2002
361—dc21   2001057741

10   9   8   7   6   5   4   3   2   1
11   10   09   08   07   06   05   04   03   02

Printed and bound in Great Britain by
Creative Print & Design (Wales), Ebbw Vale

Contents

List of Tables

List of Abbreviations

AIC	Advanced Industrial Country
AIDS	Acquired Immunodeficiency Syndrome
ASEAN	Association of South East Asian Nations
BIS	Bank for International Settlements
CSD	Commission on Sustainable Development
EU	European Union
FAO	Food and Agriculture Organisation
FDI	Foreign Direct Investment
G7/G8	Group of Seven/Eight
GATT	General Agreement on Tariffs and Trade
GEF	Global Environment Facility
GDP/GNP	Gross Domestic/National Product
HIPC	Highly Indebted Poor Countries
HIV	Human Immunodeficiency Virus
IDC	Industrially Developing Country
IGO	International Governmental Organization
ILO	International Labour Organization
IMF	International Monetary Fund
MAI	Multilateral Agreement on Investment
MEI	Multilateral Economic Institution
MNC	Multinational Company
NAFTA	North American Free Trade Association
NGO	Non-Governmental Organization
NPM	New Public Management
OECD	Organization for Economic Co-operation and Development
PPP	Purchasing Power Parity
SAP	Structural Adjustment Programme
UNCTAD	United Nations Conference on Trade and Development
UNDP	United Nations Development Programme
UNEP	United Nations Environmental Programme
UNESCO	United Nations Educational, Scientific and Cultural Organization
UNHCR	United Nations High Commission for Refugees
UNICEF	United Nations Children's Fund

List of Abbreviations

UNO	United Nations Organization
WB	World Bank
WHO	World Health Organization
WTO	World Trade Organization

Acknowledgements

Our thanks to Ian Holliday and Jan Pahl for stimulating and helpful advice on parts of the manuscript, and to friends and colleagues at the City University of Hong Kong for their responses in seminars on globalization which we presented there.

This book marks the likely end of more than thirty years of collaborative work. We like to think that it illustrates the benefits and advantages of collective endeavour over the private strivings of possessive individualism! Certainly that is how we have found it since our first joint project in 1969.

Introduction

Globalization is a long-term process which has affected all aspects of society – economic, political, cultural and social. Its pace has varied from one period to another. It certainly gained momentum during the last quarter of the twentieth century as a result of technological changes in information technology and political decisions at the national and international levels. We view globalization as the increasing and uneven interconnectedness and homogenization of the world in economics, politics and culture.

During its long history, globalization has been accompanied by different ideologies. Even in the short period of the second half of the twentieth century, it was first accompanied and driven forward by the Keynesian view of economics and welfare only to be replaced in the 1980s by its current neoliberal philosophy. Globalization can coexist with different ideologies – a fact that is often overlooked with the result that it is wrongly seen as inherently neoliberal in its approach to economic and social issues.

If there is one issue on which opinion is almost unanimous, it is that globalization has reduced both space and time. Messages can be flashed across the world in seconds; travel time has been substantially reduced; and goods can be transported from one part of the world to another faster than before. The world may not be a global village but it is certainly a more compact place.

Opinion is divided, however, about the economic and social effects of globalization on societies. Some view it as fundamentally benevolent, while others see it as a destructive, exploitative force. The evidence presented in this book suggests that the effects of globalization can be both desirable and undesirable and can vary from one country to another. Some countries have seen their economies expand while others have experienced economic stagnation or even contraction in recent years; poverty has declined in some countries and increased in others; and income inequalities have widened in some but narrowed in other countries.

On the political front, some insist that globalization has irretrievably undermined the powers of the nation state while others feel that the nation state has lost no significant powers. The reality is messier than this. This book takes the view that the forces of globalization have reduced the powers of the state somewhat but that the state remains fundamental to people's lives. There is no evidence, either, that this is the thin end of a long wedge that will see the nation state being replaced in the long run by transnational bodies.

In the cultural domain, globalization has encouraged the spread of primarily western ideas and attitudes all over the world during the past 500 years. Whether one views this as cultural imperialism or as a liberating force is a personal value judgement. The truth may well be that it contains elements of both. The recent spread of gender egalitarian ideas, for example, may well undermine patriarchy in many societies and may also increase marriage breakdown. It will be welcomed or condemned depending on one's view of the world.

The Structure of the Book

This book is concerned with, first, the effects of globalization on human welfare, that is, on employment, the distribution of income, poverty, education, health and the environment; second, with the influence of globalization on gender inequalities in various aspects of life; third, with the effects of globalization on migration and ethnicity; and fourth with the role of global institutions in dealing with the undesirable effects of globalization.

Spatially, the book looks at the effects of globalization in both the advanced industrial countries (AICs) and the industrially developing countries (IDCs) in order to reach a more balanced judgement as to the desirability or otherwise of globalization. Much of the existing writing on globalization has been confined to AICs.

The book is essentially divided into three parts. Chapters 1 and 2 are concerned with clarifying the debate on the meaning of globalization and setting out our own approach. Chapter 1 provides a typology of the various definitions of globalization and also sets out our own views on the issue. Chapter 2 takes a more detailed look at the debate on whether globalization undermines the ability of the nation state to deal with economic and social issues.

Chapter 3 looks at the effects of globalization on human welfare in AICs while Chapter 4 looks at the same issue in relation to IDCs. We take the view that employment and income from work are fundamental to people's welfare and that the social services complement this. For this reason, we examine both economic and social issues in these two chapters. Chapter 5 looks at the effects of globalization on gender inequalities in an attempt to be rather more specific about the effects of globalization and to deal with the justified criticism that much of the debate on globalization is gender-blind. Chapter 6 looks at the ways in which globalization has influenced migration in recent years and how it has affected the adjustment between immigrant communities and the receiving societies.

Chapter 7 looks at the growth of global social policy within the various United Nations institutions – the ILO, WHO, WTO, UNICEF, the World Bank and the IMF. These institutions have been concerned either directly or indirectly with improving the social situation at the global level, even though their activities have sometimes had the opposite effect from that intended. Chapter 8 puts forward our views on how globalization needs to be controlled and steered at the global and national levels in order to improve its beneficial effects and reduce its destructiveness. There is no reason to accept the argument that globalization can only benefit the strong. Political forces can shape the nature of globalization to make it a more beneficent process for all humanity.

We hope that the book will provide a much needed corrective to past debates by highlighting the social impact of globalization and the significance of social policy at the national and global level in counteracting the unequal effects of the current form of globalization. Globalization is here to stay and the challenge facing us all is how to harness its economic and social potential for the benefit of the whole of humankind.

1

The Nature of Globalization

Globalization was *the* concept of the late 1990s and remains dominant today. It has come to pervade debates in the social sciences and to be used increasingly by politicians, including many on the left, as a justification for their policies. Governments of the left, according to this view, have no option but to abandon their traditional welfare state policies. Any attempt to resist globalization will eventually fail.

Understandably, globalization is a contested concept for it has important economic, political and cultural implications at the individual, the country and the global level. The quotations in Exhibit 1.1 bring out some of these conflicting attitudes and views on globalization.

Exhibit 1.1

Attitudes towards globalization

'Every age has its defining phrases and globalization is surely one of ours.' (Kapstein, 1996a, p. 351).

'Globalization is unavoidable.' (World Bank, 1995, p. 54).

'"Globalization" is the most fashionable word of the 1990s.' (Barnet and Cavanagh, 1994, p. 13).

'"Globalization" is a big idea resting on slim foundations.' (Weiss, 1998, p. 212).

'"Globalization" is a myth suitable for a world without illusions, but it is also one that robs us of hope.' (Hirst and Thompson, 1996, p. 6).

Despite their many differences, most writers who accept the notion of globalization agree that something new is taking place in the world today which is distinct from other similar processes, such as internationalization or

1

modernization. There seems to be general agreement that globalization involves at least the processes as set out in Exhibit 1.2.

Exhibit 1.2

Main strands of the globalization process

Increasing and deepening interconnectedness of societies in different parts of the world.

Almost unimpeded flows of financial capital, news and cultural images across the world.

Rising activity and power of multinational companies (MNCs).

Rising economic growth accompanied by rising inequalities in many countries.

A global consumer culture in the making.

More travel and migration by more people from more countries to more countries; faster methods of transport and electronic communication so that time and space is increasingly being compressed.

Greater awareness by the public of what is happening in the world and of the possible implications for their own country.

The rapid growth of governmental and non-governmental supranational organizations that supplement, supplant and support the activities of the nation-state.

The numerous disagreements on globalization can be usefully discussed under five headings: the definition of globalization; its origins; the nature of its driving forces; its effects on societies; and its future direction. The various theoretical and ideological debates on these five aspects of globalization can be grouped into four main positions: the technological enthusiasts; the Marxisant pessimists; the pluralist pragmatists; and the sceptic internationalists. This will not include the views of all the writers on globalization but it has the merit of tidying up a very confused debate.

Since this book is about the effects of globalization on human welfare, more attention will be paid to the socio-economic aspects of globalization than to its cultural and political dimensions. The brief discussion that follows on these four approaches to globalization inevitably oversimplifies but, hopefully, it brings out the essentials of these positions in a form that is clear and accessible to the reader. An attempt is also made to trace the recent origin of these four positions, for contemporary ideas, however radical they may sound, always have their roots in the past.

Technological Enthusiasts

Definitions

Globalization, according to this approach, means the increasing transnationalization of the world economy that has come about during the second half of the twentieth century as a result of advances in technology and the adoption of an individualistic market ethic. Government restrictions on the movement of goods and capital have been removed so that one can legitimately talk about a 'borderless' world. Global markets rather than nation-states are now the forces shaping the course of events. National economies are a thing of the past; so, too, is an international economy for it is no more than an aggregate of national economies. What has emerged in recent years is a transnational economy, or a global economy, where markets and enterprises operate globally in a 'borderless world', free of national constraints.

What is unclear from the writings of this group is whether this transnational, global, borderless, economy exists in a fully fledged way today or whether it is in the process of coming into being at some time in the future – whether it is reality or aspiration. Many of the criticisms levelled against this approach are based on the assumption that it is reality – it exists today.

Taking the case of MNCs, it may be true that there is a greater tendency for them to operate globally today than in the past but this does not mean that they have already become totally 'footloose', that is, able to move and settle as they please. As Held *et al.*, observe, 'MNCs cannot simply locate anywhere and everywhere...the globalization of production and distribution has its limits' (Held *et al.*, 1999, p. 269).

Origins

Tracing the origins of globalization is a hazardous affair. This group of writers, however, spends little time discussing the issue of when globalization began. They tend to see it as a post-1945 process, the result of the new technologies in transport and telecommunications that made capital and markets far more mobile than before. This technological impetus was facilitated by an enabling ideology – aggressive individualism – which stressed private enterprise at the expense of state protection and provision. The new technology and the new ideology went hand-in-hand in promoting the globalization of markets and capital.

All theoretical approaches to globalization have their roots in the past and the technological approach is no exception. It has its roots in some of the theories of economic development of the 1960s and the early 1970s. On the importance of technology, perhaps the best developed account is 'the logic of industrialism' thesis put forward by Kerr and his associates in the early 1970s. Industrial technology has a certain logic that affects other institutions in society – its educational system, its labour force, its social mobility, its residential pattern, value system, and so on. Technology has a homogenising effect on society for it breaks down traditional cultures and ushers in those that are functional to an industrial society. It may be that different societies will travel at different speeds and along different paths but the direction is the same – convergence, the creation of an industrial society. This is so because 'the science and technology' on which an industrial society is based 'speak in a universal language' (Kerr *et al.*, 1973, p. 54).

On the significance of the individualistic enterprise ideology to economic development, recent antecedents are to be found in the various modernization theses of the 1960s (Hoselitz, 1960; Rostow, 1962). The basic claim was that economic aid by the West was not sufficient for the industrialization of third world countries. They had to adopt the individualistic value system of AICs before they could modernize. To become modernized, third world countries had first to be westernized. The values of many traditional institutions in the third world were considered 'dysfunctional' to the process of modernization and had to be reformed to resemble those of the AICs. Technological enthusiasts leave all this to the market. All they ask of the state is not to intervene.

Driving Forces

The central driving force behind globalization for this group is technology – particularly telecommunications and computers, that is, the information revolution of the second half of the twentieth century. It is this which propels and sustains the new financial markets that are at the heart of globalization. Wriston expresses this as follows:

> Our new international financial regime differs radically from its precursors in that it was not built by politicians, economists, central bankers or finance ministers... It was built by technology... (by) men and women who interconnected the planet with telecommunications and computers. (Wriston, 1988/89, p. 71)

Strange argues strongly that markets now exercise more power than governments and attributes this change to 'the accelerating pace of technological change as a prime cause of the shift in the state-market balance of power' (Strange, 1996, p. 7). Moreover, there is every reason to believe that techno-logical change will continue to accelerate.

This information revolution has also meant that national borders are mean-ingless for financial markets and trade. 'Markets are no longer geographical locations, but data on a screen transmitted from anywhere in the world' (Wriston, 1988/89, p. 72). This state of affairs is permanent and the global financial marketplace 'will never recede to its old national borders'(ibid., p. 72).

Technological writers do not ignore the political and social aspects of globalization. But, they insist that the technological and economic aspects of globalization are primary and determinant of the political and the cultural. There is a functional relationship between these sub-systems of society which adds a political and cultural edge to their conception of globalization.

Effects of Globalization

Globalization has certain economic, political and social imperatives, according to this group of writers. In the economic domain, it demands that labour costs be low, that management styles be mean and lean and that state expenditure be reduced to encourage enterprise and national competitiveness. In a globalized world, capital and investment can move fairly freely from one country to another choosing those with the most favourable economic conditions. Attempts by national governments to impede this economic logic of globalization will ultim-ately fail. This view of the economic imperative of globalization has been sup-ported by such international bodies as the IMF, the World Bank and the OECD. It has, as a result, been very influential in government policies in recent years.

Globalization has also two political imperatives that may at first appear con-tradictory. First, globalization means the triumph of capitalism over socialism because the economic values of globalization are in line with those of capitalism and contrary to the values of socialist central planning. Since, the economic determines the political, globalization implies the eventual elimination of social-ist authoritarian regimes. It was this technological logic that Fukuyama had in mind when he proclaimed the end of history and the triumph of capitalism after the collapse of Soviet style socialism.

> The unfolding of technologically driven economic modernization creates strong incentives for developed countries to accept the basic terms of the universal capital-ist culture, by permitting a substantial degree of economic competition and letting prices be determined by market mechanisms. (Fukuyama, 1992, pp. 96–7)

It is also this symbiotic unity between political and economic freedom that Patten, writing of Hong Kong and China, had in mind when he warned that, 'you cannot compartmentalize freedom. You may build walls between economics and politics, but they are walls of sand' (Patten, 1998, p. 181).

Second, globalization inevitably means that the nation-state will lose most of its powers to the rising might of the MNCs. The emerging global order is no longer shaped by nation states but it 'is spearheaded by a few hundred corporate giants, many of them bigger than most sovereign nations' (Barnet and Cavanagh, 1994, p. 14). At the national level, the power of these corporations is so strong that they have 'to a large extent emasculated state control over national economies and societies' (Strange, 1995, p. 298). Politicians have failed to realize this and have continued to behave as if nation states are still supreme over markets. The result has been that 'People no longer believe them' (Strange, 1996, p. 3) – and what follows is a serious lack of public confidence in the political system.

Globalization has created a 'borderless world' (Ohmae, 1990) where the state is no longer the best agency for organizing economic activities because it overlooks 'the true linkages and synergies that exist among often disparate populations' (Ohmae, 1993, p. 92). For this reason, 'traditional nation-states have become unnatural, even impossible business units.' (Ohmae, 1996, p. 5).

Peterson singles out four reasons why the nation-state will gradually surrender its authority to the rising power of global markets. First, the fact that 'the rate of global economic and financial integration is accelerating' (Peterson, 1996, p. 265); second, the fact that 'the days of segmented markets are numbered' (ibid., p. 267); third, 'the magnitude of global capital flows is exceeding the capacities of even the most powerful governments to manage the pressures they generate' (ibid., p. 268); and fourth, 'governments are increasingly incapable of keeping up with the march of technology and information flows' (ibid., pp. 269–70). Since this is an inevitable process, what is important for national welfare is the way that this surrender of government power is achieved.

On the social side, the general tendency in the writings of this group is to overemphasize the desirable consequences of globalization. The changes to the economy, the polity and culture are seen as beneficial to all in the world because they raise productivity, economic growth and living standards; they create a world of democratic societies in a global order; and they bring people together culturally speaking. Problems do exist but these are adjustment problems to be ironed out gradually as globalization matures.

The Future

For this group of analysts, globalization is an irresistible process, beneficial to the whole world, which ought to be welcomed rather than resisted. We may not yet be living in a totally globalized world but we are imperceptibly moving fast towards that happy state of affairs. It will be a world where not only do states lose their power but, according to Reich, national economies do too. They will become a thing of the past to be replaced by regional and global actors.

> As almost every factor of production – money, technology, factories and equipment – moves effortlessly across borders, the very idea of a national economy becomes meaningless, as are notions of a national corporation, national capital, national products, and national technology. (Reich, 1991, p. 8)

National states will not disappear but their main usefulness in economic terms will be to prepare the ground for the globalization of their economies, that is, to attract international investors – the 'Electronic Herd' in Friedman's words. This will depend on whether they are willing to don the 'Golden Straitjacket', that is, the liberalization of their economies – privatization, balanced budgets, low taxes and tariffs, and so on (Friedman, 1999). Failure to do this will mean economic ruin for the country.

In conclusion, the strength of this approach is that it highlights the ways in which technology and markets have influenced the nature of economic processes and transformed some of them, such as financial flows, into global forces. Its weaknesses are that it defines globalization in primarily economic terms, it makes excessive claims concerning the extent of globalization at present, and it is teleological prediction that globalization will inevitably create a fully borderless neoliberal world in the future. Its total faith in the power of the microchip is both its strength and its Achilles heel.

Marxisant Pessimists

This group includes writers of varying degrees of affinity to the Marxisant tradition. Despite their many differences, they agree on the fundamental premise that the driving logic of capitalism for constantly increased profitability has been the major force behind globalization.

During the first half of the twentieth century, most Marxists embraced Marx's optimistic view that, in the long term, capitalism would prove a liberating, modernizing force. It would spread to the whole world and would create strong working classes that would overthrow both colonialism and capitalism in order to create socialist societies. This optimism gave way to pessimism when it was realized that the collapse of colonialism in the 1950s and 1960s led neither to economic affluence or socialism. Various 'dependency theses' and 'world system theories' attempted to explain this new situation. The central claim was that the new world system was not substantially different from the old colonial world system. The economic and political power of the advanced industrial countries continued to dominate the way the world functioned. The poverty of the developing countries, and the wealth of the rich nations, was the inevitable result of the structural forms of power relationships in the world system. Poverty and wealth were opposite sides of the same coin.

Although neither the dependency nor the world-system theorists talked about globalization, their views prepared the ground for the globalization thesis of Marxian writers of the 1990s. Writing in the early 1990s, Sklair argued that the world system functions as a whole in all three of its transnational practices – the economic, political and cultural. Each of these transnational practices is dominated by a major institution that guides the drive towards globalization. As Sklair puts it, 'My contention is that the transnational corporation is the major locus of transnational economic practices; the transnational capitalist class is the major locus of transnational political practices; and the major locus of transnational cultural-ideological practices is to be found in the culture-ideology of consumerism' (Sklair, 1995, p. 6). Of the three power loci of transnational practices, the culture of consumerism stands supreme. 'The culture-ideology of consumerism is, as it were, the fuel that powers the motor of global capitalism. The driver is the transnational capitalist class. But the vehicle itself is the mighty corporation' (ibid., p. 49).

Harvey's writings provide the link with the pluralist theories that we review below. Harvey begins with the Marxisant view that capitalism is prone to periodic crises that, so far, it has been able to cope with. These periodic crises have been resolved through new material processes – inventions, reorganizations of enterprises, new labour work routines, and so on – all of which compress both time and space. The economic crisis of the 1970s was resolved through flexible production and employment policies: workers were employed in more flexible ways to produce goods that responded to consumer tastes as fashioned by international computer technology. Such a flexible accumulation process meant a compression of the time used to produce and sell manufactured goods.

The relevance of Harvey's work to globalization stems from the fact that compression of time means compression of space, that is, reduction of geographical distances. The 1970s and the 1980s, he argues, witnessed 'another fierce round in that annihilation of space through time that has always lain at the center of capitalism's dynamic' (Harvey, 1989, p. 293). This compression of time enables capitalism to operate on a world basis choosing production sites that are most advantageous to profitability. Put in a different way, production can be localized while consumption is globalized. Reebok, for example, produces shoes in different localities where wages are low but advertises, promotes and sells its products world-wide. What distinguishes Harvey's ideas on time/space compression from those of pluralist writers is his argument that it is the periodic accumulation crises of capitalism that foster time/space compression. It is capitalism's way of dealing with its periodic crises.

Definitions

There is general agreement that globalization 'is not a condition or a phenomenon; it is a process' (Sweezy, 1997, p. 1). This process has led to the latest stage of capitalism that is global capitalism or globalism. 'If imperialism is the latest stage of capitalism, globalism is the latest stage of imperialism' (Sivanandan, 1998/99, p. 5).

A typical definition commanding general support in this group is that provided by Wilkin:

> Globalization can best be seen as a process of transformation in the capitalist world-system, one that intensifies an array of structural and ideological tendencies as all aspects of the world-system come increasingly into the orbit of what we can see as a single and continuous circulation of ideas, commodities, social relations and, most important, sites of conflict. (Wilkin, 1996, p. 228)

Origins

Most writers in this group agree that globalization has its origins in the beginnings of capitalism in Western Europe: in 'the dawn of European colonial expansion and the modern world system 500 years ago: the gradual spread of capitalist production around the world and its displacement of all pre-capitalist relations' (Robinson, 1996, p. 15).

Although globalization has a long history, most writers in this group accept that it has gained speed and momentum during the post-war period because of technological inventions and the collapse of the Soviet Union. The first accelerated the globalization of capital and markets while the second made the capitalist system supreme over existing socialist alternatives.

Driving Forces

The causes of globalization are conceptualized at two different levels. At the basic level, the driving force behind the process of globalization has always been the logic of capitalism – its inherent tendency to expand, to intensify and to involve all aspects of life. At the secondary level, however, all Marxisant writers agree that the current financial, production and consumption arrangements of the world system – which are the result of the logic of capitalism – have themselves become driving forces for a globalized world-system. Similarly, the current neoliberal ideology concerning the labour process, competitiveness and consumption has become a major force in itself for the greater acceptance of the globalization process.

In addition to the discussion of the forces propelling globalization, there is a great deal of debate on the pathways and mechanisms though which these forces operate. The notion of a global capitalist class receives wide support (Sklair, 1995; Robinson, 1996; Sivanandan, 1998/99). This class is composed of the top management of MNCs, political leaders, and heads of international organizations such as the IMF, the World Bank, the OECD and so on. There is no suggestion of a conspiracy theory here; rather that such leaders by their background, their position and their outlook tend to view the causes and the solutions to social and economic issues in similar ways. It is an explanation that is very similar to the notion of a national capitalist class that was so popular in radical writings of the 1970s.

Effects of Globalization

The effects of globalization on human welfare are, at best, negative and, at worst, destructive, both in the short term and the long term.

First, there is general agreement in this group that globalization has increased poverty and inequality in both AICs and IDCs. Ironically, says Cox, 'The cure for these negative effects is generally regarded as more globalization' (Cox, 1997a, p. 27).

Second, globalization affects not only the material aspects of people's lives but their attitudes, values and behaviour through the global media dominated by large corporations. As a result, it leads to the homogenization of cultures, the standardization of lifestyles and to conformity. As de Benoist puts it 'capitalism no longer sells just commodities and goods. It also sells signs, sounds, images, software, connections and links. It does not just fill up houses: it colonizes the imagination and dominates communication' (de Benoist, 1996, p. 125).

Third, there are serious divisions of opinion on whether globalization affects the authority of the nation-state. Orthodox Marxists insist that there is little that is objectively new in globalization despite the hyperbole surrounding it. The nation-state is still central to the survival of capitalism. Capital needs the nation-state 'to maintain the conditions of accumulation, to preserve labor discipline, to enhance the mobility of capital while suppressing the mobility of labor' (Meiksins Wood, 1997, p. 12). In this case, the relevance of class struggle to achieve a socialist society is as significant as ever: 'class struggle is not only a viable option but a necessary one – maybe in some respects more, not less, because of globalization' (ibid., p. 6). Similarly, Tabb argues that globalization is neither a new phenomenon nor more widespread today than in the past. It is pure ideology to argue that globalization has weakened the state – such an argument 'ignores the continuous technical ability of the state to regulate capital' (Tabb, 1997, p. 28).

Many other Marxists disagree with this analysis because they accept that globalization does exist and it has created a new situation: a global world economy, a global capitalist class and it has undermined the authority of both the nation-state and organized labour. This is not to argue that the nation-state does not serve the interests of the global capitalist class – it does so 'through the removal of rules and regulations that in any way hinder the free play of market forces, and the privatization not only of public utilities but of a large part of the infrastructure as well. And this, irrespective of which party is in power' (Sivanandan, 1998/99, p. 9). But since capital is mobile while labour is not, capital no longer needs national labour in the same ways that it did before. Organized labour has, as a result, lost a great deal of its economic and political strength. Relying on the traditional class struggle to topple capitalism is doomed to failure as a strategy.

The political strategies that follow from this second analysis are diverse (Broad, 1995, pp. 29–31). Some stress the importance of social movements, others emphasize the significance of an organized international class struggle, several put their faith in the enforcement of labour laws on a global level, while others believe that the locus of the class struggle should move from the advanced industrial to the industrially developing countries where class and mass merge as oppositional forces to capitalism.

Writers in this group may be divided on several issues but they all view globalization with extreme pessimism.

'Social life under global capitalism is increasingly dehumanising and devoid of any ethical content' (Robinson, 1996, p. 26).

The Future

Marxisant writers accept that, regrettably, globalization is set to continue in the foreseeable future with increasing undesirable consequences for most of the world's population in terms of exploitation, poverty, environmental destruction and social breakdown. The future appears very bleak for neither a socialist revolution nor socialist reforms appear very likely. Instead, widening social division leading to social breakdown in society is a realistic possibility in the future. As Cox puts it, 'If revolution is but a dim prospect, social breakdown is a dangerous and depressing condition' (Cox, 1997a, p. 30).

In conclusion, the strengths of this approach are its insistence that the pursuit of private profit is a dominant drive of globalization; its recognition that globalization has exacerbated inequalities; and its warnings that the defeat of neoliberalism will not be easy. Its weaknesses are its neglect of other factors that have driven globalization; its refusal to accept that globalization may have positive as well as negative effects on living standards; and, for some of the writers, the utter pessimism concerning the future and the possibilities of reform.

Pluralist Pragmatists

Definitions

It is this group of writers, more than any other, which made the concept of globalization the 'buzz' word of the social sciences in the 1990s. For them, globalization is a long, multifaceted process, with diverse, at times conflicting, effects, with an assured future but whose future form is not possible to predict. The following definitions by two of the leading lights in this group give a flavour of this approach:

> Globalization can thus be defined as the intensification of world wide social relations which link distant localities in such a way that local happenings are shaped by events occurring many miles away and vice-versa. (Giddens, 1990, p. 64)

> Globalization as a concept refers both to the compression of the world and the intensification of consciousness of the world as a whole. (Robertson, 1992, p. 8)

Origins

There is general agreement that globalization has a long history though it gained momentum during the past twenty years or so primarily because of the information technology that has compressed space and time to an unprecedented extent. For some writers (Robertson, 1992; Held *et al.*, 1999) globalization, as a process of world interconnectedness, can be traced back to ancient times; others maintain that it is a more recent phenomenon coinciding with the beginning of modernity from the end of the fifteenth century onwards (Giddens, 1990; Scholte, 2000).

Irrespective of its origins, they all agree that globalization gained momentum from the 1960s onwards because of technological changes, the political decisions concerning free trade and capital flows and the collapse of the Soviet Union. Before the 1960s 'globalization did not figure continually, comprehensively, intensely and with rapidly increasing frequency in the lives of a large proportion of humanity' (Scholte, 1997, p. 17).

Driving Forces

Unlike the first and second group which tend to emphasize one major cause – technology or capitalism – this group insists that the driving forces behind globalization are diverse: they include technology, capitalist production, political forces such as the formation of nation states and their activities, and ideology. There is no attempt to stratify these forces into basic and derivative – they are considered of equal power.

An interesting exception to this Weberian interpretation of globalization is Robertson who follows Parsons's social systems theory that gives predominant position to the cultural over the other sub-systems of society. It is only with the recent reduction or elimination of the cultural cleavages between the major religions in the world, claims Robertson, that the path of globalization has been so much eased (Robertson, 1992).

Though other writers do not follow Robertson's view, they nevertheless take particular exception to the Marxist view that culture is a mere epiphenomenon – a reflection and often a justification of the existing forms of the economy and the polity. As Spybey remarks, 'it is mistaken to separate culture from polity and economy, or even to regard culture as epiphenomenal' (Spybey, 1996, p. 81). As a result, writers in this group give more weight than writers in the previous two groups to the direct influence of ideas and of social movements on changing public and government perceptions and hence influencing practice and policy.

Effects of Globalization

The central message from this group is that though 'the world is undergoing a process of ever-increasing interconnectedness and interdependence' (Axford, 1995, p. 27), it does not mean that local influences disappear from people's lives. Rather 'when people draw global influences into their lives they do so against a background of local cultural influences' (Spybey, 1996, p. 6). People are seen as active 'reflexive' agents that respond thinkingly to the globalizing influences that come their way. Reflexivity is thus central to the understanding of globalization and Giddens' definition of it is generally accepted. It is 'that quality of human action that subjects social practices to constant examination and reformation in the light of incoming information about these practices, thus constitutively altering their character' (Giddens, 1990, p. 38).

As a result, globalization does not mean westernization. It is true that many of the practices and attitudes included in the process of globalization emanate from the West but they are adapted locally when accepted in other countries. There is a dialectic relationship between the global and the local so that, in the words of Robertson, globalized institutions, their practices and values are 'up for grabs' at the local level. Japanese industrialization is the example most often cited: though it adopted the fundamentals of western industrialization, it adapted them to Japanese culture embodying many Confucian values on the way.

Despite this emphasis on 'reflexivity' and a dialectical relationship, cases where non-western values and practices have been incorporated into western culture through globalization in recent times appear to be few and far between and not basic to western civilization. Examples cited include the adoption of Chinese cooking in western diets, the increasing acceptance of alternative medicine, the influence of Indian music, and so on.

It follows from this that globalization does not mean convergence either, not even in the long run. There is no evidence, they argue, to support the technological determinism of the first approach. It is true, writes Axford, that 'the world economy is being systematically globalized, but by a process which is neither homogenizing nor symmetrical' (Axford, 1995, p. 11). Thus the economies of all the countries in the world are not likely to become alike one day. The same applies to the political and cultural systems of the world. In brief, globalization 'does not mean the inevitable, evolutionary progress toward a global spread of Western modernity' (Beyer, 1990, p. 390).

Their general position on the autonomy of nation-states is that though it is being constantly undermined by globalizing economic forces, by supranational and subnational bodies, nation states still remain important actors both within and beyond their borders. There are, however, disagreements of emphasis on the extent to which states have lost their sovereignty. On the one hand, Scholte argues that because of economic and cultural globalization, nation-state sovereignty has suffered at a rate and in a fashion that reflects the country's institutional structure. 'States have affected the manner and rate at which they have lost sovereignty in the face of globalization, but they have not had the option to retain it' (Scholte, 1997, p. 22).

On the other hand, Waters claims that because political globalization is far more difficult than economic or cultural, 'the state remains highly resistant, largely sovereign and a critical arena for problem solving' (Waters, 1995, p. 122).

None of the writers in this group envisages a situation where nation-states will become redundant or totally subservient to global forces. Indeed, all writers in this group insist that globalization has awakened nationalistic, ethnic or religious feelings either in line with or contrary to the western influences that globalization spreads to all parts of the world. Thus the break up of the Soviet Union has resulted in the formation of many new nations; and demands for political independence have sprung up in many regions of many countries in the world. At a time when the world is getting closer together, it is also fragmenting into a greater number of nation-states.

Islamic fundamentalism is often cited as an example of a reaction to the spread of western culture. Islam is not merely a religion but a way of life that, many Moslems feel, is being threatened by the incorporating pressures of western civilization transmitted through global cultural network systems.

On the political side, there is no evidence of a rejection of democratic forms of government by any popular movement in the world even though authoritarian governments proliferate in the industrially developing countries (IDCs). Democratic governance coupled with state welfare provision remains a global aspiration for many parts of the world.

For most writers in this group, globalization is inherently neither good nor bad. It spreads technology, economic growth and democracy; it also spreads crime, AIDS and environmental destruction. Beck's views on the 'risk' society are of relevance here. Globalization has created new forms of risk that know no national boundaries – environmental pollution and AIDS being the best two examples. Unlike previous risks, contemporary risks can only be dealt with on a global scale and they often have a contagion effect and a 'boomerang curve' returning to affect those who produced them. In this way 'the multiplication of risks causes the world society to contract into a community of danger' (Beck, 1992, p. 44).

The Future

Globalization is not only here to stay but it will probably intensify in the future as the website revolution spreads to the whole world. It will continue to be both a unifying and a fragmenting process; a homogenizing and a liberating force. On balance, globalization will continue to be an enriching rather than an impoverishing process. It can be made to serve the interests of humankind better through reforms at the national and international level. In Scholte's words, 'a programme of ambitious reform can counter many potential harms and increase many potential gains of globalization' (Scholte, 2000, p. 315).

Sceptic Internationalists

The sceptics' approach is essentially a reaction against the views of the first group of writers – a rejection of the view of a borderless world where markets operate on a transnational basis and where nation-states become obsolete. It is not a rejection of globalization in its milder forms for they accept that 'foreign markets have increased in importance relative to domestic ones, hence producing a greater openness and interdependence of the international system' with the result that 'the world economy is much more interconnected today than it was in the 1960s or 1970s' (Weiss, 1998, p. 170). Similarly, Hirst and

Thompson concede that 'the international economy has changed radically in structure and governance during the past twenty-five years' (Hirst and Thompson, 1996, p. 196).

They accept the increasing internationalization of the economy but they reject the claim that it has been transnationalized already. They feel that the two – internationalization and transnationalization – are substantially different and they thus reject the conclusion of a 'borderless world' and of an impotent nation-state. The extreme form of globalization, they argue, is unsubstantiated by empirical evidence.

First, they point out that many of the extreme views on globalization are based on statistics with short-time horizons, mainly post-war trends. Had the protagonists examined longer-term trends, they would have arrived at different conclusions. Using the value of exports as a proportion of GDP as a proxy for the international openness of an economy, data show that for the OECD countries this amounted to about 18 per cent in the early 1990s compared to 10 per cent in the early 1950s – which suggests greater internationalization of trade. If, however, one compares the 1990 figure with that of 1913, then the picture is very similar – 16 per cent (Weiss, 1998, table 6.1, p. 171).

A similar conclusion is drawn by Hirst and Thompson using data on trade and financial flows for the past one hundred years. Such data, they write, 'confirms unequivocally that "openness" was greater during the Gold Standard period (1879–1914) than even in the 1980s' (Hirst and Thompson, 1996, p. 28). The problem is that the figures for the period before the First World War are patchy and sometimes estimates so that any conclusions drawn from comparisons with figures of later periods must be treated with some caution.

Second, the evidence on MNCs shows that most of them are not 'footloose' – they are not TNCs; they are in fact MNCs based in their home country and operating according to the laws of their country. Hirst and Thompson thus conclude that 'MNCs still rely upon their "homebase" as the centre of their economic activities, despite all of the speculation about globalization' (Hirst and Thompson, 1996, p. 95). The question that immediately arises, however, is whether this makes any difference to the investment, trade, welfare and labour policies pursued by such companies in their different country locations. If it does not, a most likely possibility, then it is immaterial to human welfare whether one labels them as TNCs or MNCs.

Third, the extreme from of globalization, a borderless world where the nation-state is defunct, implies not only the free movement of trade and capital but also the free migration of labour. Clearly this has not happened and the state still 'remains a controller of its borders and the movement of people across them' (Hirst and Thompson, 1996, p. 181). Again this is correct but, as Chapter 6 shows, governments in AICs are finding it harder to control their borders with the result that illegal immigrants are able to come through in large numbers.

Fourth, the sceptics reject the thesis that governments have lost their traditional powers to the market. They begin by pointing out that the power of government has always been subject to constraints by both internal and external forces. They also accept that recent developments in information technology 'have loosened the state's exclusiveness of control of its territory' (Hirst and Thompson, 1996, p. 180) and its control over 'global money markets where enormous sums are traded daily' (Weiss, 1998, p. 189). This, however, does not mean total paralysis of state power. They may have had to share power with other actors 'but they have a centrality because of their relationship to territory and population' (Hirst and Thompson, 1996, p. 190). Indeed, far from being undermined, the importance of the nation-state has been strengthened in many ways by the processes of internationalization (Hirst and Thompson, 1996, p. 17).

Weiss also makes the interesting point that extreme globalists 'have not only overstated the degree of state powerlessness. They have also *overgeneralized* it' (Weiss, 1998, p. 194). In other words, they have not taken into account the different varieties of capitalist states in existence today and their differing degrees of power and regulation of the economy and society.

Finally, the notion of globalization in its extreme form has been used as an ideological tool to convey the message that governments and people should accept the neoliberal approach to the economy and the welfare state. This is an ideological statement and should be seen as such rather than elevated to some economic or political imperative. For their part, writers in this group believe that nation-states have the power to control the course of events, 'that the international economy is by no means out of control, but that the political will is lacking at present to gain the extra leverage over undesirable and unjust aspects of international and domestic economic activity' (Hirst and Thompson, 1996, p. 17). This, however, begs the question of why 'the political will' is lacking and whether this has something to do with the realization by political leaders that market forces are more powerful today than before.

In brief, the sceptics' contribution has much to commend it as a counterbalance to the Technocrats' enthusiasm for globalization. As an approach, however, it suffers from the same weaknesses as the approach it sets out to criticize: it overstates its case and it views globalization as primarily a one-faceted process, that is, economic change, that can be measured by statistical indicators alone. It under emphasizes all the evidence concerning the accelerating mobility of both capital and technology on a global basis; the speed and the ease with which news, fashion and cultural images spread across the world; the increasing difficulties which governments face in resisting the demands of MNCs; the weakening of labour; the greater public awareness of world events; and so on.

Their criticism that globalization has not advanced as far as some would have us believe is correct; their refusal to accept that transnationalization has begun is not.

Globalization: A Political Economy Approach

Exhibit 1.3

The political economy of globalization

The term 'political economy' has been widely used in the social sciences in an attempt to move away from monocausal economic or political explanations of events and processes. That, however, is as far as agreement goes about 'political economy' as a theoretical framework. Beyond that, it means different things to different people.

In this chapter, a 'political economy' approach implies the rejection both of economic determinism and of politics as single factor type explanations of the globalization process. Economic determinism – found in the writings of many in the technological and Marxisant groups – holds that economic changes are either the main, or the only force, determining the growth, spread and nature of globalization. Political explanations, in a pure form, are not favoured by any of the groups we have discussed but there are those who see globalization primarily as the result of political decisions taken at the national and international levels. There are elements of truth in both economic and political approaches to explanation but, in our view, they need to be put together. Taken separately, they are of limited value in that they inevitably oversimplify what is a very complex process. Explanations in terms of *either* economic factors **or** politics are crude and simplistic.

We use the term 'political economy' to refer to the interplay between economic, political and ideological forces in shaping the nature of the globalization process. Economic factors clearly play a central, and sometimes a dominant, role in shaping globalization and in influencing political decisions to do with globalization. Politics does matter, however, and governments in different countries respond differently to the same economic pressures depending on the nature of national institutions, political alliances, etc. Moreover, states do have the power, at certain times and in certain circumstances, to moderate and modulate the economic pressures exerted by the globalization process.

Ideological power is the third strand in our understanding of 'political economy'. Ideology can be a powerful influence on economic, political and social development. Neoliberalism is today's dominant global ideology in the same way that Keynesianism was in the 1950s and 1960s. The dominant ideology influences decisions about what should, and should not, be done, what are acceptable and unacceptable policies, what is to be encouraged and discouraged in human behaviour. Until recently, neoliberalism offered an ideological justification for a particular type of globalization even when the immediate outcomes seemed to threaten, rather than enhance, human welfare. It promoted and legitimated a particular neoliberal type of globalization – on the basis that the free market approach reflected economic, political and social realities.

This section sets out our approach to globalization under the same five headings used in previous sections: definition, origins, driving forces, effects and future direction.

Definitions

Globalization is the increasing interconnectedness of the world through the compression of time and space brought about by advances in knowledge and technology as well as by political events and decisions

Several points can be drawn from this definition. First, globalization is not a condition but a set of interrelated processes that encompasses all aspects of life: economic, political, social, cultural, military and so on. It involves both quantitative and qualitative changes with the result that globalization cannot be measured by statistical indicators alone. As a process, it coexists with other processes and forces that operate on a local, national or regional level.

Globalization, in other words, describes the development whereby an increasing range of processes operate at a global rather than at other, lower geographical levels. Capital flows, the Internet, CNN news, travel, music and so on operate on a global basis irrespective of national borders and almost irrespective of the attitude of governments. There are, however, many, areas of life and policy where the nation-state is still supreme. There are even more processes where global, international and national factors and forces coexist and where the long-term trend is uncertain.

Second, globalization involves not only an extension of activities carried out at the global as distinct from other levels but also an increase in the frequency with which such activities are carried out at the global level. Thus, not only more people today communicate with others in different parts of the world through the various electronic forms of communication but they also do this far more frequently than before. Not only has the volume of capital flowing across the world increased but the frequency with which this is happening has also increased.

Third, there is the dimension of time compression. The increase in the number and frequency of social or economic processes which can be described as global is taking place at a much faster rate than before. World travel, for example, has not only increased in volume and frequency but is increasing ever more rapidly. The spread of diseases such as AIDs has been at a much faster rate across the world than other diseases have spread in the past. Time and space have been compressed to bring different parts of the world physically, economically and culturally closer together.

Fourth, the personal perception of these changes is an important part of any definition of globalization. It is not simply that more processes today are taking place, at a faster and more intense rate, at a global rather than at other levels than before, but also that people are aware that this is happening and that it can and does affect their own lives. The world-wide televised pictures of famine or disaster stricken areas nurture a better understanding of suffering in the same way that televised pictures of affluence in the West act as magnets for would be migrants from poorer countries.

Fifth, ideology is a most important ingredient of a definition of globalization. There is no good reason to accept the claim that globalization is only compatible with neoliberal ideology. Being a long-term process, it has been accompanied by various ideologies, the most recent of which was the Keynesian view of economics and welfare. As will be shown throughout this book, the neoliberal ideology of current forms of globalization is partly responsible for the increased inequality and poverty in the world. Globalization with a more human ideology should be the aim for sustainable development in the future.

This line of analysis of the globalization process is very similar to that used by Held and his associates who list four dimensions of the process: extensity, intensity, velocity and impact. The first three are similar to our first three while the fourth refers to the impact that events occurring in one part of the world can have in another part so that 'the boundaries between domestic matters and global affairs may be blurred' (Held _et al._, 1999, p. 15). It is not included here for we discuss it in the Effects of Globalization section. Our approach differs from that of the technological enthusiasts and the Marxisant writers in the way we see globalization as a much broader process.

Origins

Globalization is an age-old process dating back to ancient civilizations because human beings have always travelled and traded beyond their borders and some governments, either directly or indirectly, have always encouraged the process of widening human geographical and social horizons. It has to be acknowledged, however, that both the reach and the depth of the globalization process during this early period were very limited. These early civilizations were largely self-contained, external trade played a very small part in people's lives, authoritarianism and theocracy were the dominant modes of government and social communication beyond the local was a rare event for most people.

The origins of what can more properly be called globalization can best be placed during the aftermath of the collapse of feudalism in Europe, the beginnings of capitalism and the discoveries of the new world. This period, around the beginning of the sixteenth century, brings together these three processes as well as the establishment of the first nation states in Europe. The mercantile period, 1500–1800, saw the gradual growth of capitalist forms of relations, a slight improvement in living standards and the looting and plundering of the new world. Capitalism was well established throughout Europe by the end of the nineteenth century, manufacturing replaced agriculture as the main source of national wealth, while trade on unequal terms with the colonies added an international dimension to investment, manufacturing and exploitation.

The first half of the twentieth century saw the further expansion of capitalist development, improved technology, the creation of democratic governments in Europe and the continued exploitation of the colonies until the 1950s when most of them gained political independence. The two world wars brought into conflict for the first time countries from all over the globe and they led to the creation of international bodies with supranational powers.

During the post Second World War period we have witnessed four major processes that have speeded up the growth of globalization: a series of political decisions that deregulated and eased the flow of trade and capital on a global basis; the collapse of the Soviet Union leaving capitalism supreme as a global economic and political system; the unprecedented technological advances in travel and communication that compressed both time and space; and the creation of regional blocs within which national governments surrendered some of their powers. By the end of the century, it can be said that a range of economic, political, social and judicial decisions are beyond the control of nation-states – the clearest sign that globalization is beginning to envelop the globe.

Our approach is similar to that of some pluralist writers. It differs from that of the first group of analysts who see it as a process of the second half of the twentieth century. It differs from the Marxisant approach which sees globalization as emanating from capitalism.

Driving Forces

Several references to the forces that have contributed to globalization have already been made in the previous section. The expansion of knowledge, the logic of capitalism, the power of technology and the policies of governments have always been the four main driving forces both singly and in combination with one another.

Scientific and other knowledge has helped to expand people's horizons, to encourage the advance and application of technology and to make communication between people more feasible. A world where ignorance prevails cannot be a globalized world.

One does not need to subscribe totally to the Marxist view of the world in order to accept the argument that the pursuit of profit by private enterprises has been a major force in the globalization process over the centuries. It was one of the reasons behind colonization and the unequal trade terms imposed on colonies; and it continues to be today a major force behind the flows of private capital, trade and investment in the world. MNCs extend their operations to different parts of the world to improve their short or long-term profitability. It may well be that the local community will also benefit as a result but this is a by-product rather than a motive for MNC expansion.

Similarly, one does not have to accept wholesale the claims of the globalization enthusiasts in order to recognize the contribution of technology to globalization. Rosenau, while rejecting the claim that the nation-state has been weakened, attributes to technology a major part in the globalization process. 'It is technology, in short, that has fostered the interdependence of local, national, and international communities that is far greater than any previously experienced' (Rosenau, 1990, p. 17).

The global circulation of news and pictures, the promotion of a consumerist culture and, above all, the compression of time and space would not have been possible without developments in technology. Some Marxists have argued that it is the logic of capitalism that was responsible for such technological advances. This may be true in some respects, but not in all cases because many advances in technology were the result of either scientific progress or government policies and programmes as the space programme of recent decades illustrates.

Technological advances have also reduced the real costs of trade and communication over the years. Thus the cost of sea freight, air transport, telephone calls and computers has declined quite substantially in recent decades. Whereas a three-minute telephone call between New York and London cost US$245 in 1920, it cost only $3 in 1990 in real terms at 1990 dollar prices; similarly, the price of computers fell dramatically between 1960 and 1990 (UNDP, 1999, Box Table 1.1, p. 30).

Government policies have played a part in the globalization process in a variety of ways. Colonization was pursued not merely for economic reasons but for political aggrandizement. Education policies have contributed to scientific discoveries that prompted globalization over the years. Decisions by governments in the post-war years to deregulate markets, to ease the flow of capital across borders, to set up supranational bodies, to legislate on migration, and so on, are just a few examples of how governments have contributed to the globalization process. It is simply not possible to exclude the nation-state from the list of driving forces behind globalization though the capitalist nature of most nation-states needs to be kept in mind.

Complex processes require complex explanations and the globalization process is no exception to this. Our approach is more in line with that of the pluralist pragmatists than the others. We see globalization as the product of a range of factors, pressures and developments. We differ from the pluralist pragmatists, however, in the greater emphasis that we place on the driving force of the logic of capitalism and, in very recent years, the accompanying ideology of neoliberalism. We differ from both the technologist enthusiasts who emphasize technology and from the Marxisant writers who stress capital-ism and ignore, or underemphasize, the other driving forces.

Effects of Globalization

We discuss the effects of globalization on societies in greater detail in the subsequent chapters. Here, we only need to state the problem and outline our position on the broad economic, political and social effects as pointers to the next three chapters. The essential problem is the classic one of attributing causation in the analysis of social change. Globalization is a useful shorthand for a number of important economic, political and social changes. But at the same time as these changes are taking place, other changes are also happen-ing, for example, the ageing of the world's population, the slowing down of the rate of economic growth in industrial economies, radical changes in the institution of the family, the maturation of western welfare states. Disentangling the specific impact of these different changes is extremely difficult and in some cases obviously impossible.

Another hazard is economic determinism – the view that globalization will change the world in certain predetermined and predictable directions. Such a view is too crude. It ignores key mediating variables – the power of culture and history, the central mediating role of politics, the likely variation arising from the variable nature and strengths of different economies and polities. What is very clear is that different countries have responded to globalization in different ways and that certain variables are important.

What of the economic effects of globalization? We see economic globaliza-tion as having four main aspects – the increased mobility of financial capital, the increase in foreign direct investment, the growth of multinational com-panies, the expansion of world trade. These economic processes have had both positive and negative effects on national economies: they helped to increase economic growth in some countries but were responsible for economic stagna-tion and even decline in others. On the whole, it can be said that it is mainly the least developed countries, most of which are Sub-Saharan, which have experienced the negative economic effects.

What of the political effects? The overall effect of the globalization process is to constrain the state's role in economic and social policy-making. States must present an acceptable face to international capital. That means privileging eco-nomic over social policy and ruling out certain policies deemed unacceptable to capital. It can also mean pressures for lower taxes and reduced expenditure on social protection. On the other hand, it can mean pressure to improve the quality of the work force by better education provision and by improved training and retraining opportunities. In the IDCs, there are the very specific pressures exerted by the structural adjustment programmes imposed by the

IMF and the World Bank which reduced social expenditure, deregulated the economy and expanded the role of the private sector.

Clearly, there has been a degree of hollowing out of the state. Power has moved upwards to supra national bodies, sideways to functional bodies and downwards through decentralization. The nation-state, however, remains much more than the shell suggested by the 'hollowing out' metaphor. It has lost a measure of autonomy and sovereignty but politics still matters a great deal.

On the socio-economic front, the major effect of globalization has been the consolidation and at times the exacerbation of uneven economic development both between, and within, countries at a time when the economies of most countries expanded. Thus the number, though not the proportion, of people in IDCs living in extreme poverty rose during the period 1987–1998. The position was far worse in Sub-Saharan Africa and in South Asia where not only the absolute numbers of the very poor rose dramatically but the proportion of the population in poverty remained static. Worst hit were the former-Soviet bloc countries, where both the numbers and the proportions of people in poverty rose between 1987 and 1998 (World Bank, 2000, table 1.1, p. 23).

Growth in poverty and inequality can lead to social tensions and conflict, particularly those of a racial kind. As the UNDP report commented, the rioting and looting of the Chinese minority community in Indonesia in the late 1990s 'shows what can happen when an economic crisis sets off latent social tensions between ethnic groups – or between rich and poor' (UNDP, 1999, p. 36).

On the cultural front, globalization has raised contacts between people and nations to an unprecedented extent as a result of the growth of television, the Internet, e-mail, tourism and so on. But behind these cultural contacts lie big business interests concentrated in the AICs, evidenced by the dominance of American films, videos, music and fashion. Entertainment in terms of films and television programmes is the largest export industry in the US (UNDP, 1999, p. 33). It is an indication that economic, political and cultural forms of dominance are interrelated.

Care must be taken, however, not to exaggerate these cultural influences because there is no reason to believe that they necessarily affect the inner core of local cultures. It is a leap into unreality to argue that every person who eats at McDonalds, wears Reebok shoes, sings western tunes and watches American films in an IDC, immediately becomes westernized in terms of such core values as gender relationships or family values. It is not so much the immediate as the longterm influence of western culture on local cultures that is the real issue.

The Future

The economic, political, cultural and social effects of globalization are clearly wide-ranging and important. They are altering the pattern and focus of national politics and of economic and social policy and the context in which the nation-state operates. Globalization has conflicting effects but clearly it is here to stay with all its pluses and minuses. The unacceptable face of globalization stems from the way it is directed and fuelled by a neoliberal ideology that extols the virtues of economic growth and private gain at the expense of broader economic and social development and the pursuit of the satisfaction of the basic needs of all as the most important concern in development. As UNDP put it

> Driven by commercial market forces, globalization in this era seeks to promote economic efficiency, economic growth and yield profits. But it misses out on the goals of equity, poverty eradication and enhanced human security. (UNDP, 1999, p. 44)

It is, however, central to the arguments of this book that the globalization process has coexisted with different ideologies over the years and there is no reason to believe that it cannot do so in the future. Indeed, the abandonment of the extreme forms of neoliberalism is a necessary prerequisite to the improvement of human welfare on a global level.

Finally, it is important to stress the point that the process of globalization is uneven. It has permeated the lives of people in AICs but has hardly touched the lives of millions of people in many IDCs – a half of the people in the world, for example, have never made or received a phone call.

In Chapter 2 we move to explore in more detail the impact of globalization on economics and politics as necessary background to chapters 3 and 4 which look more specifically at the impact of globalization on human welfare in advanced industrial and industrially developing countries.

Further Reading

Held, D., McGrew, A., Goldblatt, D. and Perraton, J. (1999) *Global Transformations: Politics, Economics and Culture* (Cambridge, Polity Press).
Scholte, J.A. (2000) *Globalization: a critical introduction* (London, Macmillan).
Waters, M. (2001) *Globalization*, 2nd edn (London, Routledge).

2

Globalization, the State and Human Welfare

Welfare states are experiments in politics, in the exercise of state power to manage the economy and to establish a range of services to meet social needs. The economic and political capacity of the state are, therefore, central to the success of the welfare state project. The impact of globalization on state capacity is an important area of enquiry because of the significance of state capacity to the promotion of human welfare. In this chapter, we explore the nature of the relationship between globalization and the nation state and the impact of economic globalization on national economic policy and on the state's capacity to pursue nationally chosen economic and social policies.

Assessment of the present and the likely future depends, of course, partly on perceptions of the past. If one believed that the state could control national capitalism, then the development of a more mobile capital and the maturation of supposedly footloose multinational enterprises may be seen as marking a major change in the chance of securing a benevolently governed capitalism. If one took the opposite view, as we do, that the state could never effectively govern even national capitalism, then the change is one of degree but not of kind. Government was never fully sovereign so what it has lost cannot be an epochal change. Equally, if one never believed that Keynesian approaches to economic management were the final solution to capitalist booms and slumps, one will not be left totally distraught by the (supposed) loss of the nation-state's capacity to pursue national Keynesianism.

Globalization raises vital questions about the state's continuing capacity to develop and deliver those national policies which make up the welfare state and promote human welfare. That is why we must explore the general impact of globalization on the nation-state before looking more particularly at its impact on the welfare state and human welfare in advanced industrial societies.

Globalization and the Nation-State: the Nature of the Relationship

To understand the nature of globalization it is very important to see it as a product of interaction between global forces and pressures, and the nation-state. States are not simply the objects of supranational forces. 'States', says Scholte, 'have played an indispensable enabling role in the globalization of capital' (Scholte, 1997a, p. 441). The way states respond to the pressure of globalization makes them important agents in the globalization process. They are not simply acted upon; they also act. They act to try to shape the globalization process because of the importance of the process to their own future. As Boyer and Drache put it 'the nation state, as mediating structure, makes the strategic difference between winning and losing in a highly volatile international economy' (Boyer and Drache, 1996, p. 4). By increasingly promoting the transnational expansion and competitiveness of its industries and services abroad and competing for inward investment, Cerny argues, the state becomes a critical agent, perhaps *the* most critical agent, in the process of globalization itself (Cerny, 1996, p. 133). Cerny sees globalization as driven not by inexorable economic forces but rather by politics (Cerny, 1999a, p. 152). Economic pressures push the state to reconsider its primary orientation. The 'welfare state' is transformed into the 'competition state' and 'the competition state is becoming increasingly both the engine room and the steering mechanism of political globalization itself' (Cerny, 1997, p. 274).

States are, then, active participants in the globalization process, not simply subjects or victims of it, because globalization need states – just as markets always have and will. Multinational enterprises, for example, need many things which only states can provide – social stability, good infrastructure, an educated workforce, a framework of law. They therefore need strong and active states. A globalized economy also needs basic ground rules and some common, coordinated policies. Development on these fronts depends, to a significant degree, on national governments.

The relationship between globalization and the state is not one between irreversible economic forces and innocent nation-state victim. The relationship is more complex than that. Obviously there are tensions but most states have, of necessity, in the past had to develop working relationships with national capital. Most have managed, and manage, an accommodation – easy or uneasy. It is also true that many states find the globalization process a useful reinforcement to their pro-capital policies and a very useful lever to jerk forward economic and social reform in the desired direction. Globalization is valuable too for politicians as an explanation, or justification, for their failures in policies which they only ever adopted with reluctance. As Sutcliffe remarks, 'I doubt that the national state has lost as much power as many of our rulers would like us to believe' (Sutcliffe, 1998, p. 325). If we believe them, our expectations are correspondingly reduced and the space for government action – and inaction – is extended.

Our argument is that, to understand the impact of globalization on the nation-state and the state's capacity to promote human welfare, it is necessary to grasp the complex symbiotic nature of the relationship. We see capital as a driving force in the globalization process. But, at the same time, we would also emphasize capital's need for the state, and the state's ability to influence the process.

Economic Globalization and the State

Economic developments in the direction of a more globalized economy clearly affect the nation-state's capacity for independent policy making in economic and social policy. The crucial question is about the nature, extent, strength and direction of that influence. To understand the issues we need to explore the pattern of economic globalization. Essentially it is made up of four connected but separate developments – the globalization of the movement of financial capital, changes in patterns of investment, changes in patterns of trade, the growth of multinational companies. We sketch the nature and significance of these developments looking very briefly at what has been happening since the collapse, in the early 1970s, of the post-Second World War Bretton Woods system of fixed exchange rates and capital controls and their significance for AICs and their governing capacity.

Globalization and Financial Capital Movements

'There is no question', says Cohen, 'that the globalization of finance is one of the most striking political economy developments of the post World War II era' (Cohen, 1996, p. 293). There are two significant aspects to the development. Aided by modern means of communication, financial capital has become truly global. It is possible to move huge sums of money from one currency or investment to another virtually instantaneously. The result is 'a functioning global financial system' (Held *et al.*, 1999, p. 189). The other huge change in the 1980s was 'the arrival of a capitalism no longer primarily industrial but speculative' (de Benoist, 1996, p. 120) – a capitalism concerned with dealing in stocks and shares and currencies not with trade or industrial investment.

Before the collapse of the Bretton Woods system, 90 per cent of all currency exchanges were commercial transactions or long-term investments. After the collapse, almost 90 per cent of such transactions were speculative in nature (Navarro, 1998, p. 628). Financial trading exceeded $1 trillion per day for the first time in 1995 which was about fifty times the total volume of world trade for the year (Baker *et al.*, 1998, p. 11).

What is the significance of the arrival of this new kind of capitalism? First, whereas there can be debate as to whether investment, trade and MNC's are truly global, there can be no debate about the global nature of financial capitalism. It is 'perhaps the most unequivocal indicator of the globalization of economic affairs' (Axford, 1995, p. 107).

Second, it puts a new pressure on companies and managers to return ever larger and quicker profits. There are no higher or longer-term loyalties. Shareholder value is all – and that is determined by short-term profits. This threatens and/or helps to dissolve the corporatist systems of partnership between state, capital and labour which depend on restraint and a longer-term and broader view. 'By internationalising, and thereby disorganising, capital and labour markets', says Streeck, 'globalisation dissolves whatever negotiated co-ordination may have been nationally accomplished between them and replaces it with the global hierarchical dominance of the former over the latter' (Streeck, 1997, p. 252).

Third, the potential return to be made from short-term investments and financial speculation on the world's currency markets can lead to a shortage of capital for productive investment – and so directly contributes to problems of employment and unemployment (Watson, 1999, pp. 60–1).

Fourth, it puts sharp pressures on governments. It is a force constraining policy makers and circumscribing the policy capacity – that is, the sovereignty – of the state. As Crotty *et al.*, put it, 'increased capital mobility within the neo liberal regime is imposing increasingly severe constraints on workers, communities and states' (Crotty *et al.*, 1998, p. 143). Governments have to conform to the assumed wishes and priorities of speculative capitalism or see their currency attacked and their reserves depleted. Any government which offends international finance's demand for unrestricted gain, says Kennedy, will find that its capital has fled and its currency has weakened (Kennedy, 1994, p. 56). Essentially this means pressures for low and lower public expenditure, low budget deficits, high interest rates and prioritizing control of inflation over measures to deal with unemployment. Small states are particularly vulnerable as recent financial and banking crises have shown. But even stronger states are not immune 'Even governments with the greatest financial resources', says Willetts, in a rather extreme statement of this position, 'are helpless against the transnational banks and other speculators' (Willetts, 1997, p. 293) – empowered by the liberalization which governments themselves have set in motion in response to capital's demands.

States want, and need, to be seen as safe places for international capital. It is the necessary desire to attract and please global financial capital which 'has put governments distinctly on the defensive, eroding much of the authority of the contemporary sovereign state' (Cohen, 1996, p. 270). Milner and Keohane's verdict is that 'the clearest effect of internationalisation has been to undermine governments' autonomy in the domain of macroeconomic policy, and this has resulted largely from rising capital mobility, rather than trade' (Milner and Keohane, 1996, p. 256).

National governments have always, of course, had to be aware of the importance of maintaining international confidence in their economic policies and in their currency. But in the judgement of Held *et al.*, a central purpose of the Bretton Woods system was to ensure that domestic economic objectives were not subordinated to the dictates of global financial capital but rather took precedence over them (Held *et al.*, 1999, p. 200). With the ending of the Bretton Woods system that has changed. In recent years the flows of international capital have become faster and greater in scale and so ever more important. National governments have, therefore, had to become ever more mindful of the presence – physical or psychological – of mobile capital at the policy-making table – a constraint and an influence which cannot sensibly be ignored but which does not necessarily determine policy in every detail. The scope for those social democratic type policies towards which capital has always been at best sceptical, and more often directly opposed, has been sharply narrowed.

Foreign Direct Investment

FDI has grown substantially since the early 1980s, doubling as a percentage of world output between the mid 1980s and the late 1990s to reach some 10 per cent of world GDP (Baker *et al.*, 1998, p. 9). The increase was dramatic but the level, as a per centage of GDP, was still only slightly above that for 1913. Predictably, as we shall see in Chapter 4, developed countries accounted for almost all the outflows of FDI. Less predictably, with about 14 per cent of world population, they absorbed around 75 per cent of the inflows. The UK is the world's second largest provider of outward FDI with 12 per cent of world stocks. The EU and the USA absorb 70 per cent of this outflow (Duffuss and Gooding, 1997, p. 31). The UK is also the world's second largest recipient of inward FDI, taking about 9 per cent of world stocks.

Five points emerge from an analysis of the significance of these patterns.

First, outward investment is driven primarily by a desire to improve profits by reducing costs (Duffus and Gooding, 1997). Countries seeking or needing such investment know what they need to do to make themselves attractive destinations for FDI.

Second, the flows of FDI are essentially regional rather than global, with funds moving between the USA, Europe and Japan. Only a relatively small proportion of FDI goes to industrially developing countries.

Third, freeing up the movement of capital for investment in other countries can have significant impacts on domestic industries and employment by depriving them of necessary investment and by giving capital a powerful weapon to use in negotiation with states and workers. Unless capital gets its way, it will threaten to invest overseas rather than at home.

Fourth, despite all the talk about FDI, productive capital has, as Watson concludes, 'remained overwhelmingly within the border of the national economy'. In 1993, for example, foreign investment in US stocks and bonds amounted to only 6 per cent of US stocks and 14 per cent of corporate bonds. Conversely 95 per cent of investment by the American people was in domestic stocks and bonds (Watson, 1999, p. 60).

Fifth, attracting FDI becomes extremely important to countries. Britain's refusal to sign up to the EU social charter was, in part at least, the product of a concern to maximise the chance of securing FDI. As John Major, the then Prime Minister, put it 'Europe can have the social charter. We shall have employment... Let Jacques Delors accuse us of creating a paradise for foreign investors; I am happy to plead guilty' (quoted in Rodrik, 1997, p. 39). The desire to attract FDI becomes a significant influence on government policy and a strong pressure to conform to dominant global ideologies.

Economic development depends heavily on investment. International investors have certain assumptions about the kind of economy and society where they will be able to secure a good return – low rates of corporate and individual taxation, modest wages, high productivity, transnational flexible labour markets, low employer social security contribution, a weakly unionized labour force, non-obtrusive environmental regulation. Obviously there is a trade-off between these – if productivity is particularly high, for example, then the level of wages may be less important. If productivity is high because of higher than average expenditure on education and training, then that may be a good bargain.

National governments are, and will be, constrained by such concerns and considerations. Securing FDI is a central concern for virtually all national governments – but not necessarily a concern which always overrides all other conerns. Creating an attractive economic environment for investors and MNCs, however, does become a key preoccupation for economic and industrial policy-makers. They have to try to tune into the beliefs, values and priorities of the key investor decision makers. In general, their beliefs and values are neoliberal rather than social democratic. So the concern, and need, for FDI becomes – generally – a force for restraint on expenditure and for retrenchment. Neoliberal approaches become a simple matter of common sense for national governments.

Multinational Companies

Most major industrial and financial corporations now hold some of their productive assets abroad. Many major companies are truly global. ExxonMobil has business interests in 200 countries. Heineken beer is drunk in 170 countries, Nokia mobile phones are used in 120 countries, McDonalds now operates in some 120 countries, the *Financial Times* is read in 160 countries, Marlborough cigarettes do their deadly work in 170 countries (Scholte, 1997b, p. 436) – and so on.

MNCs now account for some 70 per cent of world trade, 20–30 per cent of world output and control around one third of the world's private sector productive assets. The combined revenues of just two of the biggest – Ford and General Motors – exceed the total GDP of all Sub-Saharan Africa (*The Guardian*, 1 May 2000). They possess immense power and influence. As Dicken puts it 'much of the changing geography of the global economy is sculptured by the transnational company through decisions to invest and not to invest in particular geographical locations' (Dicken, 1998, p. 177). In Petrella's view, 'the globally orientated enterprise is in the process of becoming the main organisation "governing" the world economy, with the support of "the national state"' (Petrella, 1996, p. 74). Sklair sees the transnational company as 'the primary agent and institutional focus of economic transnational practices' (Sklair, 1991, p. 53).

MNCs are much sought after by national governments as sources of investment and therefore of jobs and for the prestige their presence brings. They are courted and offered large incentives to locate in particular places. They can very profitably play hard to get and seek capital-friendly policies and massive subventions and sweeteners. They can make worrying threats of withdrawal, if and when, governments pursue policies which they see as opposed to their interests.

There are three main issues relevant to our analysis.

First, there is the question of the nature of MNCs. How global/multinational are they? How mobile and footloose are they? The consensus of academic opinion is clear. Very few MNCs are fully global. Most of them hold the majority of their assets in the home country. Honda, for example, the most international of Japanese car manufacturers, has 63 per cent both of its assets and its workers in Japan (Wade, 1996, p. 79). Navarro quotes figures for US MNCs of 78 per cent of all fixed assets, 70 per cent of sales and 73 per cent of employment being in the United States (Navarro, 1998, p. 664). Power and influence are clearly related to mobility. The more mobile a company is, or can appear to be, the greater will its influence be on government. If companies are not perceived to be as mobile as they pretend to be, then governments do not need to pay as much attention to their threats to move investment elsewhere. Such movements can be major economic and political blows to governments.

Second, there is the vital question of what shapes – and is thought to shape – the investment decision of MNCs. Why do they go where they go? To what extent are they attracted by low wages, weak environmental regulation, good infrastructure, an educated workforce, social or political stability? Obviously wage levels and labour costs are factors but they are by no means always the decisive ones. Productivity and unit costs are the vital issues and there is evidence that carefully crafted domestic industrial policies can create a more attractive environment than crude liberalization because of their capacity to increase productivity (Baker *et al.*, 1998, p. 22). Goodstein's interpretation of the evidence on environmental regulation, for example, is that such regulation seems to have little impact on MNC decisions about location (Goodstein, 1998, p. 300) – because such regulation is only one relatively small element in total costs and so only one factor in the overall decision.

Third, what is the nature of MNC relations with states? All the evidence suggests a symbiotic relationship – 'both co-operative and competing, both supportive and conflictual' (Gordon, 1987, p. 25). Each needs the other so the relationship is, of necessity, both cooperative and competitive. Certainly, the pressure of international competition drives governments to offer financial inducements that cannot be justified by objective economic criteria On the other hand, MNCs rely on the government of the countries in which they establish themselves to create favourable economic, social and political conditions. MNC dependence on them gives states leverage in certain areas – though in their turn MNCs have their own bargaining counters (Holton, 1998, p. 93). Wade's authoritative conclusion is that 'most MNCs are quite susceptible to pressure and persuasion from the home country government' (Wade, 1996, p. 79) – but only up to a certain point. Governments know the risks and that there are other countries courting the same MNCs.

MNCs are *key* players – according to some analysts *the* key players in the globalization process. 'In the new era of global competition', says Drache, 'the threatening dimension is the growth of corporate power. The sovereignty of nations is in peril not on account of the international economy but because of the power of corporations to invest with less restriction, to reshape public policy in support of private wealth generation and, most of all, to appropriate the political culture of nations for corporate ends. The meaning is as clear as it is simple: national "place" has to give way to commercial "space"' (Drache, 1996, pp. 53–4). Susan Strange makes a similar judgement that 'while transnational companies do not take over from the governments of state, they have certainly encroached on their domains of power' (Strange, 1996, p. 65).

There is no denying the power and reach of the new multinational economic conglomerates. What is open to debate is the degree of their multinationality and the nature of their decision-making about location and about their priorities. Most multinational companies, in fact, have very clear roots in one country. They do have 'homes' where their headquarters and their research and development functions are located. They are not truly stateless. They are therefore subject – if there is the political will – to a measure of control from their home governments. This is not to deny their power and influence but it provides something of a counter to the suggestion of an uncontrolled and uncontrollable force before which national governments can only kow tow and concede. What they do is to exert pressure on governments by what they say and do and threaten to do, and by what governments *think* MNCs want, and expect, and may do. Nation-states need MNCs – but MNCs also need effective states and an effective state will not simply roll over at the first hint of possible MNC investment or complaint about national policies. But while MNCs do not seem to exert an inevitable pressure for a drive to the bottom, they do exert a generally downward pressure on a wide range of tax, social security and environmental policies. They stand for profit first and very foremost. The influence they exert on governments varies depending on factors such as the political complexion of the government, its authority and the strength of the economy.

Globalization and Trade

'The original and continuing fundamental of economic globalization', says Waters, 'is trade' (Waters, 1995, p. 66). In recent years, world trade had expanded rapidly and the world economy has become much more integrated. One useful index of the significance of trade is the ratio of exports to GDP. In the years between 1960 and 1990, the ratio more than doubled, from 9.5 to 20.5 per cent (Weiss, 1998, p. 170). In 1997, the OECD noted that 'in recent years' world trade had been growing three times faster than GDP (OECD, 1997a, p. 15). In comparison with the 1950s and 1960s, trade has increased dramatically but in the late 1980s, in many advanced economies the ratio of exports to GDP was still lower than in the years before 1914 (Kiely and Marfleet, 1998, p. 55).

There was, however, a striking and very important difference between the trading patterns at the beginning and end of the twentieth century. A much higher proportion of trade is now accounted for by manufactured goods – 15 per cent of world trade in the mid 1990s compared to under 5 per cent in the 1960s. Between 1970 and 1994, manufactured goods rose as a share of world exports from 60.9 to 74.7 per cent. Manufacturing exports from AICs rose only modestly but the share of manufacturing exports from IDCs increased very strikingly. This was quite new. Countries are increasingly trading each others' manufactured goods and advanced societies face new competition from low wage, newly industrialized economies (Baker *et al.*, 1998, pp. 7–8).

Why is this happening? There are the technical explanations. In certain trades larger ships and the advent of containerization have greatly reduced sea transport costs. The introduction of the wide body jet plane in the late 1960s has made for faster and cheaper air freight. Excluding Canada and Mexico, 40 per cent of US exports and nearly 30 per cent of imports are carried by air (Cooper, 1995, pp. 363–4).

There are explanations in terms of the globalization of investment and production. There are now industries which are truly global in their scale and reach – cars, consumer electronics, pharmaceuticals, tobacco and telecommunications. There are truly global products such as the Ford Focus car jointly designed by Ford Europe and Mazda Japan and to be built in Britain, Germany, the USA, Japan, Argentina, Mexico and Brazil (Holton, 1998, p. 57).

What is the significance of these developments? In the view of Held *et al.*, 'the contemporary globalization of trade has transformed state autonomy' (Held *et al.*, 1999, pp. 187–8). The most obvious and important implication is the increased and global range of goods available to consumers. In AICs, consumers have clearly gained. But increased trade puts a premium on competitiveness. More producers are in competition with producers in other countries – other advanced economies or developing economies. There are clear implications for employment and earnings – and for governments' ability to stimulate the domestic economy – when stimulating demand increases imports rather than employment.

Internationalization of the economy puts a premium on competitiveness. National industries have to compete in regional and world markets. They depend for their survival, let alone their success, on their degree of international competitiveness – so, therefore, do governments. States have to be competitive and competitive states have to have certain priorities. They are imposed, or so it is argued, by the 'realities' of the globalized economy rather than actively and voluntarily chosen by governments or electorates.

This is the way in which the increased importance of international trade constrains national governments. It is, of course, a matter of judgement as to what enhances and maintains competitiveness. There is the high road – investment in workers and infrastructure, and there is the low road – reduce production costs to the minimum. By and large, the most obvious and powerful pressures are downwards. As Peter Lilley, the then Secretary of State for Social Security in the UK, put it in 1993, linking social security costs and competitiveness, 'The increasing importance of competitiveness in the context of globalization of economic activity is also a significant pressure on social expenditure levels' (HMSO, 1993, p. 8). For our purposes the important point is that the pressures are externally generated by developments in the international economy. Competitiveness has become a, if not the, main concern of governments. How states achieve that goal is a matter of national decision but the primary and powerful direction of global pressures is very clear. What governments have to do is to calibrate their policies according to the perceived demands of the global system rather than according to their own national predilections or those of their citizens. And those demands put clear pressures on any state policies which are defined as likely to increase production costs even if they are democratically willed and seen nationally as to the long term benefit of the citizenry. Held *et al.*, see political support for welfare state type policies as being undermined by changing patterns of trade (Held *et al.*, 1999, p. 184).

Globalization and Constraints on Economic Policy

In our analysis of the key elements in the development of a more global economy we have indicated some of the ways in which particular elements affect the autonomy and capacity of the nation-state. We now draw together and summarize the argument.

What is very clear is that globalization has imposed significant constraints on the economic independence of the nation-state. The extreme position is taken by analysts such as Ohmae, whose verdict is that 'in terms of the global economy, nation states have become little more than bit actors' (Ohmae, 1996, p. 12). He sees nation-states as 'a transitional form of organisation for managing economic affairs' (ibid., p. 141) which has now been superseded.

Other writers argue along similar lines but in rather less apocalyptic terms. Streeck, for example, speaks of nation-states in Western Europe having 'progressively lost the capacity to govern their economies and impose political will on the free play of market forces' (Streeck, 1996, pp. 302–3). Despite their scepticism about globalization, Hirst and Thompson are clear that states' capacities for national macroeconomic management 'have weakened considerably' (Hirst and Thompson, 1999, p. 256). Cox's verdict is that states' 'powers of shielding domestic economies from negative effects of globalization have diminished' (Cox, 1997a, p. 27). Held and McGrew believe that 'the internationalisation of production, finance and exchange is unquestionably eroding the capacity of the individual liberal democratic state to control its own economic future' (Held and McGrew, 1994, p. 66). Tony Blair told a New York business conference in 1996 that any government had to meet the aspirations of capital – or suffer a response likely to be prejudicial to economic growth (Wickham-Jones, 1997, p. 257).

There are, in contrast, those who argue that the constraints which globalization imposes on choices in economic policy are weaker 'than much contemporary rhetoric suggests' (Garrett, 1998a, p. 788). The pressures on governments are clear but is it credible to read off a direct loss of autonomy from these changes?

Higgot, for example, argues that it is not. He sees the argument that increased globalization constrains the freedom of governments to act autonomously as 'too deterministic' (Higgott, 1999, p. 26). In his judgement the argument that 'international capital will depart economies that exhibit high tax, high deficit and big government spending is still to be proven' (ibid., p. 28). Garrett accepts that globalization does impose constraints on national governments because of the demand from global markets that states be competitive. On the other hand, governments provide collective goods important to MNCs and to international competitiveness. The essence of Garrett's argument is that there is a significant element of pragmatism in the approach of the protagonists of global capital. If intervention works, it may be acceptable. And, he argues, there is no evidence that financial markets attach interest rate premiums to higher rates of public spending as long as new tax revenues balance increased spending and such taxes are at an acceptable level (Garrett, 1998a, p. 823). Chang argues along similar lines – that the constraints imposed by MNCs on national industrial policy may be growing but are nowhere near the point at which a national industrial policy is impossible (Chang, 1998, p. 113).

These arguments are a useful corrective to the picture of national governments reduced to helplessness by the sweeping-all-before-them forces of globalization. What they contribute to the argument are three points. First, that constraints on economic policy are less than total. Second, that states can do their own thing as long as the outcomes are broadly in line with the presuppositions of the financial markets. Third, state action designed to further economic goals – for example, to improve the quality of the work force – may be defined as acceptable even if it increases public expenditure. On the other hand, the financial markets may take constraining action if the proposals for increased governments expenditure have no economic rationale – for example, improving social care services for elderly people- and/or increase budget deficits. The constraints are, to a degree, narrowed and redefined rather than denied.

If it is accepted, as we do, that globalization imposes genuine constraints on government's independence in economic policy-making, precisely how are such constraints imposed and exercised? How are national governments actually constrained? We see various types of constraints.

First, governments are constrained by the fact that 'the dominant problems of economic governance now lie in the international domain' (Hirst and Thompson, 1999, p. 219). More of the key factors which affect the health and well being of national economies lie outside the immediate control of national governments today than in the past – the health of the world economy, exchange rates, interest rates, the price of raw materials, the price of oil.

Second, they are constrained by the need for market credibility with the key players in the emerging global economy – MNCs, global capital, credit rating agencies such as Moody's Investors Services and Standard and Poors Rating Group bodies known to only a tiny minority of *cognoscenti* but with the power to impose enormous costs on governments if they reduce a government's credit worthiness. Market credibility depends, generally, on pursuing a particular range of acceptable economic and social policies. If a nation's economy and economic policies lose credibility then very nasty things can happen. The two most obvious are speculative attacks on the national currency, which have a capacity to be self-fulfilling, and disinvestment by MNCs. Just how credible such threats of disinvestment are is a matter of judgement, but the fact that they are made concentrates the government's mind on what its priorities need to be if it is to make and retain friends in high economic places.

Third, another set of constraints is to do with taxation and beliefs about it. 'Does globalization sap the fiscal power of the state?' is the key question. Kudrle's answer to the question he poses would be that states still exercise substantial powers to tax (Kudrle, 2000). Other commentators stress the constraints. As Held *et al.*, put it, 'global competition to attract FDI has now come to embrace tax measures' (Held *et al.*, 1999, p. 277). Government's preoccupation thus becomes tax reductions rather than the pursuit of desirable social programmes which might involve increases in tax.

Higgott sees a clear connection between the increase in capital mobility and the easing of the tax burden on capital to try to prevent exit. Direct taxes on capital have certainly fallen in the major economies since the 1980s (Higgott, 1999, p. 24) (Schultze and Ursprung, 1999, p. 321). In the UK, corporation tax was levied at a rate of 52 per cent in 1979. By 2000 it had been reduced to 30 per cent. In Germany, in recent years the contribution of corporation taxes to overall tax revenue has more than halved (Daly, 2001, p. 99). One obvious result which troubles the OECD is the impact of these trends, and the growth of tax havens, on the ability of governments to maintain a firm tax base (OECD, 1997a, p. 26; *The Guardian*, 1 February 2001).

Fourth, another specific example of the constraints of globalization is the influence which MNCs can exert when they are making decisions about their location and investment plans. Stopford and Strange's view is that governments have lost bargaining power to MNCs because of the way competition among states for MNC favours has intensified (quoted in Dicken, 1998, p. 276). The desire to portray themselves as potentially desirable homes for MNCs shapes governments' approach to taxation and labour market and environmental regulation.

Fifth, many countries were, in effect, forced into financial deregulation by global trends and pressures. Such deregulation had a very specific impact in certain countries – for example Sweden, Norway and Denmark. A key element in the supply side strategies of these societies, and in their success in maintaining full employment, was the privileging of borrowing by industry over other borrowers. This was, in effect, a subsidy to industry – government's contribution to maintaining a consensual model of labour–employer–government relations. Financial deregulation made it impossible to maintain this system, so constraining what had been a long standing and successful option for government.

Sixth, the development of a purely financial, speculative capitalism was a product of globalization. As we have seen, it became a powerful constraint on government policy. It also operated as a constraint in another less direct way. Globalization privileged financial capital in the sense that playing the financial markets of the world seemed to offer better returns than investment in productive enterprises. Capital therefore took that road leaving governments short of funds for industrial and technical investment.

Seventh, globalization of the last few decades embodied, was fuelled by, and propagated a particular ideology – neo-liberalism. Globalization promoted and internationalized a particular economic system – capitalism – and a particular set of beliefs about what constituted sound economic policies and the good society. 'Thanks largely to globalization', wrote Scholte, 'contemporary society is more thoroughly capitalist than ever' (Scholte, 1997a, p. 440). Nation-states were constrained by the belief system embodied in globalization.

Eighth, there is much discussion in the literature as to whether regional groupings of states as in the EU or in NAFTA, or functional groupings like the OECD, are foreshadowings of a more global future or attempts at self protection from a more globalized world economy. Be that as it may, when they join such bodies states accept certain constraints on their freedom of action in economic, industrial and social policies. The treaty constraints imposed by membership of the EU and NAFTA are well known. Membership of the WTO very clearly constrains what states may do once they are members, but states join because they think the gains outweigh the losses – or because they see no alternative.

Finally, a more globalized world constrains the nation-state by tending to prioritise the economic over the social. Contemporary globalization is about tilting the balance – temporarily or permanently – in favour of the economic over the political and the social. The social becomes more obviously and explicitly subordinate to the economic. Market considerations dominate politics and define their limits.

The triumph of the economic is evidenced in the dominance of competitiveness. and of a particular perception of how that necessary goal is best achieved. 'Competitiveness', says Rodrik, 'has become another word for labour costs, something that can be enhanced by slashing benefits and wages' (Rodrik, 1997, p. 75). Competitiveness, defined in these narrow terms, 'has become the totem of policy making' (Cerny, 1999a, p. 155). What we are seeing, is a new powerful, dominating emphasis in the role of the state, a role shaped and constrained by the demands of a globalizing world.

One of the major, if not always obvious, problems with assessing the significance of economic based global challenges to national sovereignty is establishing an appropriate bench mark. Certainly the years between 1945 and 1975 were good years for 'the state' in many countries but these were also years of growing globalization. States managed, with varying degrees of success, national economies. They created national, state-dominated welfare systems. To what extent, though, did states control markets? Was there ever a time when markets were effectively 'controlled' by states in a democratic mixed economy? Does the current world of 'disorganized capitalism' lead to a rather false depiction of a supposedly 'ordered capitalism' in the past? There were 'settlements' and 'truces' and corporatist pacts which offered a functional accommodation between state, capital and labour but there never was a day when markets were controlled by states – and continued to function effectively and efficiently.

Clearly, state sovereignty in economic, fiscal and social policy has been challenged by the development of a more global economy. Markets, the ideologies which fuel them, the need to trade internationally and competitively, the increased mobility of financial capital are all realities – new in degree if not in kind – with which national states have to come to terms. States still have national political space but it is more clearly and sharply constrained than in the past. States have to have a wary, if weary, eye on the wider, more global world, its dominant ideas and its big hitters. Sovereignty and autonomy still exist, but they are definitely constrained.

Political Challenges

The economic challenges to state sovereignty are perhaps the most obvious but there are also challenges to state sovereignty arising from political developments. At times, the line between economic and political challenges is blurred but it is worth setting out separately the challenges which are primarily political. Held and his colleagues speak of 'an extraordinary expansion' of international mechanisms to govern aspects of global affairs since the Second World War (Held *et al.*, 1999, p. 53) and argue that a very clear pattern has emerged of 'the internationalization of the institutions, practices and policy-making of the modern nation state' (ibid., p. 55). The political challenges to nation-state sovereignty are clear.

First, there is the challenge from regional bodies such as the European Union or the North American Free Trade Association. The EU is responsible for over 75 per cent of economic legislation across its member states and for 50 per cent of all domestic legislation (Giddens, 1998, p. 142). Leibfried and Pierson speak of European governments possessing 'diminished control' over many of the traditional aspects of welfare state policies (Leibfried and Pierson, 1995, pp. 73–4). The European Court of Justice is a body to which citizens of the member states can appeal on a wide range of issues to do with the legality of individual member governments' actions. Member states are bound to comply with the Court's rulings. As a result of Court rulings there has, for example, been a range of changes in British law in regard to sexual discrimination and equal pay (Holton, 1998, p. 89).

NAFTA was set up to eliminate tariff and non-tariff barriers between the USA, Canada and Mexico. It also places definite restrictions on the future development of public social protection. 'Indirectly, therefore', in Mishra's view, 'NAFTA's free trade and competition policies restrict the sovereignty and autonomy of member countries to choose their own social and economic policies' (Mishra, 1999, p. 13).

Second, national sovereignty is challenged by specific functional bodies such as the World Trade Organization and the North Atlantic Treaty Organization. Scholte speaks of the WTO as 'another striking growth of supra state governance' (Scholte, 1997a, p. 444) in that member states have to alter their national laws to make them conform with supranational trade laws agreed by the WTO. With regard to NATO, the Organization clearly imposes significant constraints on national military autonomy. It formalizes and institutionalizes the internationalization of security.

The International Monetary Fund and the World Bank can, and do, impose strict conditions on countries seeking loans or aid. The IMF's Structural Adjustment Programmes often amount to the imposition of particular economic and social policies on borrowing nations. Mishra sees such programmes as 'the supranational steering of social policy in a neoliberal direction' (Mishra, 1999, p. 124). Countries often have no effective choice as to whether or not they accept the 'solutions' held out to them whatever the likely costs to their citizens.

Third, there is an increasing slate of international conventions and protocols to which nation-states sign up and which then limit their policy options. For example, the Rio Earth Summit of 1992 established conventions on biodiversity and greenhouse gas emissions and developed a programme of action for future environmental behaviour by nation-states. The outcome was predictably less successful than the environmentalists had hoped but certain standards were established. There is now in place 'a significant if incomplete global institutionalisation of environmental protection' (Holton, 1998, p. 129) – global rather than merely national.

Fourth, in recent years there has been huge growth in international non-governmental organizations (NGOs) – voluntary bodies whose membership and concerns are truly international if not global.. There are reckoned to be some 5,000 such organizations, some of them with the resources and the standing to exert a real influence on national policy to the extent of modifying national sovereignty by the movement of international opinion – for example the Jubilee 2000 campaign for the cancellation of the debts of the poorest countries.

Fifth, globalization has also, almost paradoxically it might seem, encouraged the growth of local, regional and decentralized forms of government as particular regions or ethnic groupings struggle to preserve their identity and traditions in what they see as a globalizing and threateningly homogenizing world. There is a powerful movement in many European countries – the UK, France, Spain and Italy, for example – to create more devolved systems of government to counter the sense of democratic helplessness which globalization can induce. What this means is a loss or sharing of power by the central state as powers and responsibilities are transferred to lower levels of government.

What we are seeing, according to Paul Kennedy, is 'the relocation of authority upward and outward from the nation state' (Kennedy, 1994, p. 131) and he might also have added 'downward' to capture the decentralization which has been a parallel response to globalization and regionalization. Another depiction of what is happening is captured by Cox's phrase 'the internationalizing of the state' (Cox, 1997b, p. 253). Sovereignty is becoming in Keohane's view 'less a territorially defended barrier than a bargaining resource for a politics characterised by complex transnational networks' (quoted in Holton, 1998, p. 90). The national state is increasingly involved in what Cerny calls 'transgovernmental networks' (Cerny, 1997, p. 270) – networks which link the state with public, international non-governmental and private commercial bodies dealing with particular policy issues such as AIDS or aspects of the environment.

The result of these trends and tendencies is that nation states are coming to function 'less as "sovereign" entities and more as the components of an international "quasi polity"' (Hirst and Thompson, 1999, p. 257). Governance and regulation have become more multi layered. There are some gains from these trends. There is no hope, for example, of tackling the environmental problem or AIDS or problems of international migration without such developments. Equally, there are losses in the sense that states find it increasingly difficult to pursue policies which depart far from the neoliberal international policy norms, for example on tax or redistribution. Given the driving forces of globalization – capitalism and neoliberalism – it is social democratic approaches which get pushed into the shadows.

Even if the future of the state in a more global world is as part of a complex of interlinked bodies and powers, less obviously sovereign than in the past, it retains crucial roles. Yeates, for example, strongly emphasizes 'the resilience and continued relevance of the state' (Yeates, 2001, p. 93). States have the authority conferred by history, territorial location and democratic mandate. Only states can make the rules necessary for the development of the laws and institutions which adapt, modify and complement their re-negotiated authority. States have to use the sovereignty with which they are historically endowed to lay the basis for any new forms of global governance. This depends on them transferring some of that authority, willingly or less than willingly, to supranational bodies.

What has produced these political challenges to state sovereignty? One obvious answer is the general one 'global pressures'. The development of supranational bodies is, to an extent, a response to elements of globalization and then in turn gives its own push to the internationalization of political authority. The sense of the world as a smaller place – the global village syndrome – is another pressure. In a world of instant communication and easier travel, transnational institutions become a realistic possibility. When proliferating social problems, with no simply national solutions get firmly onto states' agendas, then another force for international, rather than national, action is in place.

Conclusion

Economic, financial, industrial and political changes interact with each other. It is hard to see what 'causes' what and to discern the precise pattern and implications of the interactions between them, but they clearly do all interact one with another. They are also a product, and part of, and forces for, the development of a new, more global frame of reference. Three interconnected processes illustrate this new, emerging and more global frame of reference.

First, there is the redefinition of certain social problems as global problems. The OECD talks of a 'growing internationalisation of many policy issues which were previously more domestic in nature' (OECD, 1997a, p. 36). Waters argues that such redefinition undermines the sovereignty of the state. It redirects individual political preferences away from the national state towards other organizations; it de-legitimizes the nation-state as a problem solver – if the nation-state cannot solve the problem it loses credibility; such a redefinition leads to the creation of new international organization to which nation-states surrender further elements of national sovereignty (Waters, 1995, p. 111).

Second, sovereignty is challenged by an increasing sense of what Falk describes as 'the porousness of state boundaries' (Falk, 1994, p. 475) By this he means a sense of the irrelevance of the national state and state boundaries to an increasing number of policy issues such as environmental degradation, drugs trafficking and financial flows. The national state seems less significant as a social and political space. Albrow talks of 'the deterritorialization of social life' (Albrow, 1996, p. 159) but the issue is actually broader. It is about the deterritorialization of economic and political life as well – with consequential effect on concepts of state sovereignty.

The third point follows closely and logically. As supranational bodies come to assume a larger role in people's lives as sources of law, courts of appeal, initiators of important policies, providers of services, so the national state becomes just one source of authority among others. Axford sees 'a frisson of global consciousness in the speeches of politicians' (Axford, 1995, p. 209). The human rights movement, the green movement, the women's movement all transcend national boundaries. Such movements hint at, and breathe, what Albrow describes as 'an incipient global citizenship' (Albrow, 1996, p. 144) which challenges and transcends traditional national citizenship and offers a broader perspective of cross cutting bonds which are transnational and even global.

What these three new perspectives feed is a novel sense of the limitations of the nation-state – its limitations as a self-contained unit and its limitations as a source of authority and a focus of loyalty. The nation-state becomes less dominant as a frame of reference. The global dimension increases in importance and, as it does so, this change of perspective is another dent in the sovereignty of the nation-state.

The central question posed by this chapter is whether globalization has affected the capacity of national states for independent action in the broad areas of economic, and social policy. And if it has constrained states' capacity for independent action, what is the nature and significance of those constraints.

Our view can be summarized in the following.

First, global economic developments – the increased mobility of finance capital, the increase in FDI, the growth of international trade, the expansion in the number and size of MNCs – have, and do, constrain national governments. Globalization does not, however, destroy all space for independent action by national governments. It does not compel nationally uniform responses. Nation-states can, and do, respond differently to the pressures which globalization imposes. The impact of globalization is mediated by history, politics and economics. States matter even in a more global world.

Second, national governments are constrained across the whole spectrum of domestic policy by the currently pervasive and dominant ideology of globalization – neoliberalism. This ideology shapes and conditions political debate and perceptions of political possibilities. More specifically, pressure to achieve the ever moving target of international competitiveness, and what that is believed to imply, have become central to the agendas of national states. But there is no reason to believe that globalization is inevitably and inherently neoliberal. There are alternative possibilities. As a long-term historical process, globalization has been accompanied by a variety of ideologies.

Third, globalization, in its many and varied aspects, compels national states to a broader view of the world at two levels. First, it has helped to create a more universal vision of human welfare and human rights which transcends national boundaries. Second, it has stimulated a perception of many key social problems as insoluble by national states acting independently but soluble only by international or supranational action. This is a powerful impetus to international rather than purely national responses and to the development of international institutions. It means a contraction of the effective sphere of autonomous state action and a corresponding erosion of the standing of the state.

Fourth, globalization establishes a new frame of reference for national policy-makers and nation-states. It brings a new psychology of politics. Even while thinking and acting locally and nationally, states have also to think and act globally – about international economic trends, about the stance of other national governments, about problems and issues which clearly transcend national boundaries and about the relative scope and possibilities of national and international problem solving capacity. In a shrinking, more interdependent world that is clearly a necessary and desirable development.

Fifth, if states are less mistresses in their own houses than in the past, this must have negative implications for democracy and the democratic rights of citizens. If global capital and MNCs are increasingly powerful influences on domestic economic and social policy then democracy loses out. Globalization does mean the emergence of what have come to be seen as 'democratic deficits'. Scholte, for example, concludes that there is a lack of mechanisms to ensure that post sovereign governance is democratic, participatory and accountable (Scholte, 2000, p. 7).

States matter in the protection and promotion of human welfare. They are key players. That is why the overall impact and implications of globalization on the potential of the state for independent action is so crucial to an exploration of the impact of globalization on quality of life. In the two chapters which follow, we move on to look in more detail at the impact of globalization on human welfare in advanced industrial and industrially developing countries.

Further Reading

Boyer, R. and Drache, D. (eds) (1996) *States Against Markets* (London, Routledge).

Cerny, P. (1997) 'Paradoxes of the Competition State: The Dynamics of Political Globalization', *Government and Opposition*, **32** (2), 251–74.

Holton, R.J. (1998) *Globalization and the Nation State* (Basingstoke, Macmillan).

3

Globalization and Human Welfare in Advanced Industrial Countries (AICs)

Our concern in this chapter is with the overall impact which globalization has had, and is having, on human welfare in advanced industrial societies. The chapter has two parts. First, we analyse the impact of globalization on a number of key social problems. Second, we explore its impact on social policies starting with a discussion of key general issues. Then we look at the impact on the heartland social policy areas, health, education and social security. We leave on one side the question of the impact globalization has had on economic growth, on culture and values and what that has meant for human welfare.

Our central concern is with the difficult question of the impact of globalization on welfare states. The question is complex for a variety of reasons – most obviously the multifaceted and contested nature of globalization, the sponginess of the concept of 'welfare state', and the other economic and social changes which have simultaneously been making an impact, for example ageing populations and changes in labour markets. Our basic position is that, to quote Daly, 'globalization creates general pressure points for policy in national settings' and 'while globalization may set up pressure points it does not predict outcomes in any one welfare state' (Daly, 2001, p. 83). National governments are crucial mediators of the effects of global pressures and particular features of welfare states render them more, or less, vulnerable to the pressures which accompany globalization.

There is considerable debate about the impact of globalization on state welfare provision. The best known position is that of those who see globalization as a powerfully constraining force. They argue their case on four main grounds.

First, because globalization gives financial capital and capital investors increased mobility, and because governments need investment, they are seen as constrained to pursue policies which will be attractive to capital. This restricts and restrains welfare spending.

Second, it makes capital international rather than national in its orientation. When national economies were relatively closed, redistribution by way of social security systems both helped to secure the support of the workers – which capital needed – and helped to avoid crises of under consumption. In a more globalized economy, capital has less need to secure workers' support because it has other location options and re-distributive policies do not necessarily feed through into increased demand for domestically produced goods.

Third, contemporary global capital is fuelled by, and propagates, a particular ideology – neoliberalism – hostile to public expenditure and state welfare and mediated through powerful international bodies.

Fourth, globalization has led to the creation of the competition state – a state whose primary concern is with international competitiveness rather than with social welfare, social justice or social rights.

In contrast to those who stress the negative impact, there are those who emphasize various positive links between globalization and the development of state welfare arguing that a more open, liberalized international economy requires a significant role for the state in social policy, that state welfare can contribute positively to globalization and that globalization can be a stimulus to social policy development.

Rodrik, for example, stresses the need for the state to counter, and compensate for, the disruptive impact of globalization on, for example, employment and domestic stability. His fear is that if the state abandons any attempt to safeguard the position of the casualties of globalization there will be a backlash against the liberalization of the world economy. He therefore sees globalization as requiring improved social protection and active education and labour market policies if states are to be economically competitive (Rodrik, 1997). Hirst, Ruggie and Garrett take the same view (Ruggie, 1994; Hirst, 1994; Garrett, 1998b). From a rather different perspective, Rieger and Leibfried argue that the development of income maintenance programmes has been a key factor in facilitating the move from protectionist policies to free trade – a central element in the globalization process (Rieger and Leibfried, 1998). Guillen and Alvarez point out a different kind of positive link, arguing that globalization exerted positive catching up type pressures in Southern European welfare states as they sought to join the EU (Guillen and Alvarez, 2001, p. 206).

In addition to these two groups, there are those who see changes in the global economy as simply one of various forces putting pressure on welfare states – and by no means obviously the most important, Pierson expresses this position very clearly. 'Changes in the global economy are important', he writes, 'but it is primarily social and economic transformations occurring within affluent democracies which produce pressures on mature welfare states' (Pierson, 1998a, pp. 539–40). These transformations are, for him, embodied in a 'triple transformation' – slower growth associated with the shift from manufacturing to service employment, the maturation and growth to limits of government commitments, and the ageing of populations and although globalization accompanied, accentuated and modified these pressures on welfare states 'it is the triple transition itself that has made the difference (ibid., p. 541).

Globalization and Social Problems

Central to a consideration of the impact of globalization on human welfare is an analysis of its impact on social problems – what Beck characterizes as 'the new globality of hazards' (Beck, 1997, p. 5). The answer has to be 'mixed'. Barber neatly captures a central element in what has happened. 'In globalizing private rather than public goods', he writes, 'we have managed, however inadvertently, to globalize many of our vices and almost none of our virtues' (Barber, 2000, p. 281) Globalization creates and exacerbates some social problems in AICs, for example, crime and unemployment. On the other hand, it helps create the resources, the policy networks, the international institutions and agreements which have the potential to provide solutions – for example, watershed type occasions like the UN Conference on the Human Environment in Stockholm in 1972 with its declaration of key principles, its Action Plan, its establishment of global and regional environment monitoring networks, and the creation of the UN Environment Programme.

We explore six social problem areas looking briefly at the size, nature and the significance of the issue and its relationship to globalization. We say nothing about gender relations or migration and immigration becaue they are dealt with in detail in chapters 5 and 6.

Work and Unemployment

One of the central issues in the analysis of the implications of globalization for human welfare is its impact on labour and employment. Does globalization contribute to a weakening of a commitment to full employment? Does the increase in world trade, and more particularly in trade with developing countries, cause unemployment in the advanced industrial economies? Or is the root cause technology rather than trade? Is a more mobile capitalism responsible for deteriorating conditions of work as nations 'race to the bottom' in an effort to increase their appeal to global investors? We explore the impact of globalization on labour and employment under four headings.

First, there is the impact on the balance of power between capital and labour. Boyer and Drache's conclusion is that the collective bargaining power of labour has weakened significantly in all industrial countries (Boyer and

Drache, 1996, p. 16). What part, if any, has globalization played in the change? Certainly, the end of traditional full employment, to which globalization has contributed, has weakened the bargaining power of labour. Capitalism's increased locational freedom in a more global world has increased its power. For example, German firms such as Daimler-Benz, Bosch and BMW, as well as multinationals such as Ford and GM Europe, have increasingly used locational threats to weaken Trade Union power and extract concessions (Rhodes and Apeldoorn, 1998, p. 417).

Globalization and the developments which it brought in its train have been a factor in the massive drop in trade union membership so weakening organised labour. In the United States, for example, union membership fell from 35 million to 15 million between the mid 1970s and the mid 1990s (Fox Piven, 1995, p. 111).

The increased mobility of financial capital has also weakened the power of labour. The risk of losing credibility with the financial markets, and so precipitating an outflow of capital, has been used by governments to counter demands for improved benefits.

Second, there is the charge that globalization has contributed to the collapse of social partnership. Labour and capital have to establish a *modus vivendi*. At one level, their relationship is one of inevitable hostility and conflict. At another level, however, their interests are complementary. Capital needs labour and labour needs capital. Sweden offers a good example of what has happened. The famous 1938 Saltsjobaden Agreement depended on the fundamentally national nature of Swedish capital. From the late 1980s, however, the Swedish economy began to internationalize. In Wilks's view, the massive outflows of Swedish capital in the late 1980s 'served to shatter the terms of the class compromise' (Wilks, 1996, p. 107). Why did this happen? 'Ultimately the Swedish model failed because it was rejected by a domestic industry which needed – or wanted – to develop more flexible production and investment strategies in a globalized economic system' (ibid., p. 108). The same trends are clearly present in Germany — a historic national consensus culture being weakened by globalization (Martin and Schumans, 1997, p. 130).

Three forces are at work undermining corporatist approaches – the weakening of labour, the international competitive pressures on capital, capital's ability to move investment elsewhere. The forces are reinforced by neoliberal ideology but globalization of the economy is clearly a powerful force for change.

As historic partnerships collapse, new forms of economic and social partnership seem to be developing. Rhodes describes new forms of "social pacts" coming into being in a range of European countries whose central concern is to improve productivity and competitiveness without straining the social bond to destruction. He describes what is emerging as "competitive corporatism" – pragmatic and productivity oriented but giving much less emphasis to the redistributive aims of traditional corporatism (Rhodes, 1998).

Third, globalization is accused of leading to deteriorating terms and conditions of work. Scholte's judgement is that 'Across most of the world pressures of global capitalism have brought a major deterioration in working conditions' (Scholte, 1996, p. 53). Standing's verdict is that 'in the past decade or so, income insecurity has become pervasive in industrialised countries' (Standing, 1999a, p. 289). The pattern is widespread – deregulation of labour markets, more use of temporary, short-term contracts, more use of part time and shift work, the proliferation of low paid jobs, the tightening of conditions for receipt of social benefits and reductions in their real value.

There are several possible explanations for the deterioration unconnected with globalization. Technology has reduced the demand for unskilled labour. The growth of a service economy has led to a proliferation of low paid semicasual work. But explanations in terms of globalization remain powerful.

Fourth, there is the impact on employment and unemployment. The late 1990s produced what Dicken described as 'a truly desperate crisis of the global state' with 34 million workers unemployed and 15 million workers in involuntary part-time employment in the industrial world. (Dicken, 1998, p. 430). There are also large numbers of workers whose early retirement conceals the shortage of employment.

There are several explanations for the crisis – overlapping, but illustrating different facets of the globalization process. Clearly the growth of international trade, and particularly the growth of trade in manufactured goods and more particularly still the growth of imports of manufactured goods from the developing world, has been a factor. Newly industrialising countries' share of world manufacturing output grew from 5 per cent in 1953 to 20 per cent in 1994. In the G7 countries, imports represented 1 per cent of all manufactured goods consumed in the late 1960s but 10 per cent by 1995 (Navarro, 1998, p. 627). What this has meant for employment and unemployment is disputed but Wade, for example, estimates that exports from the South to the North were responsible for around half of the fall in the share of manufacturing in total employment between the late 1960s and the late 1980s (Wade, 1996, p. 76). Other commentators see trade and investment flows as much less significant – in Lee's words as 'only minor explanatory factors' (Lee, 1996, p. 487).

Technological developments have meant that machines have replaced people for a range of tasks. Historically, new kinds of unskilled work have always eventually emerged to fill this employment gap but that benevolent corrective mechanism no longer seems to function as effectively as in the past. Technology seems like a factor distinct from globalization but the two factors, in fact, mesh together. Globalization ensures the rapid spread of technological innovation and, by the competitiveness which it stimulates, it pressurizes firms to a restless search for new techniques and products.

The global drive for competitiveness is also a factor in the employment problem. Elements in German and Swedish industry relocated in the 1980s and 1990s in an effort to reduce costs. In 1993, Arthuis reckoned that over a million jobs in France were at risk from the delocalization of firms in electronics, footwear and clothing to Asia and Central Europe in search of cheaper labour (quoted in Bonoli, *et al.*, 2000, p. 59). The key factor is that the market for unskilled labour has become much more international. Lower cost labour in Asia, or in central Europe, can, more easily than in the past, displace more expensive labour in advanced industrial economies.

The development of a highly mobile, rootless financial capital, and the diversion of capital from productive investment to speculation on the world's money markets, has produced a shortage of capital for investment – something which Watson sees as at the heart of the inability of Western labour markets to provide adequate levels of stable, high quality employment (Watson, 1999, p. 60). The problem has been compounded by the state's forced retreat from key past policy approaches to employment – Keynesian techniques of demand management, the state's assumption of responsibility as employer of last resort – an approach used particularly in the Scandinavian countries – and the making available of capital at preferential rates of interest by governments to national firms. As Gray puts it, 'Bond markets have knocked away the floor from under post-war employment policies' (Gray, 1998, p. 92).

Fifth, there is the effect of globalization on wages and inequality. Mishra argues that 'globalization seems to be acting as a strong force in favour of inequality of income and wealth distribution' (Mishra, 1999, p. 100). The pattern is, however, not a uniform one. In the United States, inequality increased sharply between the 1970s and the 1990s. In the early 1970s, households in the top 5 per cent of income earners earned ten times more than the bottom 5 per cent. By the mid 1990s they earned fifteen times as much (Kapstein, 1996b, p. 22). There has been a similar pattern in the UK. Wage inequality rose sharply from the late 1970s to the late 1980s but slowed down in the 1990s. In the 1980s, when inequalities were increasing most rapidly, real earnings for the top 10 per cent of male earners increased by just over 50 per cent while the earnings of the bottom 10 per cent increased by just over 10 per cent (Anderson and Brenton, 1998, p. 147). The increases in inequality were certainly widespread and particularly marked in the UK, the USA and Italy, but in France and Germany there was no such general increase (Hirst and Thompson, 1999, Table 4.3).

The main focus of the debate as to why inequalities have increased is between explanations in terms of trade and explanations in terms of technology. The consensus among economists is that trade accounts for only a small element of rising inequality (e.g., Krugman, 1995). The ILO view is that international trade has made a contribution to increasing inequality but it has not played a major role in pushing down the relative wage of less skilled workers (quoted in Dicken, 1998, p. 439). Adrian Wood is the main protagonist of the view that the expansion of trade with industrially developing countries has been the main cause of the deteriorating position of unskilled workers in industrial economies (Wood, 1995, p. 57; see also Wood, 1994).

The most obvious weakness in the argument that trade has been the key factor is its relatively small scale. As Lawrence puts it, 'to point only to trade with developing countries as the source of workers' problems is to wag a very large dog with a rather small tail' (Lawrence, 1996, p. 171). A balanced overall judgement would be that trade probably contributed only some 20 per cent of the increasing inequality of the 1980s.

Health

There are clear links between globalization and improved health care. Globalization stimulates the sense of health as a global good, a common resource. It therefore creates a new – or at least a clearer – logic of collective action because of the indivisible nature of health in a global world. Globalization also means that when a new and effective drug has been developed it will almost immediately become universally available in AICs. National frontiers are unimportant.

On the other hand, globalization exacerbates some health problems. For example, it creates a global market in trained healthcare staff – nearly a third of UK doctors were not born in the UK – and this can denude the health systems of IDCs of crucial and expensively trained staff. Increased population movement increases the spread of disease. The result is that when new diseases such as AIDS, or new strains of TB resistant to a whole range of drugs appear, they can soon spread world-wide.

Globalization can also be linked in more subtle ways to the spread of diseases. The spread of AIDS, for example, is clearly linked to the movement of population, to the increase in migrant labour, to increased international tourism, to rapid urbanization and the straining of the bonds of family and informal control. Disintegrating social structures and anomic social and sexual relations will speed up the spread of AIDS (Lee and Zui, 1996, pp. 359–60).

Globalization also facilitates the spread of health-destructive products. The tobacco industry has been immeasurably strengthened by globalization. Its poisonous products gain an international cachet and acceptability because of the sheer scale of the industry and the power over national governments which follows. The soft drinks and fast food industries have also been globalized with an expanded threat to the health of AICs, as well as IDCs.

Environment

Many commentators see the current global environmental problem as a direct result of globalization because globalization is the vehicle of an expanding industrial capitalism and the economic expansion which is the goal of that capitalism is a key factor in the worsening environmental problem. Economic growth leads to increased car and energy use with serious implications for pollution and for global warming. At the same time, globalization makes effective action to protect the environment less likely – for two main reasons.

First, the globalization of economic activity conceals damage to the environment and ecological limits to growth. It does this by separating the costs and benefits of environmental exploitation. As distanced consumers, we can enjoy the benefits of the product without ever seeing the costs we are imposing on the eco-system because the costs are often many thousands of miles away. On the other hand, in a non or pre global world, 'restricted trade keeps the consequence of our actions close to home, where we have both the community of interest and the political tools to manage them' (Goodstein, 1998, p. 136).

Second, sharpened international economic competition inhibits the development of improved environmental protection. There is no clear evidence that environmental regulations have a negative impact on investment decisions and competitiveness (e.g., Zarsky, 1997, p. 31; Jones, 1998, p. 20; UNDP, 1999, p. 86) but governments are risk-averse creatures and intensified international economic competition puts pressure on governments, irrespective of the research evidence, not to risk domestic competitiveness by imposing new environmental regulations or tightening existing ones. Chung and Gillespie do not think, however, that 'a race to the bottom' is likely. In their view 'A more likely scenario ... is that globalization will discourage unilateral environmental initiatives and force a convergence around existing environmental standards' (Chung and Gillespie, 1998, p. 13). This is a view shared by Zarsky. In his view, heightened competition for global markets causes environmental policy to be 'stuck in the mud' (Zarsky, 1997, p. 27) rather than developing in the light of experience and increasing need.

Globalization can, and does, exacerbate environmental problems. On the other hand, the environmental issue is a key one in the stumbling forward march of the evolution of global institutions. This is because it is very clear that national regulation provides no guarantee of effective environmental protection. Such protection has to transcend national boundaries if it is to be effective. So the environmental problem becomes a force for supranational government and global institutional development. As Paterson puts it, globalization can contain the seeds of a 'counter globalization' as local environmental incidents become international crises (Paterson, 1999, p. 139).

Social Order

There is considerable concern about the impact of globalization on social order, broadly defined, and on the nature of civil society. The Human Development Report 1999 spoke of globalization 'integrating economy, culture and governance but fragmenting societies' (UNDP, 1999, p. 43). Cox talks of 'the widespread but uneven tendency towards the decomposition of civil society' (Cox, 1997a, p. 27). In a recent OECD report, Michalski *et al.*, argue that 'Problems of social exclusion and a growing sense of insecurity are manifest in virtually all OECD countries' (Michalski *et al.*, 1997, p. 8).

Castells links the abuse of children, broadly defined, directly with economic globalization and the social and accompanying moral dislocation which it brings in its train. What is different in globalization, he argues 'is the disintegration of traditional societies throughout the world exposing children to the unprotected lands of mega city slums. What is different is children in Pakistan weaving carpets for world wide export via networks of suppliers to large department stores in affluent markets. What is new is mass global tourism organized around paedophilia. What is new is electronic child pornography on the Net world-wide. What is new is the disintegration of patriarchalism without being replaced by systems of protection of children provided either by new families or the state. What is new is the weakening of institutions of support for children's rights such as labour unions or the politics of social reform' (quoted in Barber, 2000, p. 282).

Globalization threatens social order by the way pressures for competitiveness and so for more flexible labour markets increase insecurity. Increasing inequality and higher unemployment strain social bonds. Globalization puts traditional family and community structures and relations under strain as patterns of work, living and gender relations change. The constraints on governments' ability to raise taxes or increase social security contributions restrict the ability of governments to respond creatively to these issues. National governments' seeming inability to solve, or ameliorate, these problems leads in turn to a weakening of faith in the potential of state action to support or reconstruct society. Finally, in the competitive state, the unproductive come to be regarded as a burden and providing for them is defined as a threat to national competitiveness so weakening the sense of collective responsibility.

Crime

Globalization has clearly contributed to an increase in international, cross-border crime and facilitated the growth of international criminal networks. In fact, there is a two way connection. As de Maillard puts it, 'The real pioneers of globalisation were the drugs traffickers of the 1960s trading inter-continentally in the world's most expensive goods' (*Le Monde Diplomatique*, April 2000). Shelley sees the growth of transnational illegal activity as 'largely due to the increasingly international scope of legitimate business' (Shelley, 1995, p. 465), to increases in air travel, technological innovations in communications and increases in world trade. 'Increasingly what drives organized crime groups', say Mittelman and Johnston, 'are efforts to exploit the growth mechanisms of globalization' (Mittelman and Johnston, 1999, p. 109).

What is the scale of organized global crime? Obviously, all that is available is estimates but its range and scale are clearly huge and most experts agree that it is a growth area. Susan Strange estimates that the heroin market increased twenty-fold and the cocaine market fifty-fold between the mid 1970s and the mid 1990s (Strange, 1996, p. 114). Brie estimates the annual profits from drug trafficking to be between $300 billion and $500 billion – some 8–10 per cent of world trade. Computer piracy is reckoned to be worth some $200 billion, counterfeit goods $100 billion. (*Le Monde Diplomatique*, April 2000). Illegal migrant trafficking – estimated to move 4 million people a year – was reckoned to be worth $9.5 billion per year in the mid 1990s and is certainly worth much more now than then (Williams, 1999, p. 224). The international trade in stolen, looted and smuggled art is estimated to be worth around $5 billion per year as is the illegal trade in animals (Williams, 1999, Ch. 9). The annual global value of criminal activities is estimated at $1.5 trillion (UNDP, 1999, p. 5) – more than 20 per cent of world trade.

What is the significance of the growth of globally organized crime? First, it is the dark side of globalization bringing fear, misery and exploitation to many – and huge profits to a few. Second, it is a sharp challenge to the established national institutions for maintaining law and order. National police systems, with a thin international presence superimposed upon them, are clearly unable to match the illegal systems which have developed. Third, Strange couples organized criminal gangs with MNCs in the way that 'their authority in world society and in world economy rivals and encroaches upon that of governments' (Strange, 1996, p. 110). Shelley's verdict is that transnational organized crime is not yet a threat to the nation state but failure to develop coordinated national policies in the face of ever growing transnational criminal activity 'may undermine the nation state in the 21st century' (Shelley, 1995, p. 463) through exposing the nation state's inability to enforce the law and supplanting the nation state as the ultimate source of authority and authoritative social values. Fourth, international crime is a potentially powerful corrupting influence on states and on state officials – customs officers, immigration officers, the police, tax inspectors (Mittelman and Johnston, 1999, p. 110). Organized crime syndicates have the power and the resources to create networks of corruption within states to facilitate their activities. Open and honest administration comes under serious threat.

Conclusion

Exhibit 3.1

The pressures globalization puts on national economic and social systems

- It is clearly a factor in the increased unemployment in AICs and in increased economic inequality.

- It exacerbates some health problems while ameliorating others.

- By the pressures for economic growth which it generates, and by the way it can distance consumers from the environmental consequences of their actions, it exacerbates environmental problems.

- In a variety of ways it fragments and fractures some of the ligatures which bind together civil society and function to maintain social order.

- As it facilitates the growth of legal international trade, so it also facilitates trade in illegal commodities and fosters a global criminal underworld.

- The exacerbation of social problems is not, of course, the whole story. There is another side to the story which stresses increased geographical mobility, increased consumer choice, the world-wide availability of life saving drugs, the internationalization of higher education, etc.

Globalization and Social Policies

Globalization has had both general and more specific implications for social policy. We look first at what we see as six of the powerful general pressures which globalization has exerted. Then we look at its more specific impact on three core areas of social policy – health, education and social security.

Ideology

Contemporary globalization expresses, promotes and legitimates a particular ideology – neoliberalism – which has had and has a profound effect on social policies. It propagates hostility to public expenditure, to public borrowing, to taxation and to collective provision of public services. It promotes a belief in private provision of services as inherently superior to public provision and in competition as the way to efficiency. It emphasizes individual responsibilities rather than social rights and argues that collective meeting of needs can be socially damaging. 'No state', says Scholte, 'has escaped the downward pressure of neoliberal globalization on government guarantees of material welfare' (Scholte, 2000, p. 141). Contemporary globalization has established neoliberalism as the dominant international belief system within which debates about the provision of public services take place. Yeates sees the 'constraints' placed on social policy development by globalization as 'primarily ideological' and powerfully mediated by key international organizations such as the IMF, the World Trade Organization and the World Bank (Yeates, 1999, p. 389 and p. 382). Yet there is no reason to believe that globalization and neoliberalism are inextricably linked. Globalization has coexisted with other ideologies and the high tide of neoliberalism seems to have passed.

Resources

The capacity to raise revenue to pursue collective welfare goals is central to the traditional role of the state in welfare in AICs. Globalization has constrained that capacity and this has been an important limitation on social policy development.

If we look at trends in taxes and social security contributions in OECD countries, their share as a proportion of GDP rose steeply in most countries between 1970 and the mid 1980s from an average of rather less than 32 per cent of GDP to more than 38 per cent. The tax take then increased only marginally over the years till 1997 when it was just under 40 per cent (Scharpf, 2000, p. 199).

If we look at levels of direct taxation, there have been widespread reductions in the highest marginal rates of tax. In 1980, the average top rate in the EC was 63.5 per cent. By 1992 it had been reduced to 50.5 per cent. Almost all EC countries cut their top rates, some very sharply. Other AICs followed the same path – for example, Austria, Canada, Japan, Sweden, USA (Owens, 1993, p. 30). In the OECD the average top rate of income tax fell from 59 per cent in 1975 to 42 per cent in 1995 (Standing, 1999a, p. 287). The OECD's conclusion in 1999 was that lowering top rates of income tax, along with broadening the tax base was 'the defining characteristic of personal income tax reforms since the mid 1980s' (OECD, 1999a, p. 39).

Cuts in the highest rates of income tax were accompanied by cuts in corporation tax. In the OECD, the average rate fell from 43 per cent in 1986 to 33 per cent in the mid 1990s (Standing, 1999a, p. 287). In Germany, the contribution of corporate taxation to total tax revenue more than halved in the 1980s and 1990s – a change justified with reference to globalization and the need for increased competitiveness (Daly, 2001, pp. 89–99).

The biggest change in the structure of taxation in OECD countries between 1965 and 1995 was the increasing role of social security contributions – from 18 per cent to 25 per cent of total tax receipts (OECD, 1997b, p. 16) – and the move to raise a larger proportion of revenue from indirect taxation. In some countries, Germany for example, there were efforts to shift the cost of social security from employers to employees. This increase in the burden of taxes to labour – the labour tax wedge – increased between 1979 and the mid 1990s in fifteen out of the twenty two countries for which there was full information available. This was a matter of great concern to the OECD which saw labour taxation as contributing to unemployment. (OECD, 1999a, pp. 39–40; OECD, 1995a, p. 97).

What has been the role of globalization in these taxation trends? As we have emphasized, globalization has been accompanied by, and has promoted, a particular neoliberal ideology which has generated a negative approach towards taxation. Clearly this has affected the stance of governments of all political complexions. This is a key factor, although certainly not the only one, in the stagnation of tax revenues from the mid 1980s. There were other factors too – higher levels of unemployment, a declining faith in the capacity of governments to spend efficiently and effectively leading to a so called tax revolt, for example, but the influence of global neoliberalism was very important.

Two aspects of globalization come together in the measures taken in many countries to reduce the top rates of income tax. Then first was the increased mobility of the very highest paid, highest skilled members of the labour force and the fear that high rates of taxation in one country would encourage them to look elsewhere for employment to the detriment of the national economy. The other factor was the neoliberal view that high rates of taxation are a disincentive, rather than an incentive, to effort. Cuts in corporate taxation were part of the global competition to attract international and highly mobile business investment – and the belief that lower rates of corporate taxation were a way to achieve this. Swank points out the absence of hard empirical evidence for this belief (Swank, 1998, p. 672) but this did not prevent it being influential.

Globalization has created an economic and political climate in which national states become more conscious of the taxes they levy and their potential economic implications. Neoliberal ideology feeds and justifies these concerns. It makes its influence felt through the reports of key global bodies such as the OECD. *A Caring World*, for example, sets out the OECD worries about labour taxation (OECD, 1999a, p. 39). In general, the OECD's stance is in favour of globalization. But in 1995 it noted the 'risk' that current levels of capital taxation could not be maintained because of the way in which competition for internationally mobile investment pushed tax rates downward and the problems which this could cause for government revenues (OECD, 1995a, p. 97). On balance, however, the OECD verdict was that 'globalization has had a positive effect on the development of tax systems' (OECD, 1998, p. 14).

Garrett points out another possible downside of globalization for tax policy – the way it increases the problems of tax collection. He writes of income-based tax evasion as 'a significant problem in the global economy' because it is harder for governments to identify and tax individual and corporate income (Garrett, 1998a, p. 159). He sees this problem as pushing governments towards taxes on consumption as less open to evasion. There are also major problems in extracting appropriate taxation from MNCs, a matter which has become a significant concern for the US and the Australian governments (Mishra, 1999, p. 44).

What are the implications of globalization for the tax system? The OECD view is very plain. 'There is little prospect of increasing taxes: the capital tax base is at risk of erosion through globalization, and increased labour taxes may harm employment especially of low skilled workers' (OECD, 1999a, p. 37) Globalization constrains nations' capacity to tax because of the increased mobility of capital which it generates and encourages. In addition, it limits the potential of raising revenue through levies on labour because of the more fragile employment prospects of the less skilled in a global economy. As one OECD report puts it, 'The potential for compensating globalization's losers through an extended social policy are limited ... because international competition restricts the power of governments to raise taxes for financing such policies' (OECD, 1999b, p. 128). Such a judgement is interesting but in our view it exaggerates the problems faced by nation-states.

Management

The so-called New Public Management (NPM) is seen by many as both a product and an illustration of globalization. Whether there are indeed global patterns and trends in public sector management is important to an assessment of the impact of globalization on public services and so on human welfare.

NPM is a break with traditional bureaucratic forms of management. It is about the introduction of private sector approaches with a strong emphasis on management skills and techniques. There is a robust emphasis on outputs and outcomes in contrast to the greater concern in traditional public administration with inputs and processes. NPM is also committed to competition as a way of improving effectiveness and efficiency. Staff will be hired on short term contracts with performance related pay. Public bodies will have to compete for tenders with private and voluntary organizations.

Commentators are divided as to whether these changes constitute a paradigm shift in the governance of the public sector. In 1995, the OECD, for example, judged that in OECD countries, at least 'the fundamental, comprehensive nature of the change represents a move to a new order' (OECD, 1995b, p. 27). In contrast, Hood's most recent verdict is that 'Public management convergence in vocabulary seems hard to deny. More problematic is what may be happening 'underneath' the shared catch phrases' (Hood, 1998, pp. 203–4). Flynn and Strehl's conclusion was that 'European cultural, political and economic diversity will continue to be reflected in public sector management' (Flynn and Strehl, 1996, p. 271).

New global paradigm or not, NPM has clearly had an impact on the provision of state social services.

Exhibit 3.2

The impact of NPM

● NPM has brought different values into public social service provision – aptly captured by the adoption of the term 'customers' for service users.

● NPM brings, and means, a much more critical approach to social service provision.

● NPM poses sharp questions about aims, costs and outcomes and asks whether value for money is being achieved.

● NPM raises questions about how goods and services can be provided most efficiently and effectively. The most obvious change which it has brought has been the initiation of competition between would be service providers.

● A more plural, competitive system of welfare, which follows from NPM doubts about monopoly public provision, leads to the rise of the regulatory state. A central state function comes to be the regulation of providers rather than the organization of actual service provision.

● NPM has ambivalent implications for the future role of the state in welfare. In one sense, NPM can function to protect the state and its core welfare role by helping it to come to terms with globalization and the competition state and by pre-empting charges of inefficiency and ineffectiveness. What is created, in Dunleavy's words, is 'a "proto" market in the public services' (Dunleavy, 1994, p. 36). To move on to full scale marketization has, however, been made much easier by NPM.

NPM is an aspect of globalizing movements, trends and forces. It expresses a global – and globalizing – ideology. It exerts pressure on states to converge on a particular model of lean, competitive and market oriented activity. Its values and techniques have been widely influential in many areas of social welfare provision. To speak of a new global paradigm is, however, to exaggerate the uniformity and coherence of state responses. But there can be no doubt that, mediated through NPM, globalization has made a significant impact on the state as provider of social services.

The Competition State

At the heart of the impact of globalization on state social welfare is the new priority it has given to competitiveness – defined in a particular way. 'Nation states in an increasingly competitive global world', says Gough, 'must accept performance competitiveness as a constraint on the pursuit of other goals' (Gough, 1996, p. 215). In the days when economies were more national, competitiveness was much less of an issue. Labour rights and non-wage labour costs were not seen as factors affecting national competitiveness (Standing, 1999a, p. 56). Greater economic interdependence has generated what Rhodes calls a 'competitive imperative' (Rhodes, 1997, p. 68). Cerny argues that the welfare state has been replaced by what he calls 'the competition state' (Cerny, 1997, p. 251). A new relation is forged between economic and social policy. Social policy is less concerned with civilizing and softening the outcomes of the free market and more with sustaining and sharpening competitiveness.

Globalization of Approaches

Globalization has meant that social policies are shaped by new global frames of reference which become a significant influence on policy development. Expectations in one country are shaped by knowledge of the situation elsewhere. Globalization means new yardsticks of comparison and so new pressures on governments. National variations in expenditure, or in other key input or output indices, become counters in domestic political debate – as did levels of health expenditure in the UK compared with EU levels in early 2000.

Globalization has also led to the growth of global policy networks, for example in health, education and New Public Management, which facilitate the development of new frames of reference and contribute to the internationalizing of the structures and patterns of policy making and to policy borrowing. Policy making can also be internationalized 'when international or supranational actors penetrate the policy-making systems of individual nations' (Moran and Wood, 1996, p. 126) as they do more frequently in a more global world. These actors might be individuals or international bodies such as the WHO or the World Bank.

Globalization of Ideas of Rights

The idea of citizens having rights which it is the duty of the state to provide for has been a strong influence on the development of state welfare. Globalization has helped to universalize such 'rights talk'. Developing ideas of rights have been a strong pressure, for example, for the further development of social security systems – rights to a minimum of civilized life, rights to appropriate benefits for people with disabilities, rights to maternity and paternity benefits, rights to a level of benefits which avoids social exclusion. Comparison of the rights which particular categories of claimants enjoy in other countries can also be used by pressure groups and new social movements to argue the case for new and improved benefits.

The last two decades have seen a re-assertion of the rights of patients in health care systems in many countries. Moran speaks of 'the development of more assertive, less deferential and more demanding patient-consumers' (Moran, 1999, p. 90). Freeman writes of a 'cultural shift...from the idea of the passive patient to one of the active health care client' (Freeman, 2000, p. 104). The same trends are apparent in education and in debates about the rights of asylum seekers which we discuss in Chapter 6. Globalization has contributed to the diffusion of these ideas.

More Specific Impacts

Our discussion of the impact of globalization on health, education and social security policy falls into three main sections. First, we explore the ways in which globalization has influenced policy. Second, we explore the globalization of agendas and policies. Finally, we analyse the significance of globalization for policy in each policy area.

Health

The ideology driving globalization exerts a powerful influence on health policy. It shapes the whole intellectual and political context in which discussion takes place. There is the fundamental hostility to public expenditure, the dislike of public provision of services as leading to inefficiency and inducing dependency, stress on value for money, economy, efficiency and effectiveness. Berlinguer links the decline in the standing of the WHO and the shifting of influence in health policy to the World Bank and the IMF with the process of globalization (Berlinguer, 1999, p. 584).

The influence of globalization

The discovery of the USA in the late fifteenth century meant, says Berlinguer, the 'microbial unification' of the world (Berlinguer, 1999, p. 582). It began the globalization of infections and so of shared concerns among nations about key infectious diseases. This concern was, of course, sharpened as travel became easier, quicker and cheaper. In the 1980s, there was a growing sense of the global nature of emerging health problems and the need for global action. The spread of AIDS was the sharpest example but other health issues also came to be seen in more global terms. A good example is the WHO report *1997 Tobacco or Health: Global Status Report* (WHO, 1997) which brought together information from 190 countries on the tobacco epidemic. Growing recognition of the significance of damage to the environment and the international nature of the issues of air pollution and global warming fostered a sense of the global nature of health problems and health policy. This microbial unification was matched in the late twentieth century by a scientific and technological unification which made new medical discoveries and new forms of treatment accessible – in theory at least – to anyone in the world as they became available.

The global emergence of the so-called 'competition state' obviously affected healthcare. In the years between 1960 and 1997 expenditure on healthcare in the OECD more than doubled as a percentage of a vastly increased GDP. Health expenditure also increased significantly as a percentage of overall government expenditure in most countries – in the USA from 4.5 to 18.6 per cent, in the UK from 9.9 to 13.4 per cent, in Canada from 7.25 to 14.1 per cent. In a word, health expenditure by the state became economically and politically much more significant and has reached a point where it can affect 'even the competitiveness of nations' (Moran, 1999, p. 7). High rates of health expenditure could easily be defined by international financial markets as threatening competitiveness and so lead to constraints and downward pressure on health expenditure.

Globalization has also contributed to the development and growth of a global healthcare industry. It has created world markets for health products as it has for other goods. This in turn has encouraged the commercialization of health care and the selling of drugs, medical equipment, services and consultancy. The result of these trends is 'to increase the extent to which all aspects of the healthcare system are considered resources in the struggle for share in world markets' (Moran, 1999, p. 161). The industrialization/commercialization of health products mediated by globalization has given the USA a dominant role both in the pharmaceutical market – a 30 per cent share – and in the global production of medical devices – 60 per cent of the world market (ibid., p. 138). This in turn helps the international promotion of US innovations in healthcare policy — for example, internal markets.

The globalization of agendas

It is possible to pick out a number of issues and areas where globalization has exerted a clear influence on health policy agendas in AICs.

First, globalization has contributed to the universal concern with cost containment and control which has been, perhaps, the central feature of health policy in AICs in the last two decades. The end of the long boom and the reduction in forecasts of future economic growth were crucial elements in this concern. So was the pressure arising from new treatments and ageing populations. But globalization was also a factor, for example, in the contribution it made to the readier availability of data showing comparative expenditure and in the emergence of the competition state. It also facilitated the spread of knowledge about different techniques and policies for cost control.

Second, globalization, and the ideology which underpinned it, has promoted a global re-assessment of the roles of states and markets in the provision of healthcare. 'Managed competition' became a central theme in healthcare reform. The separation between purchasers and providers was introduced in the UK, New Zealand and Sweden (OECD, 1994, p. 48). Several countries moved towards a contract model of care to try to reduce costs through competition (ibid., p. 50). There was a globalized faith in market mechanisms.

Third, the debate about rationing and priority setting has become a global debate fuelled by pressure on services, a desire to contain costs and the questions raised by the new public management and neoliberal ideology. In some countries – the Netherlands, Norway and Sweden, New Zealand and the UK – there have been attempts to work out principles to determine which health services should be seen as priority services to be available to all (Ham and Honigsbaum, 1998, Ch. 4). But all countries wrestle implicitly or explicitly with the same problems.

Fourth, the issue of the government of the medical profession has become a matter of international debate. Doctors, of course, decide who needs treatment and what sort of treatment. Historically they have controlled resources and decided priorities. Concern for a more efficient, more managed and more accountable service has brought the powers of the medical profession to the centre of the health policy stage. In all health care systems, reforming the position of the profession has come to be seen as central to the achievement of key current goals. Global concerns, global trends and global policy networks have fed and fuelled a movement for the closer management, supervision and audit of the medical profession.

Fifth, on a small number of issues there have been clear moves to develop global strategies. One such is pharmaceutical regulation. National regulation was cumbersome and hugely expensive – in the EU, for example, there were twelve separate registration authorities in the mid 1990s. From the early 1970s, there were moves to international harmonization. In 1994 the EU created the

European Evaluation Agency aiming to achieve common regulation and a common market (Vogel, 1998).

In recent years, AIDS has been the sharpest and clearest expression of the global nature of health problems. International networks of doctors, researchers and policy-makers and AIDS service organizations developed, but international organizations were less important in AIDS policy development in AICs than elsewhere. Europe did develop a 'Europe Against Aids' programme in the early 1990s but national programmes remained the key elements in AIDS strategies (Freeman, 2000, pp. 136–7). But we are clearly seeing here an emergent, but still embryonic, sense that 'health must be tackled as a global problem and pursued as a global goal and that its globalization is an asset' (Berlinguer, 1999, p. 581).

The significance of globalization in health policy

Clearly, globalization has been a significant influence – it has created and/or exacerbated particular health problems, it has contributed to the creation of global policy networks and so to the global diffusion of ideas about possible responses to common problems. Contemporary globalization has also promoted a pervasive neoliberal ideology which has stimulated a particular approach to contemporary problems. The globalization-induced preoccupation with competitiveness has added an additional turn to the screw of cost containment policies.

But at the end of the day, globalization has only been one factor among many affecting health politics and health policy in AICs – and it was not hegemonic in the sense of compelling particular responses or it has not yet done so. Moran emphasizes that 'health care states are still highly distinctive nationally' (Moran, 1999, p. 17). Methods of financing vary starkly between tax funding and funding from social insurance type contributions. Overall levels of expenditure on health care vary dramatically from the 14 per cent of GDP in the USA to less than 7 per cent in the UK and around 10 per cent in Germany and France. So does the public share of overall health expenditure. So do specific expenditures. If we look at pharmaceutical expenditure in the EU, for example, in 1994 Germany was spending 1.8 per cent of GDP whereas Denmark spent a mere 0.7 per cent. If we look at pharmaceutical expenditure as a proportion of total health expenditure the range in the EU is from 10 to 25 per cent (Mossialos, 1998, p. 264).

Nevertheless, the OECD verdict in 1994 was that 'The most remarkable feature of the healthcare system reforms across the seventeen countries is the degree of emerging convergence' (OECD, 1994, p. 45). National diversity and difference is still the dominant feature of healthcare systems in AICs but an emerging convergence is visible in key aspects of policy and practice. The differences are striking but so too are the buds of convergence. Globalization of ideologies and policy networks is likely to induce a pattern of convergence of responses – though obviously and inevitably mediated by the particularities of national states and national healthcare systems (Taylor-Gooby, 1996).

It is important, too, to look closely and critically at the seeming convergence of policy responses to common problems. Jacobs, for example, looked closely at the adoption of 'market reforms' to secure competition in health care in the UK, the Netherlands and Sweden. All countries set out along the same road but Jacobs' conclusion is that close analysis suggests each country actually took a different approach. The policy statements used the same terms which led to the belief that the goals were similar too. The final outcomes, however, were very different (Jacobs, 1998). As Klein puts it, 'the vocabulary of reform may be international but the way it is translated into policy remains national' (Klein, 1997, p. 1270).

What globalization has done is to foster global policy networks and create a global frame of reference in, and for, health and healthcare. This has become a significant factor in health policy and politics. International variations in policy and expenditure have become counters in domestic debates.

Exhibit 3.3

The impact of globalization on health policy

Globalization has

- contributed to a sense of the global nature of key health problems
- made health policy agendas global
- fostered the development of global policy networks
- helped to politicize health policy and health expenditure
- stimulated the growth of a global healthcare industry
- encouraged a global debate about the governance of the medical profession
- encouraged cost containment policies.

Education

Carter and O'Neill (quoted in Ball, 1998, p. 122) speak of 'the new orthodoxy' in education to do with the connection between education and government in western industrial societies. This orthodoxy has five main elements:

- A belief in improving the economy by tightening the links between schooling and employment.

- A commitment to improving student employment related skills.

- A move for more direct government control over the curriculum.

- A drive to control the costs of education to government.

- A move to increase community involvement in school decision-making and extend choice for parents and users.

The influence of globalization

What is the relationship between globalization and 'the new orthodoxy'? Clearly, there are links. Underlying the new orthodoxy is the centrality of securing international competitiveness. The result is what Ball describes as 'the increasing colonisation of education policy by economic policy imperatives' (Ball, 1998, p. 122). He sees the economic dominance of policy-making as being played out most clearly in the UK, New Zealand and in parts of Canada and with real, but slightly less dominant, versions in France and many US and Australian states. This means a change in the balance of power in education policy-making.

Another result of this economic dominance of education policy-making is that equity becomes a residual issue. (Ball, 1998, pp. 125–6). Levin points out how the case for change in education policy is today made largely in economic terms and specifically in terms of preparing the work force for competition with other countries (Levin, 1998, p. 131) The OECD reports steps to strengthen vocational education in Norway, Portugal, Spain, Switzerland, Japan, France, Italy, Austria, Finland, the Netherlands and in English speaking countries (OECD, 1997c, p. 15). The historic social engineering goals of education are superseded by an economic instrumentalism.

These new dominant concerns have given the state more power – to drive forward the changes seen as required by the gales of global economic reconstruction. The supposed requirement of competitiveness – for example, more and better skills training – justifies high level political action to drive it forward in the face of the inherent conservatism of educational institutions. Equally, national testing to raise standards and promote performance-enhancing competitiveness between educational institutions justifies increased state intervention in the secret garden of education policy-making, hitherto closely and successfully guarded by the education professionals.

The state is both taking more power to itself, particularly from the professionals, and redistributing that power. Redistribution is towards groups defined as users or customers – parents, employers and the local community. In the UK, New Zealand, the USA and Canada, powers have been decentralized in pursuit of goals very clearly influenced by globalization – a greater concern for economic considerations, more concern for competitive relations in provision and more power for consumers.

The globalization of agendas

In certain important policy areas, globalization has been a strong force for educational development and expansion. Beliefs about the importance of education to securing competitiveness have been a force for extending the length of school life in Belgium, New Zealand and Norway, for example, and in expanding mass post-compulsory education and higher education. More young people are achieving more formal educational qualifications and there are national targets for school achievement to stimulate development. In a decade, higher education has moved from an elitist to a mass system in most industrial countries and to much more diverse but common patterns with, for example, modularization and credit transfer.

Davies and Guppy see globalization as stimulating the development of what they describe as 'the international language of rights' (Davies and Guppy, 1997, p. 458). This concern has fed the school choice movement in a number of countries, for example, Canada, New Zealand, the USA, and has led to calls for education to be adapted to the needs of minorities and to local needs. Davies and Guppy see multiculturalism in education as the clear product of globalizing forces – the mass movement of populations, the globally diffused concept of rights and a concern for nation and community building in a world of greater national cultural diversity (Davies and Guppy, 1997, p. 442).

Has globalization generated a convergence in educational policy and educational systems? Clearly there are common trends and patterns – more stress on skills training, more stress on linking education with the world of work, extensions of compulsory schooling, the expansion of higher education, the introduction of mass performance testing at key ages and stages in many countries. There has been policy borrowing and a degree of policy learning.

Green's conclusion is that there is 'significant evidence of a general process of convergence in educational systems across the world' (Green, 1997, p. 174). He hastens to point out, however, that there are still marked differences even between European educational systems, for example in the balance between general and specialist and between selective and comprehensive secondary systems, between post-compulsory systems which are predominantly work based (Germany, Austria and parts of Switzerland) and those which are primarily school based (USA, Netherlands, Italy, Spain, UK, Sweden). Again, marketization has made a considerable impact in some countries, mainly in English speaking ones, whereas much of continental Europe has been resistant to this line of development. Convergence in priorities, and in some policy areas, is clear but so is continuing divergence. This is predictable. Education systems are the product of deep historical deposits. They are not going to change overnight but what we see are significant global pressures and influences which are affecting developments both at the margins and at the core.

The significance of globalization

The framework of policy debate has become more global. National performance is no longer looked at in isolation but in the context of the performance of
other countries. The availability, for example, of international data on staying-
on rates beyond minimum leaving age, the percentage of the age group going
on to higher education, achievements in mathematics, puts the spotlight on
any countries whose performance is below what politicians, policy makers
and parents see as acceptable. Globalization encourages the production of
international league tables and provides a new yardstick for the evaluation of
national achievements. Britain's poor showing in terms of staying-on rates
and in achievements in mathematics compared, for example, with some of the
newly industrializing countries of East Asia, has set alarm bells ringing in the
corridors of power.

Globalization creates international policy networks and so contributes to
policy borrowing and cross national policy learning. There is, of course, a long
history of education policy borrowing between states but, in Green's view, the
past twenty years have been an exceptional period for international traffic in
educational ideas. He sees increased economic competitiveness as 'perhaps
the most significant reason' (Green, 1997, p. 173). He shows how developments in education policy in the UK in the last twenty five years have drawn
on developments in Canada (Youth Opportunities Programmes), Germany
(industrial training), USA (competence based assessment), (Ibid, p. 174). Other
countries have also been enthusiastic borrowers. Green's verdict is that there
is a clear trend towards a convergence in general discourse and the broad
objectives of educational policy even though national policies remain distinct
(Green, 1999).

Exhibit 3.4

The impact of globalization on education policy

Globalization has

● contributed to the dominance of economic considerations in education policy

● helped to make education more work orientated

● led to the state assuming more power in education governance

● strengthened global policy networks and created a global framework of debate

Exhibit 3.4 *(cont'd)*

- encouraged a review of the power and influence of different stakeholders in education

- stimulated the expansion of provision – longer compulsory education, expansion of higher education

- contributed to divergence within convergence in education policy and systems.

Social Security Provision

The influence of globalization/the globalization of agendas

The neoliberal ideology of globalization is essentially hostile to state provided social security, hostile on principle because of its preference for individual and market solutions, hostile also because of the supposed economic and social costs of state systems. The ideology feeds through into discussions about the future of social security provision, cloaked in a seeming scientific objectivity, in publications such as the World Bank's highly influential report *Averting the Old Age Crisis* (World Bank, 1994) which argues for the privatization of main stream pension provision and a largely residual role for the state. OECD publications equally breathe anxiety and concern about the implications of social security costs for competitiveness (e.g., OECD, 1999a).

Concern about competitiveness has obviously put social security schemes under pressure given the way in which the debate about competitiveness has focused primarily on employment costs and levels of social benefits and taxation and the supposed damage they do to competitiveness. The issue is, however, rather more complex than many of the critics of state social security schemes seem to realise. Countries with high social security contributions are not necessarily those that have the highest labour costs. In many countries in Western Europe, for example, where employers' social security contributions are high, wages tend to be relatively low. In the Netherlands, on the other hand, employers' contributions are low because the larger part of contributions is paid by the workers but from wages which are significantly higher than in other countries. Simply comparing levels of social security contributions, whether of employers or employees, or wages, tells us little about overall employment costs as they are only elements in the total equation (Euzeby, 1998, p. 5).

It is possible to delineate a general pattern of changes in social security provision. Not all its elements are apparent in all countries or in relation to all benefits but a pattern is clearly visible. The essential element is one of restraint in commitment and expenditure. What is also very striking is that the changes were introduced by governments of the left, the right and the centre. It was not a simple question of a right wing assault on social security. Alber and Standing write of what they see as a 'global flight to selectivity' and 'a strong tendency' to promote a residual welfare state' (Alber and Standing, 2000, pp. 114–5). Ruggie, in 1994, spoke of 'the fraying of domestic social security safety nets throughout the capitalist world' (Ruggie, 1994, p. 10). There are five main elements in the pattern:

- Tightening of conditions of eligibility.

- Extension of means testing.

- Reduction in replacement ratios.

- A move to transfer financial responsibility from employers to individuals and the state.

- A move towards more active labour market policies rather than the simple provision of benefits for the unemployed.

We explore the pattern in relation to particular social security benefits.

Bonoli *et al.*, conclude that 'virtually every country in Europe has taken some steps towards reducing state expenditure on old age pensions' (Bonoli *et al.*, 2000, p. 30). Daly sees a convergence of European pension schemes around two core principles – a lengthening of the period to be spent in employment to qualify for a contributory pension and a general reduction of the generosity of pension schemes (Daly, 1997, p. 133). Many countries – the OECD lists eight (OECD, 1997c, p. 14) – have taken steps to raise pension ages, partly in pursuit of gender equality and partly to reduce costs. In Germany, for example, the retirement age for women will gradually increase from 60 to 65 and for men from 63 to 65. In Sweden, the retirement age is being raised from 65 to 66. In other countries the age of retirement in under active discussion. Other countries, too, have taken steps to lengthen the contribution period required for a full pension or to extend the years used to calculate entitlement.

In a range of significant, if often unobtrusive, ways, the level and value of pensions have been reduced. There has also been a widespread extension of means testing of basic state pensions – in Denmark, Norway, Finland, the Netherlands, Australia, Canada and New Zealand, for example (Bonoli and Pahier, 1998, p. 319). A number of countries have altered their methods of indexation – to the disadvantage of current and future beneficiaries. Delays in uprating have also been used. Sweden has made a more radical move to a defined contribution system rather than a defined benefit system – so the individual pensioner rather than the state bears the risk of future uncertainties.

Daly's conclusion from her review of changes in the years 1985–95 is that 'Europeans will have to work harder for lower pensions' but 'it would be difficult to argue that 'pension regimes have actually been transformed throughout Europe' (Daly, 1997, p. 135).

What of unemployment benefits? There is a clear pattern of change. In 1999, the OECD summed up the pattern as being to restrict access, limit duration and level of benefit but without substantial cuts in entitlements (OECD, 1999a, p. 91). In the 1990s, thirteen out of a list of nineteen countries introduced tighter eligibility requirements and there were reductions in initial gross replacement rates in eleven out of nineteen countries. Most reductions were small but some were significant (ibid., Table 5.1) In a number of countries – Finland, Spain, the UK – benefits were made taxable. A number of countries also introduced waiting days or increased the number – Sweden, Belgium, New Zealand – which is, in effect, a reduction in the value of benefit.

In general, the trend has been away from passive systems of income replacement towards more active labour market policies though there was only a small rise in expenditure on such schemes between 1990 and 1996 (European Commission, 1998, p. 21). In the UK, the Labour government's New Deal offered younger unemployed people a range of training and job experience options after they had been unemployed for six months. Simply drawing benefit was not one of them.

Alongside these restrictive changes, however, can be set examples of new and extended schemes. The Scandinavian response to high unemployment has, with the exception of Sweden, been 'expansionary' (Daly, 1997, p. 138). Greece, Portugal and Italy also introduced or extended schemes.

The story in relation to family benefits is a mixed one with, in general, little change. In the Scandinavian countries there were some improvements in family benefits (Kvist, 1999, p. 240). In France and Germany, some family benefits became means tested and selective for the first time in the 1990s (Bouget, 1998, p. 164; Lawson, 1996, p. 37). The area in which there was major development in the 1980s and 1990s was in parental leave. Between the mid 1980s and the mid 1990s 'all but a handful' of countries in Europe improved parental leave schemes. By 1995 ten of the countries of the EU were making some kind of cash payment to the caring parent (Daly, 1997, p. 140).

At times of high or rising unemployment, sickness and invalidity benefit expenditure always becomes an issue for governments as the number of claimants rises. The problem is clear – it is less stigmatizing to be sick or disabled than it is to be unemployed – and it frequently means higher benefits. In 1997, the OECD urged five countries to tighten the conditions of eligibility for invalidity benefits (OECD, 1997c, p. 60) and reported that Italy, the Netherlands, and Norway had already done so (ibid., p. 14). The EC reported a general tightening up in disability and invalidity benefits in member countries (European Commission, 1998, p. 23).

Another approach is for governments to make employers rather than the state responsible for sickness benefit and this has been pursued in the UK, Denmark, the Netherlands and Sweden. The aim of such reforms, according to the OECD, 'is not simply to transfer expenditures from government budgets. Doing so also gives employers incentives to ensure their workplaces are safe, healthy environments' (OECD, 1999a, p. 52). But it is hard to believe that reducing the cost to government was not the primary motivation.

Despite supposed widespread concern about non wage labour costs and their implications for competitiveness, the OECD reported that employer social security contributions increased in eight countries in the 1980s – often considerably – and were reduced significantly in only five countries (OECD, 1997b, p. 65). Elsewhere, employee contributions to social security were introduced or increased – for example, Finland in the 1990s and in Germany where workers' share of the cost of the social state increased from 20 per cent in 1979 to 30 per cent in 1994 (Lawson, 1996, p. 42). In Sweden, employee contributions also rose.

Some vulnerable groups suffered particularly from these various attempts to restrict and control expenditure. For example, the OECD reported widespread tightening of the need for lone parents to be available for work. Benefits for young people were also restricted in a number of countries, for example, the Netherlands, Australia, the UK, New Zealand (OECD, 1999a, p. 102).

Exhibit 3.5

General conclusions standing out from this review

First, the precise impact of globalization varies from state to state. Some states are more exposed than others.

Second, there has been no general 'race to the bottom' in social security. As the OECD put it 'Globalization certainly does have an impact on systems of social protection but its effects are more subtle than this unduly alarmist perspective would imply (OECD, 1999a, pp. 136–7).

Third, the pressures on systems of social protection have increased considerably for a variety of reasons of which globalization is only one. Increase in the numbers of elderly people, more lone parents, the slow down in economic growth, higher unemployment are also crucial factors.

Fourth, globalization increases the demand for social security 'while reducing the ability of the state to perform that role effectively' (Rodrik, 1997, p. 53).

Fifth, cash benefits are getting meaner and eligibility conditions for the receipt of benefits are getting stricter (Daly, 1997, p. 143).

Exhibit 3.5 *(cont'd)*

Sixth, despite meaner benefits and tighter eligibility rules, in most countries in Europe expenditure continued to rise between the mid-1980s and the mid-1990s because of increased demand.

The significance of globalization

To what extent has globalization played a part in creating or exacerbating the pressures on social security systems in AICs? Or are the key pressures the changes in the labour market, in households and in demography which are not realistically or directly attributable to globalization? In our view, globalization has played a significant part in increasing the pressures. Perhaps the biggest impact has been in the sharpened sense of international economic competition which globalization has induced, and the way in which that concern, along with globalization's neoliberal ideology, has led to a predictable focus and emphasis on social security costs.

Globalization has also played a part, but probably a relatively small one, in stimulating the rise in unemployment and under-employment which has been a significant factor putting pressure on social security. The increase in unemployment has put general pressure on social security schemes, not just on unemployment schemes. It has encouraged early retirement with heavy costs to pension funds. It has led to large increases in the cost of disability benefits – 22 per cent of social security expenditure on people below retirement age as compared with 23 per cent spent on unemployment benefits in the mid 1990s (OECD, 1997a, p. 15).

Historically, the development of social security schemes in many countries owed much to the power and influence of the organized working class, Social security was seen as an important element in the truce situation between capital and labour and as a way of incorporating the working class, We saw earlier how globalization has significantly altered the balance of power between capital and labour in favour of capital. Today, capital has less need to be sensitive and responsive to labour's aspirations and demands in relation to social security as in other areas.

If one sees the EU – as we believe one must – as both an element in, and as a response to, globalization, then one can reasonably and properly characterise the EU's impact on social policy and social security as a product of globalization, The EU's impact on both has been considerable but the strongest impact in the 1990s rose from the criteria for monetary union laid down in the Maastricht agreement. Countries wishing to join had to reduce budget deficits to below 3 per cent of GDP by 1998–9. Pierson sees this condition, given the constraints on raising taxes, as putting great pressure on public expenditure and particularly on pension provision (Pierson, 1998b, p. 789).

Clearly AICs are facing similar situations which are defined in neoliberal terms as problems – the need to be economically competitive, ageing populations, more claims for disability benefits, pressure on unemployment insurance schemes, changes in family structures. In 1998 the EC concluded that there was a significant degree of convergence in major policy developments (European Commission, 1998, pp. 8–9). In contrast to this measure of convergence, however, there is diversity in many aspects of policy and provision. In most OECD countries, for example, expenditure on public pensions will increase rapidly between 2015 and 2045 to above 15 per cent of GDP but in some countries – Canada, the UK and the USA – it will remain below 10 per cent (OECD, 1999a, p. 51). Unemployment benefit replacement rates also vary hugely in the EU from 70–80 per cent in Belgium, Denmark and the Netherlands at one end of the continuum to 30 per cent in Italy and 24 per cent in the UK (Esping Andersen, 1999, p. 124). The economic consequences of becoming unemployed 'are vastly different even among EU member countries' (Therborn, 1999, p. 554). Overall expenditure on social protection in the EU ranges from 20 per cent of GDP (Ireland) to 36 per cent (Sweden) with a group of countries bunching around the 30 per cent mark (European Commission, 1998, p. 7).

What we are seeing is a measure of convergence in approach in response to common pressures of which globalization is just one. A convergence of approach obviously has to precede any convergence in policies. These are historically determined and deeply socially embedded. Changes will provoke the anger and opposition of powerful constituencies and governments will proceed slowly and with as much obfuscation as they can manage. Genuine convergence, even in favourable circumstances, will be an extremely slow process. What we seem to be witnessing, as in education, is divergence within convergence.

In social security, details about what different countries provide and spend and how they are responding to the supposed 'crisis' in social security systems are available for anyone to suck and savour. In a situation of anxiety, comparison will tend to foster concern about spending levels and so create downward pressures rather than provide reassurance or encourage greater generosity. Governments can position themselves in the relevant league tables and see how their schemes compare with countries which they identify as key competitors. Social security systems are deeply 'embedded'. Change is slow. What we need to be alert to is pressures which are likely to prefigure future changes. Comparison has become a significant emerging pressure in a nervously competitive global economy.

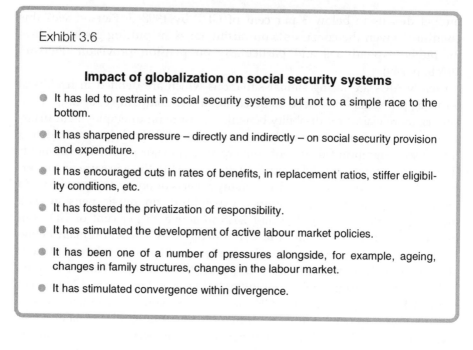

Exhibit 3.6

Impact of globalization on social security systems

- It has led to restraint in social security systems but not to a simple race to the bottom.

- It has sharpened pressure – directly and indirectly – on social security provision and expenditure.

- It has encouraged cuts in rates of benefits, in replacement ratios, stiffer eligibility conditions, etc.

- It has fostered the privatization of responsibility.

- It has stimulated the development of active labour market policies.

- It has been one of a number of pressures alongside, for example, ageing, changes in family structures, changes in the labour market.

- It has stimulated convergence within divergence.

Conclusions – Globalization and AICs

- Globalization has both positive and negative effects on the development of human welfare. It has exacerbated some social problems – drug abuse, unemployment, inequality and environmental problems, for example. On the other hand, it has increased national and global resources, facilitated the development of global policy networks, increased the amount of policy exchange, led to the development of international law, supranational bodies and transnational social movements.

- Contemporary globalization is fuelled by, and propagates, a particular ideology – neoliberalism – which stresses individual responsibility, is hostile to state service provision, believes in the superiority of market solutions and individual responsibility. The ideology of globalization is therefore a constraint on the development of state welfare.

- Globalization increases pressure to restrain taxation and public spending. It makes governments reluctant to raise taxes or social security contributions for fear of alienating international investors and undermining competitiveness. It constrains public expenditure by associating it with financial improvidence. In this way it limits and confines state welfare development.

● Globalization has exposed the limitations of the nation-state as a solver of social problems. It makes it plain that many problems — most obviously the environmental problem, the problem of drug abuse, the problem of international crime and the employment problem – can only be dealt with effectively by action at a supranational level.

● Globalization does exert pressure for convergence in social policy through, for example, the dominance of a global neoliberalism, the rise of the competition state, the growth of global policy networks, greater awareness of how other states tackle similar problems.

While exerting pressure for convergence, however, globalization does not act as a hegemonic force. Governments may be constrained but they still have room for manoeuvre. What globalization does is to create pressures for convergence within diversity.

Further Reading

Mishra, R. (1999) *Globalization and the Welfare State* (Cheltenham, Edward Elgar).

Pierson, P. (1998) 'Contemporary Challenges to Welfare State Development', *Political Studies*, XLVII, 777–94.

Sykes, R., Palier, B. and Prior, P.M. (eds) (2001) *Globalization and European Welfare States* (London, Palgrave).

4

Globalization and Human Welfare in Industrially Developing Countries

The last quarter of the twentieth century witnessed an acceleration of the process of globalization and a deeper incorporation of the industrially developing countries (IDCs) into the global economy, polity and culture. Global investment and trade with IDCs increased; a greater number of IDCs espoused western democratic forms of government or joined the various UNO bodies; and, on the cultural domain, the influence of western culture reached heights that are considered by many as a threat to indigenous cultures.

This incorporation of the developing world into the global system, however, has been very selective and uneven – high for some IDCs but low for others, high for some groups within IDCs and low for others. It has meant an improvement in economic fortunes for some countries but a deterioration for others; and within countries some groups have benefited at the expense of others. It is this uneven penetration and variable effect of globalization on IDCs that this chapter will examine.

Globalization and Financial Flows

Foreign Direct Investment (FDI)

Economic development in any country depends both on its natural resources, the quality of its people and governments and on the location of the country within the global economic system. It is this interplay between internal and external factors that determines the type and speed of economic development. Financial flows from AICs to IDCs, whether private or public, are one of the main external factors that can influence economic and social development.

Globalization has greatly facilitated the flows of FDI so that they reached high levels during the last quarter of the twentieth century though they flagged

78

a little in the late 1990s as a result of the economic crisis in several Asian countries. The amount of net FDI going to IDCs increased twelve times between 1980 and 1997 (World Bank, 1999, p. 70), but, even so, the bulk of FDI in 1997 still went to AICs – 70 per cent to AICs and the remaining 30 per cent to IDCs.

Foreign direct investment is not evenly distributed among IDCs. Rather, it is concentrated in a small number of countries. In 1997, 6 per cent of all FDI went to China, 4 per cent to Brazil, 3 per cent to Mexico, 2 per cent to Indonesia, 2 per cent to Singapore, 1 per cent to Malaysia, 1 per cent to Argentina and 1 per cent to Saudi Arabia (World Bank, 1999, Figure 3.4, p. 73). The other 10 per cent went to the remaining IDCs. Less than 2 per cent of FDI went to the least developed countries – the 48 low-income countries classified by the UN for economic vulnerability. This is not surprising, for as Todaro points out, 'private capital gravitates toward countries and regions with the highest financial returns and the greatest perceived safety' (Todaro, 2000, p. 578).

The benefit of FDI to recipient countries depends on the type of FDI, the conditions attached to it and the use to which it is being put. Long-term loans are preferable to short-term loans for the latter 'are vulnerable to sudden changes in investor sentiment' and, when withdrawn quickly, they can result in financial and banking crises, particularly in the small economies of IDCs (World Bank, 1999, p. 73), as the financial crises of the late 1990s in East Asian countries showed.

FDI in manufacturing and service plants is more beneficial to IDCs than investment used solely for the extraction of natural resources. Indeed, FDI used for mining or deforestation may benefit the economy very little and may damage the environment. Most FDI directed to Russia, for example, has been for 'mining and quarrying (primarily investment in the oil and gas sector)' with little beneficial effect for the rest of the country's economy (Martin, 1998, p. 14). The use of FDI, however, for the establishment of factories and services is more likely to bring new jobs, new technology and act as the catalyst for further economic development in a developing country, although most of the profits will leave the country. The challenge facing governments is not whether or not to accept FDI but rather 'how to navigate through this financially integrating world' (World Bank, 1999, p. 85). The difficult question is whether, when and how governments of countries with pressing needs can extract favourable terms from the investing institutions.

Multinational Companies (MNCs)

Multinational companies (MNCs), are one of the main sources of FDI, although their activities go well beyond that. They invest in IDCs for a variety of reasons: 'gaining access to domestic markets, to specific raw materials and cheap labour and to avoid state regulation which may be stronger in the First World' (Kiely, 1998, p. 56). The ultimate aim, however, is to increase their profitability in the short term or longer term. Any benefits to the host country are incidental and derivative.

A great deal of unresolved debate surrounds the effects of MNC activity on the economic and social development of IDCs. Supporters of MNCs claim that the benefits to host countries are fourfold. First, MNCs can increase the productive capital stock of the country provided that FDI is not used merely for mergers and takeovers of existing companies. Second, they can introduce technology that is more efficient than local technology, although the benefits of this will depend on the extent to which local firms are allowed to make use of it. Third, their presence can encourage or force more competitive practices among local firms. The benefits of this may be reflected in better quality products and lower prices though the other side of the coin may be more unemployment. There is also the additional danger that MNCs may take over existing companies and thus reduce competition. Fourth, they help to improve the possibilities of the country joining international trade with the potential benefits this can have on the national economy.

Opponents of MNCs claim that they export all or most of their profits; they pay lower wages compared to those they incur in AICs; they largely evade taxation; they can reduce competition by taking over existing firms; they can create new consumer demands that undermine traditional tastes and hence national forms of production; they increase inequalities by their emphasis on a small urban technical group of workers; and, above all, they distort the process of development so that it serves their interests rather than those of the host country.

In brief, the benefits of MNCs to IDCs are not as clear-cut as they are sometimes presented. So much depends on the details and the specific situations of individual countries. Governments are more likely to serve the interests of their people if they treat MNCs' intentions as exploitative rather than as altruistic. In the words of an Australian Government report, governments 'should react as if MNCs were in some sense "exploiters" of the host country's resources rather than on the assumption that the two sides had mutual interests' (Bureau of Industry and Economics, 1993, p. 130).

The MNC practice of contracting out to local firms does not absolve them of their responsibilities. A recent study of the working conditions of workers, 80 per cent of whom were women, in Reebok-contracted factories in Indonesia showed that 'employees were routinely exposed to chemicals and suffered rashes and other skin complaints'. Moreover, as little as '£1.20 from the price of a £50 pair of shoes goes to the workers who made them' (Ashworth, 1999, p. 17).

Aid and Economic Development

The least developed countries receive very little FDI and they have to rely on their own meagre savings and on aid to finance their development. In 1997,

$50 billion was granted in aid, two-thirds of which was bilateral – from the donor to the recipient country directly – and the remainder was multilateral aid channelled through the various agencies of the United Nations. There are political, social, economic, military, as well as humanitarian motives behind aid giving, particularly in relation to bilateral aid. The result is that the countries most favoured for receiving aid are not necessarily those in greatest financial need. Only 27 per cent of all aid went to the least developed countries in 1997. The rest went to countries whose financial needs were not as pressing. If the primary aim of aid is to reduce poverty where it is most widespread, then it is grossly misdirected. In 1998, aid flows per poor person was US$950 in the Middle East and North Africa, $363 in Europe and Central Asia, $70 in Latin America but only $49 for the Sub-Saharan countries where poverty is at its highest levels (Stationery Office, 2000, Figure 7.3, p. 86).

Nevertheless, if one uses a rough yardstick for aid dependency as those countries that received aid amounting to more than 10 per cent of their GNP for both 1990 and 1997, then 15 of the 19 such countries were least developed Sub-Saharan countries. Clearly these countries have relied very heavily on aid for their development projects even though in absolute terms they have received less than large countries (World Bank, 1999, Table 21, pp. 270–71). China, for example, received relatively little aid as a per cent of its GDP – 0.3 per cent compared to 59.8 per cent for Mozambique in 1996 – but it received three times as much in absolute amount.

In contrast to FDI, the real amount of aid has not increased as globalization gained pace in the 1990s. As AICs became richer, they gave less of their wealth in aid. Thus in 1960, average income per capita in AICs was $11,757 while aid per capita was $47; by 1996 income per capita rose to $27,789 while the aid per capita rose to only $59 (German and Randel, 2000, p. 14).

A great deal of concern has been expressed, and numerous studies have been conducted, over the years concerning the efficacy of aid in economic and social development. At one end are those, on both the left and the right, who see aid as detrimental to economic development. The left sees it as a form of further incorporation, domination and, as a consequence, exploitation of IDCs by the rich countries (George, 1988), while the right believes that it undermines individual initiative (Bauer, 1971). Most writers have seen aid as a positive contribution to economic development because it provides much needed capital, technology, know-how and professional help (Cassen and associates, 1986).

As in the case of FDI, the reality is far more complex. The effect of aid on the economic development of the recipient country depends on the terms attached to aid and the uses to which it is being put. About two-thirds of all aid over the years has been 'tied' aid requiring the recipient country to use the funds for the purchase of goods from the donor country. Such aid is unlikely to prove useful to economic development for it is used primarily to satisfy the needs of the donor rather than those of the recipient country.

Strictly speaking, it is impossible to assess the effects of aid on poverty reduction or on raising economic growth. Not surprisingly, the World Bank concluded that, 'A clear link between aid and the reduction of poverty has been hard to find' (World Bank, 1990, p. 128). Monitoring the success of the various projects funded by aid is an easier and more feasible task. Understandably, the World Bank claims that most such projects prove successful, at least from the short-term point of view. The reality, particularly in the long-term, may be less positive. Even projects that are assessed as successful in their own right may have undesirable effects on social development. 'Glaring examples include metropolitan hospitals that drained funds from village clinics and elite universities that starved primary schools of critical resources' (Speth, 1999, p. 16)

There is now greater awareness of the failures of aid and a greater emphasis on aid designed to promote basic social services. Thus, one of the agreements reached at the World Summit for Social Development in Copenhagen in 1995 was that donor governments should allocate 20 per cent of their bilateral aid to the improvement of social services and that this should be matched by 20 per cent of the recipient country's budget. In 1997, however, only Sweden, Denmark and Luxembourg met this target (German and Randel, 2000, p. 17).

The Debt of IDCs

Globalization is associated not only with private and public financial flows but with the higher indebtedness of so many IDCs that has resulted from these flows. Falling prices of exports, rising oil prices, higher interest rates, lower exchange rates *vis-à-vis* the US dollar and political mismanagement are the major reasons for the growth of debt. The result is that throughout the 1980s and the 1990s many IDCs have had to pay large sums of money to service their debts. Debt repayments are too high for many countries, affecting their ability both to invest and to develop as well as to provide decent public services. Eight of the eleven countries whose foreign debt exceeded their total GNP in 1997 were Sub-Saharan countries; similarly 20 of the 40 countries with foreign debts above 50 per cent of the GNP were Sub-Saharan countries (World Bank, 1999, Table 21, pp. 270–72). Not surprisingly, debt 'remains a millstone for many poor countries' and they have had to 'transfer to Northern creditors four times what they spend on the health of their people' over the last two decades (UNDP, 1997, p. 84).

The decision by the AICs in 1996, and repeated in later years, to limit the amount that is paid for debt servicing was a step in the right direction but hardly sufficient to solve this problem. It is difficult to see how low-income countries such as Angola and Nicaragua whose foreign debt exceeds 200 per cent of their low GNP can continue paying off their debt without immeasurable harm to the living standards of their people and dropping even further into indebtedness. Nothing short of a complete write-off of the debts of many IDCs can solve this problem.

Exhibit 4.1

_____

Investment, aid and debt

● Globalization has increased the volume of FDI but it continues to be directed mainly to AICs. `

● Aid has declined over the years as a proportion of the GDP of AICs. Its distribution to IDCs does not meet the challenges of globalization.

● Both FDI and aid can have positive and negative effects on economic and social development depending on the terms attached to their use.

● Globalization has been one of the reasons for the rise in the debt of IDCs.

● It is unlikely that globalization will change substantially the distributional pattern of FDI. Private capital will continue to be invested primarily in countries where there are profits to be made.

Globalization, Foreign Trade and Human Welfare

Trade has always been a major strand as well as a major catalyst of globalization by expanding contacts between different nations. Its effects go beyond mere economic matters to include cultural, political and social processes. Vice-versa, globalization has stimulated and increased trade links between nations.

Debates about the nature of world trade, whether it ought to be free or to be regulated by the state, have a long history going back to the sixteenth century, although today the free traders seem to have the upper hand. The basic premise of free traders is that 'each society can benefit from what another can offer' – the idea of comparative advantage. The pessimistic view of free trade argues that the weaker economies lose out from such contacts and the national interest is best served through either minimal foreign trade or some form of state regulation of foreign trade (Fieldhouse, 1999, p. 9). Neither of these two views is borne out by the evidence. Rather it is the terms of trade which are the crucial determinant of its distributional effects.

The volume of trade has increased dramatically over the years. In the brief period of 1985–98, the real value of world exports trebled while the real value of world imports rose three and a half times (United Nations, 1999, tables A14 and A15, pp. 276–82). An increasing proportion of this volume is not so much trade between countries as trade between different affiliates of the same MNC – an estimated one-third of world trade in the mid-1990s was of this type.

Advanced industrial countries have always dominated world trade. About two-thirds of exports were between AICs in both 1985 and 1997. Yet there have been important changes. In 1985, 61.4 per cent of US exports went to other AICs and 18.0 per cent to IDCs; in 1997, the corresponding proportions were 55.5 per cent and 43.3 per cent respectively. A similar, though not as significant, trend applies to Japan but not to the European Union. What this means is that the US and Japan increasingly depend on IDCs for their export markets and any crisis in the developing world will affect their economies more. Another important change is that a higher proportion of exports from IDCs went to other IDCs than was the case in previous decades, reflecting the growing importance of some countries in Asia as sources of manufactured goods (UNO, 1999, Table A14, pp. 276–8).

For several reasons, the prices of non-mineral primary commodities declined in both real terms and relative to the prices of manufactured goods during the 1980s and the 1990s (United Nations, 1999, Table A.17 p. 283). Indeed, the UNDP estimates that in 1990 commodity prices were '45 per cent lower than in 1980 and 10 per cent lower than the lowest prices during the great Depression, in 1932' (UNDP, 1997, p. 84).

Most IDCs rely very heavily on the export of primary commodities and some even depend on two or three such commodities – tea, coffee, cocoa, fruit, zinc, copper, etc. Thus globalization and increasing trade do not benefit all countries alike – so far they have brought more benefit to the countries exporting manufactured products at the expense of countries relying on primary commodity exports. Only the small number of IDCs that export crude oil have gained through trade.

Africa's experience in the 1990s is a good illustration of the effects of falling primary commodity prices. While the volume of its exports rose at an average of 4.4 per cent per year, the value of its total exports rose by only 1.4 per cent per year – the converse of the picture which emerges in relation to its imports: their volume rose by only 1.9 per cent per year but their total value rose by 4.5 per cent per year. In brief, this meant cheaper exports but more expensive imports for Africa (United Nations, 1999, Table A.13, pp. 274–6).

Africa's experience is interesting from another aspect. If integration into world trade is judged by the value of exports as a proportion of GDP, then Sub-Saharan Africa was more integrated than Latin America in the 1990s. Yet its economic fortunes were inferior. It is not so much the degree of integration into the global economy that is crucial to a nation's economic fortunes but the type of integration.

This picture of rising import prices but falling export prices for many IDCs is compounded by some of the rules of international trade, by some of the trade practices of AICs and by the structural bias of the international agency charged with overseeing fair play in free trade – the World Trade Organization (WTO).

Despite all the rhetoric of free trade, the tariffs on textile imports from IDCs above a certain quota are higher than the tariffs imposed on industrial country imports – a situation that disadvantages IDCs. Moreover, many AICs use unofficial quotas as a way of reducing imports from IDCs; or they provide heavy subsidies to their farmers, which not only makes imports from IDCs uncompetitive but makes possible the export of cheap agricultural goods from AICs to IDCs with the result that they undermine local agriculture as well as any small industries based on agricultural produce in IDCs (Elliott, 1999, p. 16). It is now recognised that opening up the markets of AICs to the products of poor countries is a top priority. As the managing director of the IMF put it at the WTO conference in Seattle, 'Providing unrestricted access for all exports from the poorest countries should receive priority and be brought to an early resolution' (quoted in Bayne, 2000, p. 145).

The tightening up by the WTO of the rules on patents (the Trade-Related Aspects of Intellectual Property Rights – TRIPS) in 1994 has meant that IDCs have to pay more for new technology since '97 per cent of all patents worldwide' are held by AICs, mainly by the USA (UNDP, 1999, p. 68). This strict regulation of patents is in stark contrast with earlier stages of development when the USA or Japan industrialized without much attention to patent ownership.

The function of the WTO, set up in 1994, is to make the rules for international trade and to examine complaints brought to it by member countries about trade rules violation. Its decisions are final and can lead to trade sanctions against countries found guilty of trade rule violation. Most countries are members, even though many IDCs do not maintain a mission in Geneva where the WTO has its offices, and some have failed to pay their subscription fees. Moreover, IDC missions are small and the costs of hiring international law firms are so high that IDCs cannot pay them. It is, therefore, not surprising that until 1997 no African country and no least developed country had complained to the WTO. It is the AICs and the larger IDCs that make use of the WTO's services – a clear reflection of the fact that structural inequalities of power are key factors in the daily work of the WTO as indeed of any other UNO body.

It is extremely difficult to quantify the losses incurred by IDCs through the various handicaps that they experience in world trade and finance. One such estimate by the UNDP put the losses at the beginning of the 1990s 'at $500 billion a year, 10 times what they received in foreign assistance' (UNDP, 1997, p. 87).

Despite all of the trading handicaps suffered by IDCs, it is not possible for them to cut themselves off from world trade. Even a country with the size and the population of China has decided to abandon its policy of relative trade isolation and to join the global market and the WTO. The only solution that will benefit IDCs is to change the rules, the practices and the overseeing of world trade. This, however, begs the question of how weaker countries can force the more powerful states and the MNCs to change a situation that at present works to their obvious advantage.

Exhibit 4.2

Globalization and trade

- Globalization has increased world trade but most of it is between AICs.

- World trade has benefited exporters of manufactured goods.

- The rules of world trade disadvantage IDCs because of their reliance on primary goods exports.

- Globalization of trade has benefited AICs more than IDCs.

Globalization and Economic Growth

During the 20-year period 1975–95 the world economy grew at an annual average rate of 2.8 per cent. The economies of IDCs as a group grew at a faster rate than the economies of AICs – an annual average rise of 4.4 per cent *vis-à-vis* a low 2.6 per cent for AICs.

Different groups of IDCs, however, witnessed different rates of economic growth. The Sub-Saharan countries experienced the lowest rates – a mere 2.0 per cent per annum; East Asia showed a remarkable rise of 8.8 per cent per annum; and Latin America experienced rates that were in between those of Africa and Asia – a 2.8 per cent annual rise. Within each of these groups of countries there are substantial variations and indeed the economies of six Sub-Saharan countries experienced a contraction during the 20-year period (UNDP, 1999, Table 11, pp. 180–84).

The picture that emerges from the former Soviet countries of Eastern Europe is quite depressing:

> In over one third of the 27 countries in transition, measured output in 1998 was still 40 per cent or more below the 1989 figure ... only three countries in the region, Slovakia, Poland and Slovenia, had managed to exceed the GDP levels of 1989. Both the Czech Republic and Hungary were just below their 1989 levels. (UNICEF, 1999, p. 3)

In brief, the effects of globalization on economic growth, as in investment and trade, have been uneven. They have raised rates of economic growth in many countries, they have done little for others and they have had a negative influence on a few others.

Globalization has meant a greater role for manufacturing in economic growth in many IDCs but this has not been accompanied by a corresponding increase in industrial employment. A good deal of it was jobless growth. The same applies to the growth of agro-business which has benefited so much by the process of globalization. Productivity on the large commercial farms, usually owned by foreign firms and servicing AIC markets, increased but without a corresponding increase in employment. The result has been a large exodus to the cities of rural labourers, many of whom became unemployed or found employment of a kind in the informal sector which usually means insecurity and low wages. Robinson estimates that 'four out of every five new jobs in Latin America are in the informal sector' (Robinson, 1999, p. 119).

The neoliberal thesis that the process of globalization should be accompanied by small government, by liberalization and privatization measures if the economy is to benefit is not supported by the experience of different countries during the past three decades. Many countries – the former East European and several countries in Africa – followed the path of liberalization and privatization without achieving even modest rates of economic growth or indeed experienced contractions of their economies. However, South Korea and Taiwan witnessed remarkable rates of economic growth even though their governments intervened substantially in industrial investment and education.

The World Bank, which in the mid-1980s stressed the virtues of liberalization and privatization, has now come to accept the weakness of this position. 'Some countries followed policies of liberalization, stabilization, and privatization but failed to grow as expected. Other countries intervened to a relatively large extent in markets and enjoyed rapid growth' (World Bank, 1999, p. 16).

It has now come to accept that while markets have a role to play in economic growth so do governments. The actual combination of state and market policies will vary from one country to another to reflect their particular socio-economic position. Globalization can proceed and economic growth can be achieved without the neoliberal ideology.

Exhibit 4.3

Globalization and economic growth

- Globalization has helped to expand the world economy.
- The economies of IDCs expanded faster than the economies of AICs as a group.

Exhibit 4.3 *(cont'd)*

- Within the IDC group, several countries have seen their economies shrink.
- The attempt to incorporate the economies of the former Soviet countries into the global economy has resulted in reductions of economic growth.
- There is now abundant evidence that economic globalization is quite possible without the current neoliberal ideology.

Globalization and Incomes Per Capita

Rates of economic growth give a very general picture of the rise or fall in living standards. Incomes per capita provide a slightly more accurate picture, although still general. Several conclusions can be drawn from the statistical evidence covering the period 1975–97 (UNDP, 1999, Table 6, pp. 151–5).

- First, during the 22-year period incomes per capita of the 100 or so IDCs as a group grew from $600 in 1975 to $908 in 1997 at 1987 prices. Incomes per capita in the poorest IDCs, the 48 least developed countries, dropped from $287 to $245 during the same period.

- Second, despite the fact that economic growth rates have been faster in IDCs than in AICs in recent decades, the gap in incomes per capita between the two sets of countries has not narrowed because of differential rates of population growth. The population of IDCs comprised 70 per cent of world population in 1950, 82 per cent in 1998 and it is estimated that by the year 2050 it will reach 88 per cent. Clearly, countries with low rates of economic growth but high rates of population growth have witnessed sharp drops of income per capita. However, China's income per capita grew at an annual rate of 7.7 per cent – very close to its rate of economic growth – as a result of its population control policy.

- Third, the relationship between economic growth and population growth is both complex and reciprocal and it is beyond the scope of this chapter. What cannot be claimed is that population growth is such that it outstrips food production and inevitably leads to starvation. Agricultural productivity is so high that the issue is not the adequacy of food supply but its distribution. Today, four fifths of total world GNP is in the hands of the minority of world population living in AICs – a little redistribution to the IDCs would go a long way in alleviating the food shortages in IDCs.

● Fourth, the gap in incomes per capita between the two sets of countries is vast and it has not changed much over the years. The income per capita in AICs in 1997 was 21 times greater than that of IDCs – a figure that was exactly the same as in 1975. The income gap, however, between the least developed countries and the AICs widened: it was 44 times smaller in 1975 but 79 times smaller in 1997. A slightly more hopeful picture emerges in the case of the two most populous countries in the world – China and India. The figures for China are 116 times smaller in 1975 but only 34 times in 1997; for India, the corresponding figures are 50 times and 42 times respectively. These comparisons are based on the exchange rates of local currencies *vis-à-vis* the US dollar and may well exaggerate the differences between IDCs and AICs.

● Fifth, a second method used to compare incomes between different countries is the purchasing power parities (PPPs) of different currencies as the basis for comparisons. This refers to the amount of money needed in a country to buy the same quantity of goods and services in the local market of a country as $1 would buy in the USA. While the income per capita in the USA in 1997 was 79 times higher than that in India and 34 times that of China using the official exchange rates, the corresponding figures based on PPPs were only 17 and 8 times respectively. It is hard, however, to believe that the spending power of the average American was only eight times greater than that of the average Chinese. Thus if the first approach exaggerates income inequalities between rich and poor countries, the second method underestimates them. As Todaro observes, 'The truth is probably somewhere in between' (Todaro, 2000, p. 44).

● Sixth, globalization has had variable effects on incomes per capita in different IDCs: it has raised them in some and reduced them in others. On present evidence, the income gap between AICs and most IDCs looks unbridgeable.

Globalization and Income Inequalities in IDCs

Although incomes per capita give a better idea of the prevailing living standards in a country than economic growth rates, they do not take into account the patterns of income distribution in the country. For this reason, a look at income inequalities is necessary.

If one uses the proportion of national income accruing to the bottom and top 20 per cent of the population as a yardstick of income inequality, the following conclusions emerge from the evidence (World Bank, 1999, Table 5, pp. 238–240).

● First, there are substantial variations in the degree of income inequalities between IDCs. In Africa, Zimbabwe and South Africa stand out as the most unequal – both countries with strong racial stratification systems; in South America, Brazil stands out with Chile and Paraguay following close behind; and in Asia, it is Thailand that exhibits the highest rates of inequality. However, several Asian countries stand out for the relatively high proportions of national income going to the bottom quintile of the population – Bangladesh, India, Pakistan and Sri Lanka. All this is evidence of the importance of national factors to the prevailing degrees of income inequality.

● Second, the figures for the former Soviet bloc countries best illustrate the effects of globalization on income inequalities. Globalization was at its highest for many of the former Soviet bloc countries during the 1990s with the privatization of public industries and the application of neoliberal labour market policies. Yet, as pointed out earlier, economic growth did not benefit but income inequality rose substantially. During the period 1989 to 1997, the gini coefficient rose from 0.26 to 0.37 in Rusia; in Poland from 0.26 to 0.34; in the Czech Republic from 0.21 to 0.26; and in Hungary from 0.23 to 0.26 (Flemming and Micklewright, 1999, Figure 9, p. 64 and Figure 11, p. 68).

● Third, there is no evidence to support the claim that income inequalities reflect the prevailing levels of income per capita. There are always national factors – social, political and historical – that override purely economic factors. Several examples illustrate this point: the Czech Republic and Brazil had similar incomes per capita in 1997 but their income distribution profiles were very different; Mexico had higher incomes per capita than India but higher rates of income inequality; and so on.

● Fourth, increased globalization does not necessarily result in either higher or lower rates of income inequality. In some countries inequality over the years increased while in others it declined. Even within the same country the direction of income inequality over the years is not unilinear.

● Fifth, the data suggest that the structural adjustment policies (see Exhibit 4.4) imposed on governments of IDCs in the 1980s and the 1990s increased inequality in the short term in many countries – but not all – depending on the severity of these policies and the country's political and socio-economic situation (Stewart and Berry, 1999, p. 185).

Globalization and Poverty in IDCs

The effects of globalization on economic growth, incomes per capita and income inequality have been variable. If the same applies to its effects on poverty, then its underlying philosophy is seriously flawed and needs to be changed. Poverty, of the kind that exists in IDCs, has never had any defenders in political circles because of its abject nature – it is almost identical with star-vation or the lack of very basic needs. It is essentially different from poverty as it is known and measured in AICs.

A Tale of Changing Post-War Policies on Poverty

The rhetoric about the need for poverty reduction in IDCs has always been strong, even though the policies considered necessary to achieve this have changed over the years. Four such changes stand out over the post-war period.

First, during the 1950s and 1960s, the general view among international bodies was that economic growth was the road to economic salvation and the general improvement of human welfare. It was felt that as the economy grew, and the country became westernized, the poor would benefit. By the late 1960s, however, there was enough evidence that this was not happening – economies did grow but the 'trickle down' effect was noticeably absent.

Second, this realization signalled the beginnings of the second paradigm. The ILO in 1972 called for a new approach to poverty reduction – redistribution with growth. The World Bank followed suit and called for a 'basic needs' strat-egy. Both approaches emphasized the importance of directing policies and aid to the improvement of the living conditions of the poor in the rural and urban areas through employment projects and better social services. The market itself, it was assumed, could not adequately deal with poverty reduction.

Third, the rise in third world debt signalled the beginning of a new approach that dominated the 1980s – the Structural Adjustment Policies which attributed indebtedness to 'big government', to central government planning, regulated labour markets and over-expenditure on the social services. In line with the neoliberal thinking that came to dominate government policies in the USA and the UK, the new approach called for small government, cuts in social services, lower taxes and deregulation of labour markets so as to encourage economic growth. The World Bank explained the new approach as the better of two evils. On the one hand, economic growth had to be encouraged for without it poverty 'cannot be reduced in the long term' (World Bank, 1990, p. 106); and on the other hand, adjustment policies 'necessitate cuts in public expenditure which are in conflict with two essential parts of the strategy advocated in this Report – delivering social services and providing transfers and safety nets' (ibid., p. 103). The poor had to pay the price for higher rates of economic growth, which did not materialize in many cases.

Fourth, by the mid-1990s there was enough evidence that SAPs needed to be toned down for they were leading to greater levels of poverty and deprivation without necessarily raising economic growth. The World Bank began to advo-cate a more flexible approach to development and poverty reduction. Public services were seen in more positive terms and the market in a less messianic light. The new view was that both governments and markets have a role to play in equitable development; the issue is to decide on the appropriate blend and balance between the two and this can vary from one country to another. The World Bank has come to accept that 'growth, equality, and reductions in poverty can proceed together, as they have done in much of East Asia' (World Bank, 1999, p. 15).

This approach was extended further in the Bank's Report for 2000. To abolish poverty, countries need to promote economic growth, reduce inequality, improve the delivery of services to benefit the poor, encourage the political empowerment of the poor, and abolish discrimination against women and ethnic minorities – all these policies to be pursued at the local, the national and international level. If such policies are pursued, 'the 21st century will see rapid progress in the fight to end poverty' (World Bank, 2000, p. 12).

Exhibit 4.4

Structural adjustment policies (SAPs) in IDCs

During the late 1970s, the USA and the UK witnessed a movement away from Keynesian ways of managing the economy towards monetarist methods as well as a gradual shift from universal provision of social services towards more targeted and private forms of provision. Other AICs followed suit, albeit at different speeds and in different ways.

The debt crisis of the early 1980s hastened the spread of monetarist or neoliberal policies, as they are better known, to the IDCs. The World Bank and the IMF insisted that before any aid was paid, or any debt was rescheduled, the government of the country had to apply neoliberal policies in three areas of government activity. First, the economy should be managed in monetarist ways that emphasized the control of inflation, the repayment of government debt, and the reduction of tax levels, government employment and government expenditure, even if this meant a rise in unemployment. Second, public utilities such as water, electricity, gas and telephones should be privatized. Third, government social expenditure should be reduced even if this meant lower standards in social services and a rise in poverty. These structural adjustment policies were imposed mainly on African and Latin American countries, while many Asian countries introduced them voluntarily.

There are serious difficulties in calculating the effects of SAPs. Most of the evidence suggests that SAPs did not always lead to higher rates of economic growth as the World Bank and the IMF expected. Similarly, however, the evidence does not support the conclusion that SAPs always led to a rise in income inequality. The distributional

Exhibit 4.4 *(cont'd)*

effects of SAPs differed across regions and countries depending on the severity of the policies, the country's levels of indebtedness and its political stability. Stewart and Berry (1999) reached the following conclusions: in Africa 'the impact on income distribution has been mixed' (p. 162); in Latin America, 'a deterioration in income distribution was most marked and extensive' (p. 168); in Asia, 'the varied structure of the economies make it difficult to generalize' (p. 174); and in the ex Soviet countries income inequality increased though more in some countries than in others depending on the severity of the SAPs (p. 181).

SAPs have been subjected to a great deal of criticism from many quarters, including UNICEF and the ILO, because of their adverse effects on the poor. Structural adjustment, it is argued, may be necessary to encourage economic growth but this should be accompanied by strong compensating measures to protect the poor. The World Bank, more than the IMF, has taken these criticisms seriously and has begun to move away from general structural adjustment lending towards 'project lending' related to labour and health standards, the environment, women's concerns and other issues which are directly related to poverty. The severest critics of the World Bank, however, remain unconvinced, for they believe that the reduction of poverty (widely defined to include health, education, housing and income) rather than economic growth should be the primary aim of any aid package.

Income Poverty: Its Extent and Depth

As with income inequality, data on poverty have to be treated with caution particularly when used for historical or comparative debates. The data presented in Table 4.1 measure the extent of subsistence poverty and comparative relative poverty in IDCs. The subsistence poverty line used by the World Bank is less than $1 a day in Purchasing Power Parity (PPP) dollars at 1985 values. People below that level are counted as poor; those above that line are not poor. Despite the crudeness of this definition, it does provide a rough index particularly for comparative purposes.

The comparative relative poverty line used in Table 4.1 is income that is equivalent to less than one-third of the average national consumption level for 1993 if that figure was higher than the $1 a day poverty line. In countries where this figure was lower, the $1 a day poverty line at 1993 prices was used. This has the advantage of being both relative and constant in comparative terms. The net effect of this relative approach was that the poverty levels were higher.

Table 4.1   Percentage of population living on less than $1 a day; or at a constant relative poverty level*; at 1993 Purchasing Power Parity (PPP).

Region	$1 a day poverty line at 1993 PPP			Less than one-third of average National consumption for 1993		
	1987	1993	1998	1987	1993	1998
East Asia and Pacific	26.6	25.2	15.3	33.0	29.8	19.6
Excluding China	23.9	15.9	11.3	45.1	30.8	24.6
Europe and Central Asia	0.2	4.0	5.1	7.5	25.3	25.6
Latin America and Caribbean	15.3	15.3	15.6	50.2	51.1	51.4
Middle East and North Africa	4.3	1.9	1.9	18.9	13.6	10.8
South Asia	44.9	42.4	40.0	45.2	42.5	40.2
Sub-Saharan Africa	46.6	49.7	46.3	51.1	54.0	50.5
Total	28.3	28.1	24.0	36.6	36.7	32.1
Total in millions	1,183	1,304	1,199	1,530	1,703	1,603

Adapted from: World Bank, 2000, tables 1.1 and 1.2, pp. 23, 24.
*One third of average consumption level in the country at 1993 PPP provided that figure was higher than $1 per day: otherwise the absolute poverty line of $1 per day was used.

Several conclusions emerge from Table 4.1:

- First, the numbers of the severely poor and the relative poor increased between 1987 and 1998 because of the rise in population.

- Second, the proportion of the population in both subsistence and relative poverty showed a slight decline.

- Third, the vast majority of the poor – about three-quarters – live in Asia, a reflection of the fact that most of the world's population lives in Asia, mainly in India and China.

- Fourth, the risk of poverty is at its highest in South Asia and Sub-Saharan Africa.

- Fifth, though the poor in the IDCs of Europe constitute a very small proportion of the world poor, their numbers increased far more than the rise in the poor of any other region – a reflection of neoliberal globalization policies.

- Sixth, the depth of poverty as measured by the poverty gap was at its highest in Sub-Saharan Africa and it increased over the years. The poverty gap refers to the extent that the income of the poor falls below the poverty line of $1 a day. Clearly, the more it falls below the poverty line, the more money is needed to raise the incomes of the poor above the poverty line. Countries with low rates of poverty and narrow poverty gaps possess the economic resources to abolish poverty but they lack the political will to do so. Countries, however, with high rates of poverty and wide poverty gaps may not have the financial means to abolish poverty even if they have the political will. Many of the least developed countries fall into this category.

- Seventh, the prospects for a substantial reduction in world poverty – in absolute or relative terms – in the near future appear very slim in view not only of the financial crisis that hit Asia in 1997 but also because of the continuation of the neoliberal ideology that underpins globalization and the work of the IMF. These prospects become even dimmer if a poverty line of $2 PPP per day is used as the poverty line – a benchmark that is ludicrously low by Western standards. Using this standard, the extent and the depth of poverty increase very substantially. In India, for example, it would mean that 87.5 per cent of its population would be in poverty and the poverty gap would reach 42.9 per cent – so serious a problem that it is truly beyond the financial capabilities of the country to solve.

- Eighth, and more controversially, it is difficult to see how even major country political reforms can reduce poverty in the short term in the absence of structural economic changes at the global level. The apartheid system was a major reason for the high levels of poverty among the black people in South Africa. Its abolition has not, however, led to any reductions in poverty. Its 'legacy' still lives on to influence the extent of poverty in the country (Carter and May, 1999) – evidence of the argument that global as well as national factors influence the extent of poverty in today's increasingly globalized world. Government policies, demographic factors, family break up rates and other national factors as well as the external terms of trade, the volume of FDI, the amount of aid and other external factors all coalesce to create poverty scenarios that can vary from one country to another.

The Human Poverty Index

Income has been widely used as the index for poverty in both the AICs and the IDCs because it affects, and reflects, many other aspects of a person's life. This relationship, however, is never perfect and there have always been voices calling for a broader definition of poverty. As far back as 1980, the World Bank argued that 'absolute poverty means more than low income. It also means malnutrition, poor health and lack of education – and not all the poor are equally badly off in all respects' (World Bank, 1980, p. 35).

More recently, Sen has argued that there are good reasons 'for seeing poverty as a deprivation of basic capabilities, rather than merely as low income' (Sen, 1999, p. 20). Seen in this broader perspective, the unemployed will be considered as poor despite the fact that the cash benefits they receive may lift them out of monetary poverty. Similarly, premature death, illiteracy, malnutrition and other such human risks will be seen as part of poverty. He illustrates the usefulness of his approach by citing the fact that 'African Americans as a group have no higher – indeed have a lower – chance of reaching advanced ages than do people born in the immensely poorer economies of China, or the Indian state of Kerala or in Sri Lanka, Jamaica or Costa Rica' (Sen, 1999, p. 21)

It was such considerations that led the UNDP to develop the Human Development Index in 1990 and the Human Poverty Index (HPI) in 1997 – one for AICs and another for IDCs to reflect their different stages of economic development. The HPI is a measure that reflects deprivation in four aspects of life: 'a long and healthy life, knowledge, economic provisioning and social exclusion' (UNDP, 1999, p. 132). The indicators used for these four deprivations for IDCs are: percentage of people who die before age 40, adult illiteracy, and a decent standard of living as measured by the percentage of people without access to safe water, without access to health services, and the percentage of children under five who are under weight (UNDP, 1999, Table 1, p. 127).

The advantage of the Human Poverty Index is that it brings together different types of deprivation into one figure and this can be a useful tool for public policy purposes; it shows that economic growth by itself is not always the best way to reduce poverty broadly defined; and it can more easily show development trends. Its disadvantages are that the HPI can compensate one form of deprivation against another; it can lead to false conclusions and hence mistaken policies unless the index is disaggregated. Two countries with the same HPI may be suffering from different forms, even degrees, of deprivation and would be in need of different types of policies.

Using this approach, the 1999 UNDP Report concluded that the five countries among the IDCs with the lowest HPI and hence the best provisions were Barbados, Trinidad, Uruguay, Costa Rica and Cuba. The worst five countries with the highest HPI were the Central African Republic, Ethiopia, Sierra Leone, Burkina Faso and Niger (UNDP, 1999, Table 2, p. 128). The order would have been different had they been ranked according to their income poverty rates. What this does not tell us is the rank order of the various types of deprivation in each of these countries and hence the policy requirements.

In brief, the human poverty index can supplement, but cannot supplant, the monetary definition of poverty. The two approaches complement each other and serve rather different social policy purposes.

Rural versus Urban Poverty

People in the rural areas of IDCs are more likely to be in poverty than urban dwellers for at least four reasons. First, unemployment is higher as a result of many reforms that have resulted in increased landlessness in recent decades; second, the urban bias of public policy where hospitals, universities, government offices and the like are sited in the cities creating a good deal of professional employment and concentrating service provision; third, the demographic imbalance with a higher proportion of older people residing in the rural areas as a result of rural migration to the towns; and fourth, the far lower coverage of rural people by the social security system.

It is, however, important to disaggregate this picture for urban centres contain pockets of affluence as well as slums of unspeakable misery. Life in the urban slum areas can be worse than in rural areas. The national figure for infant mortality in Bangladesh, for example, was 94 per thousand live births compared to 97 for the rural and 71 for the urban areas but a high 134 for the urban slums in 1991 (World Bank, 1999, Table 7.1, p. 142).

Globalization, however, is likely to change this poverty profile. It is estimated that by the year 2025, the urban population of IDCs will almost double from its current 1.99 billion to 3.73 billion while the rural population will rise only marginally from 2.92 billion to 3.09 billion. Moreover, the poverty risk of urban dwellers may also increase so that the majority of the poor will be urban dwellers (Haddad *et al.*, 2000).

Globalization and Social Security

In AICs, social security cash benefits provide protection against poverty for the majority of those not in paid employment – the unemployed, those with disabilities and the retired. This is not the case in IDCs. Very few countries provide any cash benefits for the unemployed; sickness and disability benfits are only slightly more common; and pension schemes for the retired are inadequate in many ways despite the fact that they consume most of the expenditure on social security. In 1990, state expenditure on pensions for old age, disabilty and survivors amounted to a mere 1.4 per cent of GDP in Africa, 2.1 per cent in Latin America and the Caribbean and 3 per cent in Asia. In Europe, the proportion was 12.1 per cent (ILO, 2000, Table 14, p. 312). The contrast was even greater in relation to other benefits. Inevitably, only a small minority of the population is covered by state social security systems – 'no more than 20 per cent' in many IDCs and 'no more than 10 per cent' in much of Sub-Saharan Africa (ILO, 2000, p. vi).

Globalization has exerted a predominantly negative effect on social security protection systems in IDCs. It has, on the one hand, helped to increase the number of vulnerable people and, on the other, it has been a negative influence against expanded social protection because of its neoliberal ideology. It has increased the number of those in part time employment and in the informal labour market; it has reduced the number of those in the employment of the state; it has encouraged the rural exodus to the cities where family support systems are weak; and, in many countries, it has increased the number of the unemployed as a result of the financial crises to which it has contributed in recent years. On the other hand, many of the institutions and governments as well as the MNCs and the neoliberal ideology propelling the globalization process during the past twenty years have pressed for limited state social security protection. The result has been that the coverage of social security sytems in IDCs has remained very low and will remain so until globalization is underpinned by a more pro-welfare set of forces.

Exhibit 4.5

Globalization, economic growth and poverty

- Globalization has increased economic growth in IDCs.

- The number of people in absolute poverty in IDCs has increased in recent years.

- The proportion of people in IDCs who are in poverty has declined a little.

- Globalization has increased both the risk and the numbers of people in poverty in many IDCs but reduced them in others.

- The effects of globalization on the geographical distribution of the population will mean that in the future most of the poor will live in the urban rather than the rural areas.

- Social security systems in IDCs are rudimentary.

- On current evidence, poverty will continue to be massive in IDCs for the foreseeable future. Only a change in the economic and social philosophy underlying globalization and the work of international and national bodies, particularly in relation to aid and debt, can change this.

Globalization and Health

The health of any nation depends largely on two sets of factors: the prevailing living conditions and lifestyles; and the nature of the health services. The first acts to prevent or exacerbate disease while the second performs a primarily curative function. Adequate nutrition, safe water and good sanitation are the main preventive factors while access to primary and technological medicine are the curative factors.

Globalization has had an effect on both sets of factors and has, therefore, influenced health standards in IDCs in both positive and negative ways. Its influence on economic growth, income inequality and poverty is pivotal since many of the diseases in IDCs are so closely associated with poverty. Thus the influence of globalization on nutrition, clean water and sanitation is crucial to the prevention of disease and premature death. However good preventive services may be, there will always be a need for curative health services. The level and distribution of public expenditure on health is a rough indication of the level of a country's health services. Globalization has played an important part in this. Finally, globalization spreads western ideas of medicine not only because so many doctors are trained in AICs but also because of the imposition of health management methods by the various international agencies on the health services of IDCs.

Undernutrition

Nutrition is vital to good health while malnutrition and undernutrition cannot but be a central reason for illness and disease. The FAO estimates that 918 million people, 35 per cent of the total population in IDCs, were undernourished in 1969–71; 839 million or 21 per cent of the population in 1990–92; and 828 million or 19 per cent of the population in 1994–96 (FAO, 1996, Figure 13, p. 271; and FAO, 1998, Table 1, p. 3 and chart p. 373).

The situation improved in some countries but deteriorated in others. Of the 98 IDCs for which the FAO provides information, 54 witnessed an improvement between 1969 and 1996, 35 countries saw an increase in the proportion of their population who were undernourished and nine witnessed no change. The two most populous countries saw an improvement: China's proportion of undernourished people fell from 48 per cent in 1969 to 15 per cent in 1996; India's rates were 36 per cent and 20 per cent respectively (FAO, 1998, chart, p. 373). It was mainly Sub-Saharan countries that witnessed rises, not only in the number but also in the proportion of undernourished people.

There is a strong, though by no means perfect, relationship between incomes per capita in a country and its level of undernutrition. Thus the rate of undernutrition in Sub-Saharan countries is the highest in the world: it is double that of all IDCs, double that of Asia and three times that of Latin America. Historically, too, the relationship between income and undernutrition stands. While most IDCs managed to reduce their degree of undernutrition between 1969 and 1996, 'the poorest group of countries has not been able to reduce the number or percentage of undernourished since 1969–71' (FAO, 1998, p. 8). There are, however, several IDCS with low incomes but lower than expected rates of undernutrition because of the egalitarian distribution of income.

The proportion of children who suffer from undernutrition has declined but 'the absolute number of malnourished children worldwide has grown' (Bellamy, 1998, p. 10). A tangible manifestation of undernutrition is the proportion of young children who are under-weight. Of all children under five in the IDCs in the late 1990s, 31 per cent were under-weight; the proportion reached 40 per cent for the least developed countries; and 48 per cent for South Asia because of the high percentage in India – 53 per cent – and Bangladesh – 56 per cent (UNDP, 1999, Table 4, pp. 146–9).

Undernutrition among young children can be more devastating than among adults. It not only affects their physical, mental and emotional development but it is also a major cause of death. 'Of the nearly 12 million children under five who die each year in developing countries mainly from preventable causes, the deaths of over 6 million, or 55 per cent, are either directly or indirectly attributable to malnutrition' (Bellamy, 1998, p. 11).

Sanitation and Safe Water

The majority of the population in the developing world have no access to sanitation or to safe water. During the 1990s, in only 15 IDCs was the situation so good that less than 10 per cent of the population had no access to sanitation; in 30 countries the proportion of the population with no access to sanitation was 10–29 per cent; in 25 countries, 30–49 per cent of the population were without access to sanitation; in 27 countries the proportion rose to 50–69 per cent; and in 21 countries a staggering 70 per cent or more of the population had no access to sanitation.

The picture for access to safe water is equally grim: 24 countries with less than 10 per cent of the population having no access to safe water; 34 countries with a proportion of 10–29 per cent of their population having no access to safe water; 31 countries with 30–49 per cent; 21 countries with a proportion of 50–69 per cent; and 5 countries with 70 per cent or more of their population having no access to safe water (UNDP, 1999, Table 4, pp. 146–9).

Unsafe water and insanitary conditions are major causes of illness and death, particularly in children. Typhoid fever, diarrhoea, cholera and other serious diseases could be controlled with improvements in water supply and sanitation. It is an urgent problem for all developing countries but particularly for the poor and those living in the urban slums.

Much has been said about the power of the mass media in the modern world. Television, radio and newspapers can bring news to every corner of the globe within minutes and thus influence public opinion and public policy.

The record of the mass media on undernutrition has been worse than inadequate – it has been harmful. They have concentrated on scenes of famine that account for only a small proportion of the total suffering from malnutrition and the deaths which result. They have given hardly any publicity to the ongoing, and seemingly permanent, chronic and widespread undernutrition with the result that it remains 'not just a silent emergency – it is largely an invisible one as well' (Bellamy, 1998, p. 9).

Health Services

Health service provision in IDCs is woefully inadequate. Public expenditure per annum on health during the period 1990–98 was a mere 1.3 per cent of GDP for the lower income countries and 1.9 per cent for all IDCs compared to an average of 6.2 per cent for the AICs. There were also wide variations in the expenditures of different IDCs: Brazil, 3.4 per cent, China 2.0 per cent, and a mere 0.6 per cent for India, and 0.2 per cent for Nigeria (World Bank, 2000, Table 7, pp. 286–8).

Low expenditure on health is translated into fewer doctors and nurses, hospital beds and other health services. What is more, most of the doctors, nurses and hospital beds are located in the urban areas making the situation far worse in the rural areas where the majority of the population live. In brief, the level and distribution of health resources does not fit the level or pattern of demand for health care. Redirection of health resources to immunization programmes would achieve better health standards. In 1995, only 60 per cent of all one-year olds in the least developed countries were immunized against diphtheria, polio or measles and this was with wide country variations.

Life Expectancy

There has been a general improvement in survival rates over the years. Life expectancy at birth has risen from 54.5 years in all IDCs in 1970 to 64.4 years in 1997; in the least developed countries the corresponding figures are 43.4 and 51.7 respectively; and in the industrialized countries, 71.4 and 77.7 respectively (UNDP, 1999, Table 8, pp. 168–72). This overall improvement, however, masks a deterioration of rates in some countries: In the Russian Federation, life expectancy in 1997 was the same as in 1980 at 67 years; in Zambia, it declined from 50 to 43 years; in Uganda from 48 to 42 (World Bank, 1999, Figure 12, p. 26). Infant mortality rates per 1,000 live births dropped from 111 in 1970 to 64 in 1997 for all IDCs; from 149 to 104 for the least developed countries; and from 20 to 6 in the AICs.

Despite the improvements, the figures show that the gap between the rich and the very poor countries has not narrowed much in the case of life expectancy and has widened considerably in relation to infant mortality (UNDP, 1999, Table 8, pp. 168–72). Perhaps, the starkest statistic showing the gap in survival rates between rich and poor countries is the percentage of people not expected to survive to age 40 years – in 1997 it was 3.1 per cent for the AICs and 30.8 for the least developed countries.

AIDS

Globalization has facilitated the rapid spread of AIDS throughout IDCs in a variety of ways. Globalization undermined traditional sexual practices particularly in the urban areas; it increased poverty in some countries; and it reduced expenditure on health in several countries. Breastfeeding provides a grim illustration of the problems involved. Though it is more beneficial to babies than artificial feeding, it also runs the risk of passing on AIDS to the baby when the mother is HIV positive. The use of artificial feeding, however, is not only expensive but it can be just as dangerous to the health of the child if it involves the use of unsafe water.

The rate of AIDS in IDCs in 1997 was lower than in AICs – 28.9 officially diagnosed as against 99.1 per 100,000 people. Only in the Sub-Saharan countries was the rate higher standing at 111.1. In several African countries, however, the rates were far higher: 564.4 in Zimbabwe, 505.4 in Malawi and 420.6 in Namibia compared with the highest figure in AICs of 225.3 in the United States (UNDP, 1999, Table 9, pp. 172–6). What is more worrying is that the speed at which AIDS is spreading is so rapid that it is likely to make Africa the AIDS continent with catastrophic effects on the economy and the welfare of its people. Already, Sub-Saharan Africa contains 'over 90 per cent of all AIDS orphans – children who have lost their mother or both parents to AIDs' (Bellamy, 1999, p. 34).

Western Medicine

Finally, globalization has also influenced the nature of health care in IDCs through the spread of western ideas on medicine. It has encouraged the belief that western medicine is always superior to traditional medicine; it has promoted the sale of western drugs in sometimes unethical ways and at always high prices; and it has created a situation where western and traditional medicines are used together in complex ways to partially reflect local cultures. Western practice has penetrated but has not replaced, traditional practice for the majority of people, particularly in the rural areas, rely on it even though many aspire to western medical practices. 'In a variety of often inappropriate ways, traditional and modern medicines are combined, thereby offering both the reassurance and the familiarity of local traditional practice and the "magic bullet" effect of the modern' (Larkin, 1998, p. 101).

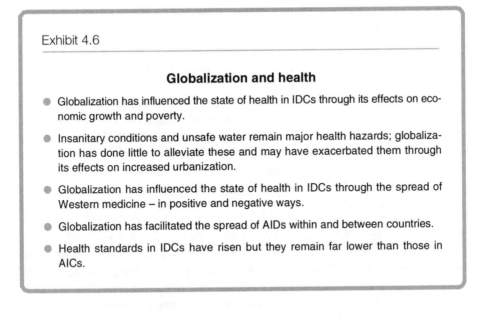

Exhibit 4.6

Globalization and health

- Globalization has influenced the state of health in IDCs through its effects on economic growth and poverty.

- Insanitary conditions and unsafe water remain major health hazards; globalization has done little to alleviate these and may have exacerbated them through its effects on increased urbanization.

- Globalization has influenced the state of health in IDCs through the spread of Western medicine – in positive and negative ways.

- Globalization has facilitated the spread of AIDs within and between countries.

- Health standards in IDCs have risen but they remain far lower than those in AICs.

Globalization and Education

The spread of western ideas has always been an integral part of the globalization process. Directly and indirectly, they have been presented as superior to the traditional ideas in the developing world. National elites have given credence to this process by accepting them and incorporating them into their life styles and into government policies. Education very clearly illustrates these trends and processes.

Globalization has affected the structure and ideology of education of IDCs in a variety of ways:

- First, the claim by many social scientists in the west that education is the most fundamental prerequisite to both economic growth and individual advancement became the cornerstone of government planning in post-colonial IDCs. In this way, individual and national living standards benefit.

- Second, if it is to succeed in its mission, it was believed, the educational system of a country must be selective and meritocratic. Through a process of selection, only a minority of pupils should be able to reach the higher echelons of education – university education.

- Third, as the world economy became more globalized and competitive, higher education was to become less exclusive, more open to private funding and subject to more evaluation in its outcomes (Green, 1999).

- Fourth, the effect of globalization on public expenditure on education has been positive in some countries but negative in others.

- Fifth, globalization has encouraged an increasing number of students from IDCs to pursue their studies in the universities of AICs.

Governments in IDCs placed tremendous emphasis on raising educational standards with the result that today public expenditure on education is often greater than expenditure on any other government activity. Public expenditure on education in all IDCs was 4.1 per cent of their GNP in 1997 as compared to 5.4 per cent in AICs. Some IDCs spent as much as some AICs on education. Interestingly, too, public expenditure on education did not decline over the years: for IDCs as a group it rose from 3.5 per cent of GNP in 1980 to 4.1 per cent by the end of the century; and for the Sub-Saharan countries from 3.8 per cent to 4.1 per cent (World Bank, 2000, Table 6, pp. 284–6).

Enrolment rates in primary and secondary schools have risen everywhere even though published figures exaggerate the extent of improvement since they do not take into account absenteeism and drop out rates that are very high. Nevertheless, there is no denying the substantial progress made in this area, despite the fact that millions of children still do not go to school and even larger numbers are educated in the most unsatisfactory schooling conditions. The relationship between poverty, school standards and education is brought out graphically in the following quotation about life in a school in Zambia:

> The average pupil walks seven kilometres every morning in order to go to school, has not eaten, is tired, undernourished, malnourished, suffers from intestinal worms, is sweating and lacks concentration on arrival. He or she sits with 50 other pupils in a similarly poor condition.... The teacher is poorly educated, badly motivated and underpaid. (Bellamy, 1999, p. 79)

Illiteracy rates have dropped everywhere but a major problem still remains: 'an estimated 855 million people – nearly one-sixth of humanity – will be functionally illiterate on the eve of the millennium' (Bellamy, 1999, p. 7). Though we discuss gender issues in Chapter 5, it is worth mentioning here that illiteracy rates for women are higher than those for men – 19 per cent of men and 34 per cent of women aged 15 and above in 1997 were illiterate in IDCs. The rates are much higher in Sub-Saharan countries – 34 per cent and 50 per cent – and in South Asia where the figures are 36 per cent and 63 per cent respectively (World Bank, 1999, Table 2, pp. 232–4). Moreover, this gender gap is set to continue for girls represent 'nearly two of every three children in the developing world who do not receive a primary education' (Bellamy, 1999, p. 7). Despite the improvements over the years, the recent economic crisis in Asia and the collapse of Soviet governments have had an adverse effect on schooling standards.

Following the western model of education, IDCs have expanded their university sector considerably and send many of their students to universities in western countries. Since the cost of a university student is many times greater than the cost of a primary student, the result is that the minority of university students consume a disproportionate share of their country's educational budget. The world-wide process of educational certification has meant a continuously rising level in the educational qualifications needed to fill jobs; an expansion in university places; and, in some countries, graduate unemployment.

Although no one denies the importance of education to economic growth, there is now greater understanding of the other factors involved in raising rates of economic growth. Similarly, some researchers report disenchantment among the poor concerning the human capital potential of education to help individual people because of falling educational standards. Writing of poor communities in Zambia, Kelly concludes 'In the past, people saw education as their great hope and promise for the future. Many no longer do so' (quoted in Jellena, 2000, p. 28).

Moreover, it is now acknowledged that education has done little to reduce income inequalities, an essential step if all sections of the community are to benefit from economic growth. Indeed, 'the educational systems of many developing nations sometimes act to increase rather than to decrease income inequalities' (Todaro, 2000, p. 343). This is the inevitable result of the twin processes whereby middle class young people are more likely to enter universities than other youngsters and to occupy the professional jobs that command higher salaries than other jobs. It also stems from the growth of private schooling in many IDCs which is leading towards a two-tier system: 'one for the rich, another – underfunded, mismanaged and ineffective – for the poor' (Jellena, 2000, p. 29).

As in health, there is a strong urban bias in education. It is not simply that institutions of higher education are sited in the cities but also because of the strong urban bias in the curricula of even primary schools which in turn reflects the influence of western ideas. As Todaro put it, 'The formal primary school system in most LDCs is, with minor modifications, a direct transplant of the system in developed countries' (Todaro, 2000, p. 349).

Such a bias neglects the needs of the rural population and makes the fight against illiteracy more difficult. Some feel that if illiteracy is to be abolished soon, many IDCs would be best advised to spend more on primary education and less on the university sector. This will not be easy bearing in mind the political pressures against such a policy.

As in health and poverty alleviation, it is difficult to see how highly indebted countries can deal with the educational problems facing them. Often, servicing their debts takes priority over providing adequate services. In 1998, '10 per cent of Zambia's GDP went to the servicing of debt while spending on primary education did not exceed 2 per cent of the GDP. Other examples include Ethiopia and Niger whose debt servicing expenditure is twice that of primary education' (Mwengo, 2000, p. 194).

The neoliberal ideology accompanying the current stage of globalization is responsible for the reductions in public expenditure on education imposed by the SAPs mentioned several times in this chapter. Since educational budgets were often the largest government budgets, they also suffered more from the cuts. It is estimated that between 1980 and 1987, real spending on education per person fell by 65 per cent in Sub-Saharan Africa and by 40 per cent in Latin America and the Caribbean (Colclough and Lwein, 1993, p. 20). Similarly public spending on education in the ex-Soviet countries fell dramatically during the 1990s – 'by one third in the Russian Federation and by three quarters or more in Azerbaijan, Bulgaria, Georgia and Kyrgyzstan' (UNICEF, 1999, p. 7), at a time when family incomes had fallen and inequality had increased.

In brief, the effects of globalization on public expenditure on education have been variable. Comparing expenditure on education in 1980 and 1996, one finds that in Africa it rose in eight countries and declined in fourteen; in Latin America, it rose in ten and declined in eight countries; in Asia, it rose in nine and declined in three; and in AICs, it rose in twelve and declined in seven (World Bank, 1999, Table 6, pp. 240–42).

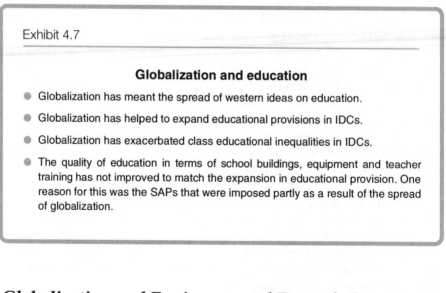

Exhibit 4.7

Globalization and education

● Globalization has meant the spread of western ideas on education.

● Globalization has helped to expand educational provisions in IDCs.

● Globalization has exacerbated class educational inequalities in IDCs.

● The quality of education in terms of school buildings, equipment and teacher training has not improved to match the expansion in educational provision. One reason for this was the SAPs that were imposed partly as a result of the spread of globalization.

Globalization and Environmental Degradation

Globalization has the potential for both destroying and protecting the environment. On the one hand, it facilitates the spread of aggressive industrialization and of rapacious consumerism both of which lead to environmental degrad-ation in direct and indirect ways. On the other hand, it can improve the quality of the environment by spreading technologies and practices that are environ-mentally friendly and by encouraging international action on environmental issues. So far, its destructive force has outweighed its protective potential.

A small number of environmental problems are national in character in the sense that they can be solved by policies at the local or national level. Urban slums, traffic congestion, overcrowding, insanitary conditions and dirty beaches are examples of this type of environmental problem.

A larger number of environmental problems, however, are global in character in the sense that they require national and international action. Gas emissions from different sources and from different countries polluting the atmosphere; destruction of tropical forests by different countries; desertification brought about by the activities of people in different countries; and reductions in biodi-versity, whether of the oceans, the forests or the countryside are examples of global problems which require both global and national action.

All environmental problems, however, have implications for the national and the global environment. From the perspective of the affluent world, it is the latter group of problems that are most pressing. These are 'the problems of the "global commons" which will place all countries at risk if no collective action is taken' (World Bank, 1999, p. 87). This is understandable for AICs have either largely solved their national environmental problems or, at least, have the capacity to do so. In the case of global problems, however, AICs are not masters of their own environmental fate.

For people in IDCs, however, it is poverty, slums and other local environ-mental problems that are the most pressing for it is they that directly result in immeasurable suffering and death. For the IDCs, a more equitable distribution of world resources is the key to a better environment; for the AICs, environ-mentally friendly policies provide the solution. Both the perception and the solution to the problems of the environment between IDCs and AICs are differ-ent (Redclift and Sage, 1999).

Increased urbanization brought about by globalization in IDCs has so far had adverse effects on the environment. The early stages of urbanization are always characterized by deteriorating environmental problems: the influx of large numbers of rural immigrants combined with the inability of local gov-ernment to provide adequate regulation and public services result in over-crowding, insanitary housing, unsafe water, lack of sanitation, rotting garbage, industrial waste and emissions from factories and vehicles. Central and local government in IDCs cannot afford clean technologies and the municipal services needed to prevent such problems reaching degradation levels. It is, therefore, not surprising that the worst polluted cities in the world are in IDCs today.

Deforestation is a major environmental problem. It is the result of many factors – commercial logging for global markets, road building, urbanization and extension of agriculture. The scale of deforestation has been very high in recent years: an annual loss of 15.5 million hectares of natural forests during 1980–90 and a slightly lower figure of 13.7 million hectares per annum during 1990–95 (FAO, 1997, p. 53). Only a small part of this can be attributed to the behaviour of the rural poor. The rest is the result of global commercial forces. Consider, for example, the consumption of paper on a world scale: while the average per person consumption of printing and writing paper in 1996 amounted to only 5.5 metric tons for the developing countries, the corresponding figure for the affluent countries was 104.6 metric tons and for some affluent countries far more than that – Finland 240.1 and the USA 136.8 metric tons per person (UNDP, 1999, Table 18, pp. 205–9). Deforestation will continue to worsen, because demand for wood and wood products will accelerate. Even a country such as China, which has managed to expand its forest area, may still be faced with severe shortages of wood in the future (Yin, 1998, p. 2153).

Carbon dioxide emissions are the most serious form of air pollution contributing to global warming and ozone depletion. Until recently, the affluent world with a small proportion of the world population produced most of the gas emissions; in recent years this has changed so that today it is the IDCs that produce most of these emissions though still far less than the size of their population warrants. In 1980, 36.1 per cent of such emissions came from IDCs and the remaining 63.9 per cent from AICs; in 1996, the corresponding proportions, however, were 52.6 per cent and 47.4 per cent respectively. If one looks at emissions per capita, however, the dominance of AICs is still overwhelming. In 1996, emissions per capita were 12.3 metric tons – the same figure as in 1980; for IDCs the corresponding figures were 2.5 tons in 1996 and 1.5 tons in 1980. The USA leads the world with 20.0 metric tons per capita in 1996, the same as in 1980. Indeed, the total carbon dioxide emissions from the USA in 1996 were far greater than the volume of such pollution from China though the gap was not as wide as in 1980 (World Bank, 1999, Table 10, pp. 248–50).

Globalization has also affected the environment in adverse ways as a result of its encouragement for more travel, more tourism and more trade. These are mostly pastimes of people from affluent countries but they have brought economic benefits to some groups in IDCs.

At the beginning of this section, reference was made to the positive potential of globalization for the environment by stimulating economic growth, spreading environmental technology and by promoting international action on the environment. There are numerous examples of environmentally friendly technologies – catalytic converters in cars, the replacement of CFCs in fridges and aerosol sprays, the use of solar and wind power, and so on. It is, however, unlikely that such technologies will be widely used in IDCs partly because of cost reasons and because of entrenched business opposition to such measures – a well-known problem in AICs, too.

The increased environmental pollution has been paralleled by a corresponding rise in Green parties, in non-government organizations (NGOs) concerned for the environment and by a succession of UNO conventions on different aspects of the environment. Green parties and NGOs have done a great deal of good in pressurising governments and in enlightening the public – more in AICs than IDCs – on the environmental dangers created by modern industrial and commercial practices and, to a lesser extent, encouraging industry to adopt sustainable practices.

International conventions on the environment involve complex economic, technical and political issues and they have met with varying degrees of success. Their low legal standing is shown by the fact that 'No mechanism exists for forcing recalcitrant states into line' (Held *et al.*, 1999, p. 411) – another indication that the national state has not been overrun by global forces. It may have lost some of its power but it has not been made redundant.

The Montreal Protocol in 1987, designed to reduce CFCs, has proved relatively successful because it was technically easy to implement, there was general agreement on its necessity, the interests of big business were not threatened and the big powers – notably the USA – were strongly supportive.

On the other hand, the Kyoto Protocol of 1997 that focused on gas emissions, particularly from cars, in order to reduce global warming has proved far less successful. Support for it from governments was either lacking or lukewarm and opposition to it from big business was strong. The result was that AICs simply agreed to try and reduce their greenhouse emissions to the level prevailing before 1990 by the year 2010; IDCs declined to do anything; China refused to sign the accord; and the US first pleaded for special case status and more recently declined to sign the protocol.

The Rio Convention on Biological Diversity in 1992 has also proved of little value but for different reasons. It relies heavily on the active cooperation of IDCs because they harbour most of the world's plants, fish and animals that need to be protected. Though support for the convention was strong, there were conflicting interests in its implementation. The large pharmaceutical companies, for instance, would gain a great deal because many of their drugs depend on plants in IDCs. At the same time they pass on little, if any, of their profits to the countries where the plants are to be found. The World Bank cites the example of the rosy periwinkle plant in Madagascar used by pharmaceutical companies to prepare a drug for treating childhood leukaemia. Sales of the drug net the companies $100 million a year but 'None of these proceeds, it should be noted, goes to Madagascar' (World Bank, 1999, p. 102).

Multinational companies were prepared to benefit from the Convention but not prepared to compensate IDCs for this. It was a convention that 'was conceived far too narrowly within the European tradition of conservation and emphasised environmental concerns at the expense of economic and development needs' (Biggs, 1998, p. 117). As pointed out earlier in this chapter, the most immediate environmental problems for governments in IDCs have to do with safe water and sanitation so they will naturally worry less about issues of biodiversity – an issue that is dear to people in the affluent world. Efforts to protect the 'the global commons' will never succeed until they are seen in AICs as part of the wider issue of economic development and poverty eradication in developing countries.

Globalization in AICs and IDCs:
A Brief Comparison

In this section we compare and contrast the effects of globalization on the two groups of countries we have been considering, although we are well aware that such an account inevitably simplifies what is a nuanced and complex picture. The wilder assertions of both supporters and opponents of globalization about its positive and negative impacts and potential need to be looked at carefully in the light of all the evidence.

First, globalization has penetrated AICs more than IDCs. No AIC has been unaffected by the globalization process, although many IDCs have yet to experience even modest effects of globalization. In terms of external trade, foreign direct investment, and the use of electronic forms of entertainment and communication, IDCs lag far behind AICs.

Second, overall, globalization has boosted economic growth far more in IDCs than in AICs – although obviously IDCs were starting from a much lower base line – even though several IDCs have performed far worse than any AIC. Differential rates of population growth, however, have meant that the differences in average incomes per capita between the two groups of countries have changed very little in recent years. The small proportion of the world's population living in AICs still consumes most of the world's resources.

Third, there is some truth in the claim that the export of jobs to IDCs – a process much facilitated by globalization – is one of the many reasons for the rise in unemployment among the unskilled and the semi-skilled in AICs. This, however, must be set against the creation of jobs in AICs as a result of the rise in exports to IDCs.

Fourth, globalization has boosted international trade but it has not changed the rules of trading with the result that AICs have benefited more than IDCs. The prices of primary agricultural goods – the main exports of IDCs – have not kept pace with increases in the prices of manufactured goods – the main export of AICs.

Fifth, the political effects of globalization have been felt far more in IDCs than in AICs. To begin with, governments of AICs possess more power to oppose some of the unwanted aspects of globalization than governments of IDCs.

Additionally, many of the globalization pressures on IDCs emanate from sources within AICs or are controlled by AICs. The pressure for democratic governments in IDCs stems largely from within AICs, while the pressure for neoliberal policies exerted on IDCs comes from agencies – the World Bank and the IMF, for example – which are controlled by the AICs.

Sixth, the claim that globalization has ushered in a 'borderless world' where the nation state has become an anomoly is a gross exaggeration. There is no doubt that governments have lost, or ceded, some powers to international bodies and to MNCs but national governments still possess the power substantially to influence and control events within their borders. Clearly, governments of AICs are in a stronger position to do this than governments in IDCs.

Seventh, there is much to support the view that globalization has involved the transmission of western culture to the whole globe. What is difficult to assess is whether this simply undermines local cultures or whether it creates new forms of hybrid local cultures. It is often a value judgement whether this type of cultural globalization is a form of enlightenment or of simple cultural imperialism.

Eighth, globalization has, on the whole, resulted in increased inequalities in both AICs and IDCs during the past twenty years or so. There are, however, countries in both groups where the reverse has taken place, evidence of the policy space left to national states. Many countries have become more affluent but also more unequal.

Ninth, the fundamental weakness of globalization has been its failure substantially to reduce poverty in either AICs or IDCs during recent years. Poverty declined in some countries but it increased in many others. In relative terms, the poor in both groups of countries may justifiably feel their deprivation equally strongly. In objective terms, however, the starvation poverty of the IDCs is a much more inhumane violation of human rights than the poverty found in AICs. Also, as Buttel points out, 'hunger is one of the ultimate yardsticks according to which the legitimacy of social institutions can be gauged' (Buttel, 2000, p. 16).

Tenth, we argue throughout this book that the neoliberal ideology underpinning current globalization is largely responsible for the misallocation of resources between, as well as within, countries. Globalization can coexist with other ideologies as it has in the past. Until a more welfare-friendly ideology supplants neoliberalism, globalization will continue to stimulate economic growth and, at the same time, to generate and tolerate increased poverty in both AICs and IDCs.

Finally, the destructive potential of globalization has outpaced it as a constructive force in relation to the physical environment. In the same way that earlier phases of industrialization and globalization witnessed the deterioration of the environment in AICs, the current phase has damaged the physical environment in IDCs. MNCs and consumerism have played havoc with the physical environment of IDCs. In an increasingly globalized world, however, the costs of environmental degradation know no national or regional boundaries.

Further Reading

Hoogvelt, A. (2000) *Globalization and the Postcolonial World* 2nd edn (Basingstoke, Macmillan).

Hurrell, A. and Woods, N. (eds) (1999) *Inequality, Globalization, and World Politics* (Oxford, Oxford University Press).

Kiely, R. and Marfleet, P. (eds) (1998) *Globalisation and the Third World* (London, Routledge).

5

Globalization and Gender Inequalities

The effects of globalization on women are mixed: they can be positive and negative, direct and indirect. It is a matter of fine judgement, laced with a touch of ideology, as to whether or not the evidence points, on balance, towards a positive rather than a negative influence. Although no contemporary society treats its women as well as its men, gender inequalities are less severe today than they were half a century ago. There are many reasons for this improvement; globalization is just one of them.

On the positive side, globalization has contributed to the expansion of employment for women; it has helped to improve women's educational prospects; it has made contraception more widely available; it has facilitated the creation of the international women's movement; it has helped to improve, even if only slightly, attitudes towards women; and it has popularized a more egalitarian set of gender relationships. In these, and in other ways, globalization has contributed to the reduction of gender inequalities. On the other hand, the negative impact of globalization on state welfare provision, the growth of low-paid, insecure jobs, the rise of sex tourism and the increase in lone parent families have had an adverse effect on the welfare of women.

This chapter examines the effects of globalization on a number of key interrelated issues – women's employment, women's caring tasks at home, progress in women's education, women's health issues, poverty and gender, the progress women have made in the political arena and the thorny question of culture and gender.

Treating women as a monolithic group oversimplifies what is a far more complex situation. Incorporating class and ethnicity in the analysis makes for a more realistic appraisal but an impossible task in the space of one chapter. An attempt, however, is made to bring out the differences between the position of women in IDCs and AICs because they are so striking. In the area of maternal mortality, for example, 'An African woman is 180 times more likely to die from pregnancy complications than a Western European woman' (UNDP, 1995, p. 36).

Globalization, Gender and the Labour Market

It is generally agreed that women's participation in the labour market strengthens their status in society at large. Behind this general consensus, two slightly different views emerge on how much women's participation in the labour market affects gender equality.

First, there is the very enthusiastic view that sees paid employment as self-evidently fundamental to women's standing in society. Paid employment provides women with an independent income and hence strengthens their influence and power within their family, their community and society. As Fajth and Foy put it, 'Economic power is the foundation of women's equality and the muscle which helps women exercise their human rights' (Fajth and Foy, 1999, p. 5).

The second position adopts a more cautious stance. It argues that the economic does not necessarily change the cultural or the social constraints on women's independence. Thus there are still countries where women workers are expected to hand their pay packets over to their husbands and to continue to play the usual submissive role in the family and in society. There is evidence from Bangladesh, Pakistan, India, Sri Lanka and elsewhere that one-third to one-half of women workers in agriculture and in industry give their wages to their husbands or other family members. Paid employment is a necessary but not a sufficient condition for gender equality (Agarwal, 1994, p. 71).

Such evidence, however, needs to be treated with caution because in many instances women give part of their wages to their parents not out of compulsion but voluntarily as a form of 'parent repayment'. This 'is not viewed by the women or their families as coercive or exploitative; rather it is voluntary, natural, logical, and a rational act of reciprocity' (Foo and Lim, 1989, p. 218).

Globalization has influenced both the quantity and the quality of work available for women. It has increased the number of jobs available and it has altered the nature of the jobs – for the worse in many situations. Several strands of the globalization process are responsible for these two rather contradictory effects on women's employment.

On the quantitative side, globalization encouraged both a rise and a decline in the number of jobs for women though the net effect was positive. To begin with, the nature of technological change in recent years has meant a decline in the traditional manufacturing and other heavy jobs that were the domain of men and a rise of the service sector where women have been able to compete very effectively with men. Second, foreign direct investment by MNCs in several developing countries has led to the creation of Export Processing Zones where women provide 'up to 80 per cent of the labour force' (ILO, 1998, p. 142). Third, in the light manufacturing sector, such as textiles, clothing and footwear, women have gained an advance over men because of the lower wages that they command. This is true for IDCs where this type of employment has increased but less so in AICs where there has been a contraction in recent years.

On the other hand, the reduction of employment in public services affected women more than men because these sectors were major employers for women. These effects were more strongly felt in IDCs and ex-Eastern European countries because the reduction of public sector employment was not compensated by an expansion of private welfare employment – as was to some extent the case in AICs. Standing, however, provides evidence that suggests that the female share of public sector employment in most of the small number of IDCs where data were available rose during the 1990s (Standing, 1999b, table 7, p. 594).

The qualitative changes stem from the strong emphasis that modern enterprises place on work flexibility. It has led to an increase in the number of part-time jobs, of contract work and low-paid jobs. The quality of these jobs in terms of security, wages, and welfare benefits is not as good as it is in the traditional 'standard' work model. Women have occupied most of these jobs – sometimes willingly because it suits their family circumstances and sometimes against their better judgement because there is nothing better available.

Using ILO data for 124 countries, Tzannatos shows that male participation rates in the labour force declined between the 1950s and 1990s from 93.7 per cent to 90.1 per cent while women's participation rates rose from 35.9 per cent to 47.9 per cent. Inevitably, there were significant variations between different regions in the world. While women's rates declined in only two regions – West Africa and South Asia – men's rates declined in all regions (Tzannatos, 1999, Table 1, p. 553).

Although the gender gap in labour force participation has narrowed significantly over the years, women are still the minority in the paid labour force in the world. They made up about one-third of all workers world-wide in the 1990s with significant regional variations – 11 per cent in the Middle East but 48 per cent in Central and Eastern Europe.

The rise in women's labour force participation rates is due not just to the forces of globalization but to a number of other interacting factors. Improvements in education, reductions in fertility rates, rising divorce rates, more social acceptance of women working outside the home, and rising male unemployment rates have also played their part. Political ideology, too, has been important for despite the demise of Soviet socialism, the female participation rate as a proportion of the male continued to be one of the highest in the world – 82.4 per cent in 1997 (UNDP, 1999, table 26, p. 236).

Official figures on gender and paid employment, however, underestimate women's participation in the labour market (Greenwood, 1999; Beneria, 1999) particularly in relation to two groups: those employed in the informal sector of the economy – a vast and growing sector in many IDCs; and home-based workers who are also a large group in many IDCs. Evidence suggests that most of these workers are women and including them in the official statistics could change the picture of gender participation rates and our understanding of women's contribution to economic growth. 'Perhaps no other category of workers better illustrates the limitations of official statistics and mainstream understanding of the informal sector than that of homebased workers' (Chen *et al.*, 1999, p. 605).

Sectoral trends in women's employment have not been too dissimilar from those of men. Historically, there has been a movement away from agriculture towards manufacturing and recently towards the service sector. This general trend, however, varies considerably from one region to another. In general, men are likely to be the majority in the manufacturing sector, women to dominate in the services while the position in agriculture varies from one region to another. All these trends have on the whole benefited women since 'the non-agricultural sectors generally offer higher-wage and more stable and secure employment' than agriculture (Mehra and Gammage, 1999, p. 538).

While women's participation rates in paid employment rose in most countries, they declined in most of the former Soviet bloc countries. At the beginning of the transition to capitalism in the early 1990s, they all had very high partici-pation rates – higher than most West European countries. The liberalization of the economy with its emphasis on privatization and reduction of public services meant a drop in labour participation rates for both men and women – although more for women that for men. Fourteen of the 26 million who lost their jobs during the transition were women (Fajth and Foy, 1999, p. 6).

The rise in women's paid employment has been mostly of the part-time type. The ILO speaks of the feminization of part-time employment. Of the twelve countries which it examines, in only two – Mexico and Turkey – is the part-time employment rate equal between men and women; in the other ten, women dominate with the UK showing the highest rate – women made up 87 per cent of part-time workers in 1996 (ILO 1998, Figure 6.4, p. 142). The importance of part-time work varies not only between the main world regions but also within the same region. Thus in the European Union, 18 per cent of men and 68 per cent of women in the Netherlands worked part-time as com-pared to only 4 per cent of men and 20 per cent of women in Italy, Greece and Spain in 1998 (European Commission, 1999, graphs 28 and 29, p. 34).

There is ample evidence that part-time employment is inferior to full-time employment in a number of ways: median hourly earnings, job tenure, training opportunities and social security benefits (OECD, 1999c, pp. 21–2).

Evidence from EU member countries suggests that the majority of women working part-time do so out of choice. Only 16 per cent in a Union wide survey in 1998 said that they worked part-time because they could not find a full-time job. The growth of part-time working among men, however, seems to be the result of employers wishing to increase flexibility since a high proportion of men in part-time employment, some 40 per cent, said that they did so because they could not find a full-time job (European Commission, 1999, p. 38).

Occupational segregation by gender has always been a feature of labour markets. It has declined slightly over the years but it is still a major feature of employment in both AICs and IDCs. Sex segregation occurs by both occupational sector and within the same occupation. Occupations such as teaching, nursing and social work, that is, the caring professions, as well as clerical and secretarial work are feminized occupations. Even in occupations where women do not dominate, they are concentrated within the lower strata of the occupation rendering those sections feminized. Thus, although women do not dominate the manufacturing sector, they overwhelmingly dominate garment production on a global scale. Occupational sex segregation tends to result in worse working conditions, lower pay and inferior career opportunities.

Tzannatos shows that sex segregation during the second half of the 20th century declined slightly and, surprisingly, it declined faster in the developing world so that in the 1990s sex segregation was less pronounced than in advanced industrial countries. Indeed, sex segregation in the industrial countries of Europe was higher than in Asia or Africa by both industry and occupation in the 1990s (Tzannatos, 1999, Table 5, p. 556 and Table 6, p. 557). Declining gender work segregation means the penetration of male dominated occupations and strata within occupations by women – something that improves the chances of gender equality.

One has to look, however, not just at pay but at the other conditions surrounding employment. As Perrons and Gonas point out, gender inequalities in employment may have narrowed at the general level but 'when employment categories are examined in more detail – in terms of status, degree of security and actual hours worked – then it becomes clear that gender inequalities remain' (Perrons and Gonas, 1998, p. 9).

Sex segregation is one of the major reasons for gender inequality in wages. All the evidence from across the world indicates that 'women typically receive less pay than men' (Elder and Johnson, 1999, p. 458). This applies to both part-time and full-time employment in all occupations. Earnings inequality between the sexes is not simply due to such personal characteristics as age, levels of education or experience. As Mehra and Gammage put it, 'Controlling for age, education and labor market tenure persistent differentials remain between rates of remuneration for men and women' (Mehra and Gammage, 1999, p. 545).

Earnings differentials between men and women declined slightly in most AICs during the last quarter of the twentieth century; in those IDCs where long-term data are available, earnings differentials declined in some but not in others; and over its last quarter, the twentieth century witnessed both rising and falling inequalities. Economic growth by itself does not reduce earnings differentials between the sexes since in two of the richest developing countries – Hong Kong and Singapore – earnings differentials between the sexes increased between 1975 and 1994 to become higher than those in many other less rich societies (Standing, 1999b, Table 6, p. 593).

Surprisingly, the transition to capitalism in the former Soviet bloc countries has not been accompanied by a widening of the gender pay gap. The difference in earnings between men and women was small under most of the Soviet regimes and it has remained so in the 1990s. The average monthly earnings of women as a proportion of male earnings in 1997 ranged from 88 per cent in the former Yugoslavia to 69 per cent in Bulgaria – figures that are very similar to those prevailing before 1990 (Fajth and Foy, 1999, Figure 4, p. 8).

Statistics on unemployment are notoriously unreliable particularly when used to make comparisons over time between countries. Nevertheless the data show that women's unemployment rates are higher than those of men in most developing as well as in most advanced industrial countries (Mehra and Gammage, 1999, p. 546).

In the European Union, the unemployment rate for women in 1997 stood at 11.8 per cent compared to 8.6 per cent for men; the figures for long-term unemployment were 5.8 per cent and 4.1 per cent respectively (European Commission, 1998, p. 127). Of the ten ex-Soviet countries where data were available for 1997, five had higher unemployment rates for women, three showed higher rates for men and two had the same rate of unemployment for both men and women (Fajth and Foy, 1999, Figure 3, p. 7).

Gender trends in unemployment show an improvement in women's position. During the twenty-year period from the mid-1970s to the mid-1990s, women's rate of unemployment in relation to that of men fell in 73 per cent of AICs and 83 per cent of IDCs (Standing, 1999b, Table 9, p. 596). Government data, however, may underestimate women's rate of unemployment more than men's because of the official definition of unemployment.

Exhibit 5.1

Globalization, women and employment

- Globalization has increased women's participation in the labour market and has narrowed the gender gap in employment rates.

- Occupational sex segregation has declined slightly but it is still a feature of labour markets.

- Women's pay is lower than men's even though pay differentials have narrowed slightly in many countries.

Exhibit 5.1 (*cont'd*)

- Globalization has encouraged the growth of 'feminized' employment, that is, low-paid, insecure, part-time or contract work.

- Women's rate of unemployment is higher than men's in most countries despite recent improvements.

- The main driving force behind the growth and changing pattern of women's employment has been the changing nature of the labour market brought about largely by the forces of globalization. Social, cultural and political factors have also played a part.

- The evidence does not support the thesis that globalization has marginalized women in the labour market (Horton, 1999). It has improved, but has not equalized, women's position in the labour market *vis-à-vis* that of men.

Globalization, Gender and Caring

Paid employment and unpaid caring at home are intertwined in the lives of most women in all societies. What happens in one domain has implications for the other. The state, however, sees them as two separate areas of activity and only reluctantly intervenes in the latter because it considers caring a private duty. It is this gender-blind approach to paid work and unpaid caring that many feminists consider as an institutional form of sex discrimination. Labour markets, too, operate on the basis of this approach with the result that they are both institutionally sexist and 'reinforcers of gender inequality' (Elson, 1999, p. 613).

The feminist perception of labour markets is distinct from that of most traditional labour economists who view the operations of the labour market in isolation from household caring work and who consider sex discrimination as a residual phenomenon resulting from the decisions of individual employers. In contrast, the feminist approach insists that 'gender equality in work and income can only be achieved if there is a complementary policy on (unpaid) care' (Plantenga and Hansen, 1999, p. 378). Labour markets occasionally make allowances for women so that they can carry out their twin roles of employees and carers but this is done largely on the employers' terms.

The contemporary form of globalization with its strong neoliberal ideology has, on balance, exacerbated the difficulties of women as carers. First, it has, on the one hand, created many more jobs for women, albeit part-time in nature, while on the other it has militated against occupational or state provisions that make it easier for women to carry out their dual roles. At best, globalization has meant that state provision in child care, community care and social security did not expand to meet the rising needs of growing female paid employment. At worst, it has resulted – as in the SAPs and welfare retrenchment reforms – in a reduction of these services that inevitably made the burden on women even heavier. Connelly sums up the situation, 'What the World Bank, the IMF, governments and companies regard as efficiency is simply a shifting of costs and workload from the paid workforce onto the unpaid household economy and the shoulders of women where it cannot be seen' (Connelly, 1999, p. 26).

Second, the reduction of state services and the rise in female employment has not only meant a greater burden for women but in many cases a reduction of caring. This is particularly the case with poorer households that cannot afford to make up the deficit in care from the private sector. In IDCs, this will apply to the majority of the population. As the 1999 UNDP Report puts it 'Globalization is putting a squeeze on care and on caring labour' (UNDP, 1999, p. 77).

Third, globalization has strengthened women's independence and encouraged more liberal attitudes to sex and marriage. It could be claimed that the downside of this has been a sharp rise in divorce and in the number of one-parent families headed mostly by women in all parts of the world. State provisions for one-parent families are non-existent in most IDCs and, where they exist in AICs, they are grossly inadequate. It is not surprising that the extent and depth of poverty among these families is far greater than among two-parent families.

Fourth, globalization has not had the same impact on the caring load of men. While men in AICs may have taken on a few more caring tasks than before, the belief that men's main role is in the labour market persists in many countries, even advanced industrial countries. An EC study of attitudes in the 15 member countries found that although in general men and women respondents agreed that it is just as important for a woman to have a job as for a man, a sizeable minority – 36 per cent of men and 29 per cent of women – believed that men should have priority over women when jobs are scare. As expected, there were wide country variations in this with Sweden at one end and Belgium and Greece on the other (Plantenga and Hansen, 1999, Table 2, p. 366). Such state provision as state paternity leave is rare and only a paltry 5 per cent of male workers in the EU took paternity leave in 1995 and a similar proportion worked part-time (UNDP, 1999, p. 82).

Fifth, globalization boosted male rural migration to the towns in many parts of Africa and Asia leaving women behind to care for the children and the elderly as well as till the land. In the absence of state support, and sometimes with no financial assistance from their husbands, women have to bear a triple burden – caring, paid employment and farming.

Sixth, globalization has encouraged work practices – contract work, unsocial hours of work, competitive practices, payment by results, and so on – that have had undesirable effects on people's physical and mental health. It is difficult to establish whether this has affected men more than women though all the evidence shows that women work longer hours than men when paid and unpaid work are taken into account. A survey of men and women in manufacturing in Bangladesh in 1995, for example, showed that women worked 87 hours a week compared to men's 67 taking account of both paid and unpaid work (UNDP, 1999, Box 3.3, p. 81).

Flexible employment, women's paid employment and greater gender equality are here to stay. Current government and occupational policies in the labour market, in support of the family and of caring in the community place an excessive burden on women. This means that 'the family – the main institution for ensuring social cohesion – needs help in an age of flexible production and changed gender roles' (Carnoy, 1999, p. 428). Changes in government and occupational policies as well as a more active role by men in caring are necessary.

The increasing burden of caring placed on women can be and is alleviated for those women who have the financial means to purchase labour-saving devices in the home and to pay for private services to carry out domestic or caring roles. The proportion of such women is small in AICs and far smaller in IDCs but it is an indication of the significance of class in gender debates.

The development of good pension systems in AICs has enabled older people to live independent lives and to rely less on their families. Financially, most pensioners are well provided for and many have enough income to pay for care assistance. It is the elderly of IDCs that are in greatest difficulty and globalization has done little to help them. To the extent that women live longer than men, this lack of pension provision has affected women more than men.

Exhibit 5.2

Impact of globalization on caring

- Globalization has increased the need for caring in society.
- Globalization has reduced the supply of women who traditionally do caring.

Exhibit 5.2 (*cont'd*)

- Globalization has thus increased the burden of caring on women.
- Globalization has made imperative the need for changes in government caring policies and for a greater caring role for men.

Globalization, Gender and Education

Education is not only a form of human capital investment raising the employment and earnings prospects for all; it is also a way of reducing gender inequalities in earnings. A study of nine AICs in 1994 showed that university education narrowed the earnings gap between men and women with the exception of France where women's earnings stood at 65 per cent of men's for both university and non-university educated workers. In the UK, the annual earnings of women with only secondary education amounted to 40 per cent of men's while the earnings of women graduates totalled 60 per cent of men's. The corresponding figures for the USA were 60 and 63 per cent respectively while those of the Netherlands were 43 and 52 per cent respectively (ILO, 1998, Figure 6.5, p. 145).

Globalization has influenced the education of women in a variety of ways. First, it has been one of the forces that have been undermining the traditional cultural belief that women's education is not important since their place is in the home. This attitude still persists in some countries but its strength has weakened making the education of girls more possible.

Second, the constant stream of technological changes associated with globalization has meant that the education of girls is more important since many of the jobs resulting from these changes will be suitable for both sexes. Brain rather than brawn is the essence of most jobs created by modern technology. Moreover, employers prefer women as employees because they find them more adaptable to the demands of a flexible labour market. Women's education is more necessary today for purely labour market reasons.

Third, the contemporary phase of globalization spreads information and knowledge around the world more rapidly than before. The connection between parental education and children's educational achievement has been known for decades but the evidence linking the mother's education level to her children's health is more recent. There is an inverse relationship between the level of women's education on one hand and the size of their families, as well of child mortality rates, on the other. In brief, 'educating women has been shown to be a critical ingredient in breaking the vicious multigenerational cycle of poor child health, low educational performance, low income, high fertility, and poor child health' (Todaro, 2000, p. 348).

Fourth, education has long been seen as the main path to professional, technical and managerial jobs. Globalization has both increased the number of such jobs and may have reduced the gender bias in professional careers by promoting images of successful career women in the global mass media. Although women are still under-represented in these positions, they are more visible today than in the past.

Fifth, international bodies – part of the globalization process – have assisted the cause of women's education. The UNICEF Girls' Education Programme in more than fifty countries, for example, attempts to stimulate gender sensitivity in both the contents of the curricula and the methods of teaching so as to encourage girls' enrolment in schools and close the enrolment gap with boys (Bellamy, 1999, p. 56).

On the negative side, the neoliberal ideology accompanying the most recent stage of globalization may have hindered women's education as a result of the SAPs policies forced on governments in IDCs by the IMF and the World Bank. Reductions in public expenditure can reduce education budgets and they may also raise the costs falling on parents for the education of their children. Although all children's schooling suffers as a result of education cutbacks, girls' education suffers more than boys' in those countries where schooling for girls is not considered as necessary as that of boys.

Several indicators can be used to measure trends in the education gender gap in recent years. Beginning with adult literacy rates, that is, the percentage of people aged 15 and over who can read and write, the gender gap has narrowed in all regions. The rates for all the developing countries were: 68 per cent for men and 46 per cent for women in 1980; the corresponding figures for 1995 were 79 and 62 per cent respectively. These overall figures conceal wide variations. The least developed countries had much lower figures: in 1980, 47 per cent of men and 24 per cent of women were literate; in 1995, the figures were 59 and 38 per cent. East Asian countries had fairly high figures for both years – 80 and 58 per cent for 1980 and 91 and 76 per cent for 1995. Latin America had even better literacy figures for both sexes so that by 1995 there was almost gender parity with figures of 88 and 85 per cent for men and women. The same, however, cannot be said of South Asia, which includes the Indian subcontinent: for 1980, the figures are 52 and 24 per cent while for 1995 they are 63 and 36 per cent. Clearly, most women in this region are illiterate and bearing in mind the population size of the region, this constitutes a very major problem (Bellamy, 1999, Table 4, pp. 106–9).

Literacy rates in advanced industrial societies have been almost universal for both men and women for the period under consideration here. The same applies for the ex-Soviet societies despite the fact that they are not rich – another indication that political factors can override economic obstacles.

Reductions in illiteracy rates may underestimate the volume of progress made in recent years because they cover the entire adult population. Concentrating on primary school attendance may well provide a more accurate picture. In Sub-Saharan Africa, twice as many boys as girls attended primary school in 1960; in the late 1990s, the proportions were almost the same: 57 per cent for girls and 61 per cent for boys. Progress was even better elsewhere. By the late 1990s the gender gap had closed in four regions: AICs with universal primary school attendance for both sexes; the ex-Soviet countries with almost universal rates; East Asia with rates of 94 and 93 per cent for boys and girls respectively; and Latin America and the Caribbean with rates of 89 per cent for boys and 90 per cent for girls. Only South Asia still presents a problem despite the narrowing of the gap with 74 per cent for boys and 62 per cent for girls (Bellamy, 1999, Table 4, pp. 106–9).

A similar picture emerges with regard to both secondary and tertiary education. Girls' net enrolment in secondary schools rose faster than that of boys so that by 1997 it was the same in the industrialized countries, in the ex-Soviet countries, in Latin America and the Caribbean and in East Asia even though the proportion of girls and boys attending secondary schools varied among these regions. The gender gap closed considerably in the other regions so that in even the least developed countries it reached 66 per cent, though only 25 per cent of girls enrolled in secondary schools (UNDP, 1999, Table 25, pp. 229–33).

Data for tertiary education is available for only some regions. They show that the numbers of female students exceeded those of male students in 1996 in the AICs and the ex-Soviet countries; they were 73 per cent of male students in the Arab countries; 61 per cent in South Asia; and 57 per cent in East Asia (UNDP, 1999, Table 25, pp. 229–33).

Despite the very substantial progress made in recent decades in closing the gender education gap, the problem is still of sizeable proportions at all levels of education in IDCs. Only in AICs has the gender gap disappeared and education at the primary and secondary level has been made a reality for all boys and girls. The paramount reason behind the gender gap is the cultural belief in many countries that education is not so important for girls as it is for boys. Until this cultural belief is changed, the gender gap in education will continue.

Exhibit 5.3

Globalization, gender and education

- Globalization has contributed to narrowing the illiteracy gap and the school enrolment gap between the genders.

Exhibit 5.3 *(cont'd)*

- In many countries, school attendance and school performance by girls has exceeded that by boys in recent years.

- Yet, most of the illiterate people and those not attending school are female.

- Globalization has improved women's educational standards though they still lag behind those of men in IDCs.

Globalization, Gender and Health

The ways in which globalization affects health standards across the world is discussed in chapters 3 and 4. In this section, we set out, in brief, the effects of globalization on women's health beginning with the two most commonly used health indicators – life expectancy and infant mortality rates by gender. They may be blunt yardsticks of health but are useful nevertheless.

Life expectancy at birth and at age sixty has increased for both men and women over the years. Only two groups of countries have witnessed a reduction in life expectancy in recent years – some of the ex-Soviet countries and some of the Sub-Saharan countries. Between 1989 and 1997 female life expectancy at birth in the ex-Soviet countries decreased for both men and women as a result of the collapse of the economy, the rise in poverty and the decline in health services brought about by the strong neoliberal policies adopted (Fajth and Foy, 1999). In some of the Sub-Saharan countries, life expectancy is also decreasing because of the heavy death tolls resulting from AIDs.

Although life expectancy has improved for both sexes across the world, it rose more for women than for men so that by 1997, only one country – the Maldives – showed a higher life expectancy at birth for men than for women. There were, however, several countries where women's life expectancy in relation to men's was not as high as one would expect from the experience of most other countries.

It could be legitimately argued that the real problem today is not so much the gender gap in life expectancy but the gap between rich and poor countries. Life expectancy at birth in Sub-Saharan countries in 1997 was 52 years for women and 49 for men; in the AICs, the corresponding figures were 81 and 74 respectively. The gap is even wider when comparing individual countries: Sierra Leone in 1997 had a life expectancy at birth of 38.7 years for women and 35.8 for men; the corresponding figures for Japan were 82.9 and 76.8 respectively (UNDP, 1999, Table 2, pp. 138–42).

The rate of infant mortality is another blunt but equally useful health indicator. As with life expectancy, the general picture has been one of steady improvement over the years. Infant mortality rates declined for both sexes and in 1992 only one country, Egypt, had higher infant mortality rates for baby girls than for baby boys – 37.3 per thousand live births of baby girls compared to 35.3 per thousand live births of baby boys (UNO, 1998, Table 22, pp. 498–517).

Child mortality before the age of five years highlights the discrimination against girls in some societies. In most countries, more boys than girls die before the age of five but in 13 countries – which interestingly did not include either China or India – more girls than boys died before that young age in 1992 (UNDP, 1995, Table 2.4, p. 35). Again this represents an improvement over the years but is hardly enough to deal with the problem.

There is general agreement that women are biologically 'hardier' than men and, given the same degree of care as men in society, one would expect them to live longer than men, to outnumber men in the general population and to dominate men among the elderly groups. This generally applies in the world with the exception of some countries in Asia and North Africa where the gender ratio favours men. This has come to be known as the problem of the 'missing women' that has attracted a great deal of debate in recent years. It is estimated that had girls and women been given the same degree of attention and care as boys and men in these societies, there would have been between 60 and 100 million more women (Klasen, 1994). The main reason for this 'disappearance' of women is not the much-publicized incidence of female infanticide but 'the comparative neglect of female health and nutrition, especially – but not exclusively – during childhood' (Sen, 1999, p. 106).

Despite the seriousness of the problem of the 'missing women' the evidence suggests that it is amenable to improvement. Looking at trends in the four countries where the problem exists – Bangladesh, China, India and Pakistan – while life expectancy at birth in 1965 was higher among men in three of the four countries, by 1997 female life expectancy surpassed that of men in three and equalled it in the fourth – Bangladesh – a welcome improvement but not of the magnitude that would eliminate the problem altogether. Even if life expectancy among women *vis-à-vis* men improves considerably in these countries, a new problem is emerging in recent years – high rates of abortion for female pregnancies. The one-child policy of China has resulted in anti-female baby practices, the most serious of which is selective abortion 'which has become quite widespread in China with the progress of technology' (Sen, 1999, p. 107). Medical advances, which can ascertain the gender of the foetus, have resulted in more abortions of baby girls in various parts of Asia in recent years.

The main causes of mortality for women vary considerably between AICs and IDCs. While in affluent countries, the main causes are diseases of the circulatory system and cancers (European Commission, 1997, Figure 5.1, p. 53), the major causes in poor countries are pregnancy complications and poverty with its effects on nutrition, housing and so on. 'It would be hard', says Smyke, 'to exaggerate the influence that poverty has on people's health, because poverty restricts choice in so many areas that are basic to good health' (Smyke, 1991, p. 26).

Women are more likely than men to be in poverty and to be undernourished, particularly in IDCs. This has always been the case and globalization has in some ways reduced the problem by providing employment for women, by raising education standards and by changing social attitudes concerning the position of women in society. There are, however, instances where globalization has increased the health risks for women in IDCs. The rural exodus by men to the towns has meant that women are left behind with the triple burden that we discussed above – a sure combination to endanger health. Where globalization has led to local deforestation, women have had to walk longer distances to bring fuel exposing them to increased dangers. It brings them into frequent contact 'with contaminated rivers and exposes them to water-borne diseases like schistosomiasis (sometimes called snail fever, or bilharzia)' (Turshen, 1995, p. 240).

Structural Adjustment Programmes (SAPs) forced on so many governments in IDCs affected women more than men when they led to reductions in state health care provisions. This may have been the result of the lower status of women, their lower political power, their preoccupation with caring duties, and so on. The fact that most health care facilities are in the cities while many women stayed behind in the villages in many third world countries exacerbates the situation particularly at times of reductions in health provisions.

Globalization has encouraged the rise in female-headed families in many IDCs for a variety of reasons. It has encouraged freer sexual attitudes and hence higher rates of family breakdown with the women usually left to care for the children. In IDCs globalization has encouraged a male rural exodus to the cities and in many cases this has meant more one parent families. In AICs, many women would rather look after their children on their own than live in oppressive family situations. They would not have been able to do this without the existence of employment opportunities which globalization has helped to create.

These changes in family patterns have not only increased the burden borne by women but they have also increased the health risks run by these families. Jacobson gives figures that show that the proportion of female-headed families in rural areas of IDCs in the 1980s is very high – ranging from 21 per cent in the Dominican Republic to 40 per cent in rural Namibia (Jacobson, 1993, p. 17). Though female-headed families in AICs, too, are disadvantaged and run higher health risks than two-parent families, the depth of disadvantage suffered is not of the same seriousness as that endured by their counterparts in IDCs where social security benefits and social service provision is either absent or minimal.

Violence against women is ingrained in all societies – it is part of the patriarchal system that characterizes all societies to a greater or lesser extent. It is very difficult to disentangle the effects of globalization on this problem, as evidenced by a brief look at the situation in China. Traditional Chinese culture stresses the obedience of women to their father, their husband and, when widowed, to their son. Globalization has been undermining this cultural tradition through its employment, technological and cultural effects and it has made possible the emergence of a modicum of awareness of the seriousness of the problem of gender violence in recent years. This has meant that more cases of violence against women, including rape, are being reported; more public discussion of the problem takes place; and it is beginning to be seen as a gender problem rather than a problem of general lawlessness, as the Criminal Code of China defined it. Despite all of this, evidence seems to suggest that violence against women is still 'a problem which may be largely condoned' (Tang *et al.*, 2000, p. 207).

Globalization has encouraged the growth of sex tourism on a large scale. Visitors to several Asian countries – Thailand and the Philippines – arrive specifically for easily available cheap sex. Young girls work in brothels and massage parlours earning high incomes for their employers and pittance amounts for themselves. Escaping from prostitution is not easy because these girls come from impoverished large families in the rural areas. They are a major source of income for their families. Sex tourism 'also shades into the mail order bride business' (Cohen and Kennedy, 2000, p. 220). Men arrive on package tours to look and select a bride often under the belief that Asian women make more docile wives. On a smaller scale, there is also the sex tourism in European cities with girls from the former Soviet bloc countries working as prostitutes. Poverty is the main reason behind sex tourism and until this underlying problem is dealt with, sex tourism will continue.

Finally, the technological and international aspects of globalization have facilitated the growth of women's social movements across the globe. Local, national and international campaigns on women's health, either on their own or with the support of international bodies such as the WHO, have had some effect in highlighting women's health issues and in improving services (Doyal, 1996). This, of course, applies to other areas – violence, education, discrimination and so on.

Exhibit 5.4

Globalization, gender and health

- Globalization has contributed to the rise of life expectancy – slightly more for women than for men.
- Globalization has contributed to the reduction of infant mortality – slightly more for baby girls than for baby boys.

Exhibit 5.4 (*cont'd*)

● Despite these improvements, the problem of the 'missing women' remains.

● Globalization has encouraged sex tourism.

● Globalization has made it easier for the women's movement to influence health events.

● Globalization has reduced the vast disparities in health between women in AICs and IDCs. These disparities, however, remain distressingly wide.

Globalization and the Feminization of Poverty

The feminization of poverty thesis refers to the twin and related claims that the majority of the poor are women and that women run a higher risk of poverty than men. This section examines how globalization has affected the various reasons behind the feminization of poverty.

First, there are the labour market reasons discussed earlier in this chapter. Women are more likely than men not to be in paid employment, to be working part-time and to be earning lower wages. This is less so today than fifty years ago – a trend that suggests that globalization has improved the position of women in the labour market and hence has reduced the risk of poverty arising out of low wages or the absence of wages. Indeed, one recent study found that the risk of poverty among women of working age is becoming similar to that of men in a small number of European countries (Casper and McLanahan, 1994).

Second, there are strong demographic reasons. Women's weak position in the labour market is reflected and reinforced in old age. Women not only live longer than men in most countries but they are also less likely to have adequate pensions arrangements or substantial savings. Inevitably, they are more likely to be in poverty than men at a time in their life when health or disability needs are at their highest. The increasing urbanization and geographical mobility of the population encouraged by globalization have made it increasingly difficult for the extended family to provide adequate support to elderly members.

Third, the recent sharp rise in one-parent families headed by women weakens women's economic position because of the inadequate financial and child care provision by the state and the low wages for those who decide to go out to work. All the evidence shows that the financial situation of one-parent families is weaker than that of two-parent families and the risk of poverty that they run is higher. As mentioned earlier in this chapter, globalization has played its part in the growth of one parent families.

Fourth, there are cultural reasons that influence the distribution of family income to the detriment of women. We saw earlier in this chapter how women give some of their wages to their husbands either voluntarily or against their will. There is also abundant evidence that in married households in AICs, the husband consumes more of the family income than the wife. Pahl's pioneering study in the UK, supported by subsequent studies in other countries, found that women in couples are less likely than men to have income of their own, spend less on themselves than their husbands and, in the case of the poorer households, are more likely to be responsible for the family budget than men (Pahl, 1989). Globalization, however, has encouraged a more egalitarian distribution of family income through the empowerment of women which is discussed in the next section.

Fifth, government and occupational social security policies discriminate against women because of their reliance on the insurance principle and full-time paid employment. As a result, caring at home is largely or wholly ignored for social security purposes; and benefits for those in part-time employment are either non-existent or inferior to benefits for those in full-time employment. Moreover, the generosity of state and occupational retirement pensions depends on the individual's previous earnings and length of employment – both of which factors militate against women. The situation is worse in IDCs where only a small proportion of women are in full-time paid employment to qualify for insurance benefits. Not surprisingly, one study of the situation in Africa concludes that formal social security systems in the region 'target males and disadvantage females' (Kasente, 2000, p. 32). Globalization has reinforced this through its emphasis on competitive employment policies.

Sixth, IMF restructuring policies in several IDCs involved the reduction of government subsidies for basic commodities and hence a rise in prices. Though all people on low incomes suffered as a result, it can be legitimately argued that women suffered most because of the well-known tendency for women to give priority to the welfare of their families over their own welfare.

In view of the above analysis women will continue to run a higher risk of poverty and, given their numerical superiority, they will also outnumber men in the poverty population.

In 1997, real GDP per capita in PPP$ was substantially lower for women than for men in all countries. In the AICs, the figures were 17,660 for women and 30,050 for men; in the IDCs, they were 2,088 and 4,374 respectively; and in the least developed countries, they were 731 and 1,258 respectively (UNDP, 1999, Table 2, pp. 138–42). The figures also show the glaring income inequalities between AICs and IDCs that are referred to in Chapter 4. Women's incomes in AICs were eight times greater than those of women and four times greater than those of men in IDCs.

Poverty studies in several AICs support the feminization of poverty thesis. In the UK, 22 per cent of two-parent families, 60 per cent of one-parent families and 32 per cent of single pensioners – most of whom were women – were in poverty in 1995 (George and Wilding, 1999, Table 5.7 p. 140). In France, during the late 1980s and early 1990s, 14.9 per cent of all households were in poverty; 18.3 of lone parent families; and 31.0 per cent of those aged 75 and over. In Spain the corresponding proportions were 17.5 per cent, 22.8 per cent and 34.1 per cent respectively; in Portugal, 26.5 per cent, 34.5 per cent and 49.3 per cent respectively; in Italy, 22.0 per cent, 36.6 per cent and 41.4 per cent respectively; and in Belgium the percentages were 7.5, 23.6 and 12.7 respectively. The majority of both lone parents and those aged 75 and over are women (Ramprakash, 1994, Table 2, p. 121)

In the USA in the late 1990s, children in female-headed households had poverty rates 'nearly five times those of children in married-couple households' (White House, 1998, p. 94). Also, in the USA during the same years 'Poverty rates for elderly women are nearly twice as high as those for elderly men, and 72 per cent of all elderly living in poverty are women' (White House, 1999, p. 164).

In West Germany in 1994, the proportion of women in poverty using household income as the yardstick was 12.4 per cent while for men the figure was 9.8 per cent. If one used individual income rather than household income as the basis for the calculation, then the corresponding proportions were 21.4 per cent and 4.5 per cent respectively (Ruspins, 1998, Table 1, p. 296)

Thus, despite the existence of fairly comprehensive welfare provision in AICs, women are more likely than men to be in poverty. The position is worse for women in IDCs where their status in the labour market and in the welfare state is inferior.

Exhibit 5.5

Globalization, gender and poverty

- The majority of the poor in any country are women.

- Women run a higher risk than men of being in poverty.

- Globalization has increased the risk of poverty for some groups of women and reduced it for others.

- Globalization has weakened the feminization of poverty in some ways but strengthened it in others.

Globalization and Gender Empowerment

The power that individuals and groups have stems from the command that they have over material, social, political and ideological resources *vis-à-vis* other individuals and groups in society. A great deal has already been achieved in empowering women in AICs but a great deal remains to be done, particularly in the IDCs. A number of factors, all linked with globalization, have affected women's empowerment.

First, women's entry into the labour market, and into positions previously closed to them, has been a major force in improving their position within their household, community and society. Having their own income gives them more freedom as well as more power even if this has to be viewed within the cultural context of their society.

Second, the advances in education achieved by women in recent decades have contributed immensely to their empowerment. Education enables women to be more independent, lifts their status in society and enables them to have a greater say in decision-making even in the most traditional of societies.

Third, the spread of birth control techniques has enabled women to be more in control of their reproductive functions. Numerous pregnancies inevitably take their toll on the independence and health of women particularly in societies where their status is already low. Reduced and planned pregnancies enable women to fulfil other roles in society apart from reproduction. Birth rates are declining the world over even though the decline is far greater in AICs than IDCs. Many factors have contributed to this and globalization is simply one of these.

Fourth, the spread of democratic forms of government, spurred on by globalization, has been another factor that has contributed to the rise of women's power. Only a handful of countries today have either no democratic government elections or no enfranchisement for women. The right to vote and the right to be elected to political office are now almost universal for both men and women

Generally, however, women's progress in being elected to political office has been far slower than their advances in employment, education or health. Indeed, the higher the level of the political office, the lower the representation of women. Thus female representation at the local council level is higher than at the national level and this in turn is higher than at the cabinet level. It is at its lowest at the head of state level.

The percentage of seats in parliament held by women in 1999 was 17.3 for the AICs, 10.0 for the middle-income countries and 8.9 for the low-income countries (UNDP, 1999, Table 3, pp. 142–6). Until 1995, only 21 women had been heads of state or prime minister and some of these followed their father into the job. So far, no Secretary-General of the United Nations has been a woman. In voluntary organizations and in social movements, however, women have fared better in securing high office.

In brief, globalization has not greatly assisted the representation of women in the national assemblies of their countries even though it has encouraged the spread of democratic forms of government. This is best shown by the experience of the former Soviet bloc countries. Globalization was one of the forces behind the replacement of Soviet forms of government by elected democracies but it has resulted in a reduction in the percentage of women in national assemblies from 30 per cent to 10 per cent (Pettman, 1997, Figure 25.1, p. 486).

Fifth, changes in the legal system concerning gender issues in a country can make a contribution to women's empowerment. As early as 1947, the General Assembly of the United Nations adopted the Convention on the Elimination of All Forms of Discrimination Against Women. By 1995, 139 countries had signed it while 41 countries did not sign it, 6 signed it with reservations, and 43 ratified it with reservations (UNDP, 1995, p. 43).

Despite these improvements, there are still countries where open discrimination against women is not illegal in several aspects of life: countries where the right to own property is subject to their husband's guardianship, where women's employment outside the home needs the husband's consent, where women are not able to transfer their citizenship to their husbands and countries where women are not able to obtain a passport without their husband's agreement.

Sixth, the undermining of the traditional gender ideology that is examined in the next section has strengthened the forces for women's empowerment. Traditional gender ideologies consider women as inferior to men and have been used to justify all sorts of discriminatory practices against women. Undermining such ideologies can but help the empowerment of women, even though this may be seen by some as a form of cultural imperialism.

These are strong forces making for the increased empowerment of women. But the process is neither irresistible nor inevitable. When the Taliban gained power in Afghanistan in 1996, for example, it demanded that women should stay at home and closed girls' schools (Chinkin, 1999, p. 308)

Exhibit 5.6

Globalization and gender empowerment

- Globalization has made a positive but modest contribution to gender power equality.
- Women's advances in the labour market and in education have enhanced their power.

Exhibit 5.6 (*cont'd*)

- Reductions in birth rates have had a positive effect on women's social power.
- Progress in political empowerment for women has been slow.
- Similarly, progress in reducing legal discrimination against women has been slow.

Globalization and Gender Ideology

Gender ideology refers to the cluster of values, attitudes and beliefs that societies uphold concerning the relative position of the two sexes in different aspects of life in both the public and the private domain. These values and attitudes constitute one of the many forces that influence gender inequalities.

All contemporary societies were heavily patriarchal in premodern times and, as a result, they all carry different packages of gender discrimination today. All religions today, for example, are patriarchal in different ways and degrees simply because they all emerged during premodern times. It was only recently with the advance of industrialization that women began to challenge their inferior position in society and to win gradual concessions from male-dominated governments and institutions.

Patriarchal ideology is made up of several closely interwoven strands and it is necessary to identify them in order to discuss the extent to which globalization has affected it. There is no agreement on these constituent strands of anti-feminist ideology but Afshar's and Agarwal's concise list based on research in Asian countries is a useful statement for the purposes of this discussion. They identify four such strands (Afshar and Agarwal, 1989, p. 2).

First, there is the ideology of female seclusion found in many countries. The most common practices of this ideology are the veiling of women and the restriction of women's movements both in the house and outside. Inevitably, female seclusion makes it difficult for women to obtain outside employment or political office and thus increases women's dependence on men. Where economic necessity demands that the woman should be gainfully employed, working from home or working in an all-female environment are some of the compromise solutions used.

Second, there is the related ideology of women's exclusion from certain types of employment because of ideological reasons acquiring the strength of taboos. The recent acrimonious debates in the Church of England about the ordination of women as priests, as well as the current arguments about the deployment of women in the armed forces, are indications of the strong feelings aroused.

Third, the traditional construction of femininity emphasizes such values as docility, submissiveness and modesty in contrast to such values as aggressiveness, independence and self-assuredness that are seen as male characteristics. Such values have deep roots in the culture of all countries and, though they are changing, progress is slow and markedly uneven between countries.

Fourth, most cultures consider unpaid domestic work and caring to be the responsibility of the wife and paid employment the responsibility of the husband. Most cultures also accept that the wife can engage in paid employment in addition to her basic role as housewife while the husband can help out with household duties. Several inequalities flow from this role demarcation: the wife becomes dependent on the husband financially; women's level of wages suffers because employers treat them as if 'working for lipstick' (Joekes, 1985).

This traditional gender ideology has come under increasing pressure in recent years from a variety of directions: the rise in women's paid employment, the improvement in women's education, the work of several UN bodies, the Women's Movement and the influence of cultural globalization. We have already discussed the importance of employment and education. Here we will briefly outline the influence of the other factors.

The United Nations' role on gender issues was peripheral until 1975 when it organized the First World Conference on Women in Mexico City. This was followed by three other such conferences: 1980 in Copenhagen, 1985 in Nairobi and 1995 in Beijing. The conferences were attended by women's delegates from many countries and they acted as platforms to publicise women's serious problems and to put forward programmes for change. They also led to the creation of specific projects to deal with specific issues in different countries.

The United Nations, however, tends to put political issues above gender equality. Despite the liberation of Kuwait from the Iraqi invasion by UN forces, the UN did not insist that the rulers of Kuwait should introduce reforms to enfranchise women.

The growth of the Women's Movement, often assisted by the activities of international bodies, has raised the profile of women's issues, particularly in AICs. It has also demonstrated that though women in AICs and IDCs have many common problems, they also have different agendas stemming from their very different socio-economic conditions. Feminists in IDCs would be interested in such issues as 'repressive forms of birth control' or 'dowry deaths' that are of no direct concern to feminists in AICs (Cohen and Kennedy, 2000, p. 309). On the other hand, women everywhere would be interested in issues of rape and poverty even though the incidence of these problems varies both by country and by region.

Cultural diffusion has been a feature of globalization from ancient to present times. What distinguishes present from previous forms of cultural diffusion is its intensity, geographical spread and commercial ethos. The intensity of cultural diffusion is best measured through the number and efficiency of media that promote it. Until the nineteenth century, cultural globalization took place through the written word and human travel. Now, news, information, images and sounds are transmitted across the whole world in record time and these carry with them western attitudes, beliefs and values on all sorts of issues including gender relationships. The drive behind this global enterprise of cultural diffusion is primarily commercial profit. The effects, however, are complex and difficult to estimate but they do question the autonomy of national cultures on gender issues.

Various views surfaced during the second half of the twentieth century concerning the desirability of this cultural diffusion. It was warmly welcomed in the 1950s by the modernisation theorists who saw it as essential to economic, political and social advancement in the third world. The traditional cultures of third world countries had to be modernized by incorporating the value system of the advanced industrial countries. This was a view that was heavily criticized, however, in the 1970s as being nothing more than cultural imperialism, a more subtle form of colonialism.

Mainstream globalization theorists of the early 1990s distanced themselves from this dichotomous debate by positing that what takes place is not a simple diffusion of western culture that undermines national cultures but rather a diffusion of ideas and values that 'fragments as it co-ordinates' (Giddens, 1990, p. 175). Cultural ideas and values transmitted by western media are interpreted and reformulated to suit local conditions with the result that though there is a broad overall cultural framework in the making, there are also manifold local cultural variations. It is most unlikely that this will lead to cultural homogenization in the foreseeable future.

The images and ideologies of gender relationships transmitted through western media to all corners of the globe are not strictly speaking gender egalitarian. They are still male dominated but are, nevertheless, far more egalitarian than the gender ideologies that prevail in most IDCs. The effects of this cultural diffusion on local cultures is inevitably variable and uncertain but, over a long period of time, they are likely to encourage an image of womanhood that is less inferior and less dependent on men.

Many have welcomed this cultural process that brings about greater equality between the sexes but some have seen it as a threat to local cultures – a fear that has given rise to fundamentalist movements, particularly in Islamic cultures. It is a mistake, however, to view fundamentalist movements as opposed to all western values concerning gender relationships. Referring to one of the most visible expressions of this fundamentalist movement – the veiled women in Turkey – Kaya rightly points out that the veiled women 'are mostly urbanized and educated' and they do not reject the emphasis of western culture on women's education, health or employment (Kaya, 2000, p. 196). What they do object to is, what they consider, the excesses of western culture, particularly in the area of gender sex relations.

Exhibit 5.7

Globalization, gender and ideology

- The culture of all societies is patriarchal in varying degrees.
- Globalization spreads western ideas about the rights of women to all parts of the world and, hence, promotes a more egalitarian gender ideology.
- Cultural diffusion is not synonymous with cultural homogenization but it is still a force for gender equality.
- The Women's Movement and the UNO have encouraged gender equality.
- Despite this, cultural values in many countries help to perpetuate women's inferior position in society.

Conclusion

The effects of globalization on gender equality have been mixed. On balance, however, the evidence suggests that they have strengthened rather than weakened those forces and processes which advance gender equality.

First, women's progress in employment has been spectacular during the second half of the twentieth century. Not only has the proportion of women in employment risen but gender inequalities in earnings and access to occupations have narrowed.

Second, the growth of women's employment, however, has not been accompanied by a corresponding decline in women's unpaid caring work in the home. Women bear a double burden in all societies.

Third, there is no doubt about the advances of women in education. In many AICs women's education achievements today are equal and even surpass those of men. Yet, the majority of illiterate people and those dropping out of school in IDCs are women.

Fourth, health standards have improved for all and gender inequalities have declined in both life expectancy and infant mortality rates. The problem of the 'missing women' still remains and maternal mortalities in IDCs are unacceptably high.

Fifth, the feminization of poverty is still a fact of life even though gender inequalities in earnings and wealth have narrowed. Globalization forces have, on one hand, improved women's economic position but on the other, because of the preoccupation with competitiveness, they have hindered the development of those government policies that are necessary to deal with women's poverty.

Sixth, progress in the political field has not been as strong as in the economic, education and health fields. Though women have the right to vote in most countries, they hold a disproportionately low proportion of senior government positions.

Seventh, globalization has encouraged the spread of western culture to all parts of the world. This has benefited the position of women in society but it has also undermined local cultures. The hybridization of local cultures in IDCs is in the direction of a wider acceptance of western culture.

Finally, the position of women in IDCs is inferior to that of women in AICs. Globalization may have helped to narrow this gap somewhat but a great deal remains to be done.

Further Reading

Marchand, M.H. and Parpart, J. (eds) (1995) *Feminism, Postmodernism and Development* (London, Routledge).

Peterson, V.S and Runyan, A.S. (1999) *Global Gender Issues*, 2nd edn (Boulder, CO, Westview Press).

Yuval-Davis, N. and Werbner, P. (eds) (1999) *Women, Citizenship and Difference* (London, Zed Books).

6

Globalization, Migration and Ethnicity

During the second half of the twentieth century, migration became truly global. Multi-ethnic immigrant communities from around the globe were firmly established in all AICs with important political, economic, social and cultural implications. As a result, migration has become a high profile political issue and, as globalization proceeds to include more fully all countries, migration and its effects will gain even greater prominence at both the national and the international level. As migration gains momentum, it will also become clearer that the current adversarial philosophy underlying migration movements is unhelpful and that a new approach is necessary – one that brings together sending and receiving countries in an effort to find solutions to migration issues that are to their mutual advantage.

This chapter examines three interrelated issues:

● the effects of globalization on migration movements;

● how globalization affects ethnic inequalities today in AICs;

● the influence of globalization on the adjustment patterns between ethnic communities and the receiving society.

Globalization and Migration

Migration has been an integral part of globalization in much the same way as trade or investment. The movement of populations, goods and capital across countries is an age-old process – it has been a feature of the globalization process for centuries now, as we pointed out in Chapter 1. It can, therefore, be claimed that historically speaking 'we are all migrants because our ancestors have all travelled to the places where we have come from' (Pieterse, 2000, p. 392). Such an approach has the advantage of reminding everyone that being a native of a country is an accident of birth and not an individual achievement. It runs the risk, however, of glossing over the difficulties that arise when newly arrived immigrants come into contact with members of the 'host' society.

Migration takes many forms. It can be voluntary or involuntary; local, regional or global; temporary, permanent or semi-permanent; economic, political or religious; legal or illegal; or several combinations of these. Often these are not distinct categories – they are ideal types which in real life merge into each other. The difference, for example, between voluntary and involuntary migration is not always as clear as first appears. Though it is customary to label people who leave their country because they cannot eke out an existence as voluntary economic emigrants, one could justifiably argue that their decision to emigrate was not completely voluntary and that it was imposed on them to a certain extent by their circumstances. In other words, they are to some extent involuntary economic emigrants. As the discussion later in the chapter will show, the distinction between political refugees and economic migrants is hotly disputed. Many political asylum seekers are rejected because they are seen by government authorities as economic refugees attempting to gain entrance through illicit means. The difference between regional and global migration can be a matter of opinion particularly when viewed in a historical context. When the ancient Greeks established settlements in Italy and France, they probably viewed their migration as a global feat while in the eyes of the modern jet age the distances involved are a mere hour's flight!

These different types of migration, bar the legal/illegal, have always existed, as any cursory look at migration history will show. The legality of migration, however, has only become an issue since the establishment of nation-states in Europe from the fourteenth century onwards claiming sovereignty over their geographical boundaries. Even then, it was not until the end of the nineteenth century that anti-immigration laws barring people from entering a country were passed. There was no need for such legislation before that because migration between the nation-states of Europe was limited. Most European migrants during this period, 1500–1900, headed for the New World, mainly for the United States, although a small proportion emigrated from one European country to another as in the case of the Irish migration to Britain or the Jewish exodus from Russia at the end of the nineteenth century to many countries within and outside Europe.

This multifaceted nature of migration also suggests that no single explanation can adequately explain either its origins or its impacts on society. There are several reasons for the rise and fall of migration over the years. Globalization is only one of them even though it features strongly in this chapter because we are dealing with post-war migration when the globalization process intensified. Before we look at the theoretical debates linking globalization and migration, it is necessary to sketch out the pattern of post-war migration with more emphasis on the advanced industrial societies since they were the major receivers of international migration movements.

Post-War Migration

In a period of less than fifty years, migration has transformed the nature of advanced industrial societies, particularly those of Europe. It has enriched their human and cultural capital but it has also intensified potential social tensions. In Europe, it has transformed largely mono-ethnic into multi-ethnic societies while in the US, Canada and Australia it has expanded even more the multi-ethnic nature of their society. 'Thirty years ago', says Togeby, ' almost no foreign citizens lived in Denmark' but by the 1990s, 'Denmark has become a multi-ethnic society' (Togeby, 1998, pp. 1137, 1138).

Two major periods of migration stand out during the post-war years. The first coincides with the expansion of the welfare state – the period of high economic growth, full employment and improvement of the social services – 1950 to 1975. The second begins with the economic recession of the late 1970s down to the present day.

During the first period, demand for labour in Europe was high and could not be satisfied by national resources. Industry and government went out of their way to recruit foreign labour, mainly from the developing former colonial countries but also from the periphery of Europe. It was a mixture of regional and global migration – the first time that Europe had ventured outside its boundaries in search of labour in a big way.

In Britain, immigration from the Commonwealth started in the late 1940s and continued throughout the 1950s. It involved both men and women mainly from the Caribbean, the Indian subcontinent and Africa and immigrants were treated as permanent residents with full citizenship entitlements. The ethnic minority population of the country increased from 1.5 million in 1950, to 4.1 million in 1975 totalling 7.8 per cent of the population but with concentrations in the large cities (Castles and Miller, 2000, Table 4.1, p. 72). The Immigration Act of 1962 and the downturn of the economy meant an almost total cessation of immigration involving new workers, although families of immigrants were allowed to join them until this, too, was restricted by legislation in the early 1970s.

France, too, experienced substantial immigration from its former colonies in West Africa, from North Africa, from the Caribbean but also from Southern Europe. Economic as well as demographic reasons lay behind these migrations for population growth in France had been low for many decades. As in Britain, immigrants filled mainly low-skilled and low-paid jobs in the cities. Its minority population rose from 2.1 million in 1950 to 4.2 million in 1975 amounting to 7.9 per cent of its population (Castles and Miller, 2000, Table 4.1, p. 72). Belgium and the Netherlands experienced similar patterns of immigration from their former colonies so that by the mid-1970s they, too, had visible ethnic minority communities in their cities.

Immigration to Germany was of a different nature. It was made up of 'guestworkers' who were recruited by the government from Greece, Turkey and North Africa for specific sectors of the economy with explicit contracts of employment for specified lengths of time. The principle behind this type of immigration was that workers should stay as long their labour was required and then they should voluntarily return or, if necessary, be repatriated to their country of origin. Family members were not expected to join them though gradually this was relaxed, first in practice and then in law. Immigrants, however, were treated as foreigners with restricted citizenship rights unless they were granted German nationality – something that was done with great reluctance. The rise of the minority population in Germany was sharper in absolute terms than in either Britain or France – from a mere half a million in 1950 to 4 million in 1975 making up 6.6 per cent of the total population (Castles and Miller, 2000, Table 4.1, p. 72). Switzerland adopted a very similar policy to Germany's and by 1975 it had the highest proportion of minority population – 16.0 per cent of its population – in Europe.

Immigration to the United States in the early part of this period was at a low level because of the preference given to European immigrants and the discrimination against Asian immigrants. The expansion of the American economy, the scarcity of European immigrants and the rise of the civil rights movement led to the legislation of 1965 that abolished discrimination against Asians and relaxed the criteria for family immigration. The result was a substantial rise in immigration from Asia and Latin America in the 1970s and afterwards. Similar patterns of immigration were experienced by Canada and Australia. Their preference for European immigrants was abandoned in the mid-1960s so that the number of both the immigrants and their countries of origin rose in the 1970s and after. As all three countries were traditional countries of immigration, they viewed immigrants as permanent residents with full citizenship rights – not as 'guestworkers'.

In brief, the first period of migration was driven predominantly by economic criteria. Immigrants in Europe were recruited 'for menial jobs in the public services and dirty jobs in the manufacturing sector' (Held *et al.*, 1999, p. 304). The process of migration, however, took different forms with important legal differences to the citizenship entitlements of the immigrants involved. By the mid-1970s, European societies became multi-ethnic and multicultural beginning to resemble those of the US, Canada and Australia.

From the mid-1970s onwards, all European countries began to experience economic difficulties as a result of changes in the world economy. They had, therefore, no further need for more immigrants of the unskilled type. Indeed, a high proportion of their unskilled nationals became long-term unemployed. Not unnaturally, every European country tried to reduce immigration by more restrictive legislation and by more stringent policing of its borders. Countries with 'guestworkers' encouraged their immigrants to return to their countries of origin but very few took up the offer apart from those who were returning to countries that were themselves becoming more affluent – Greece, Portugal, and Spain. Indeed, during this period, these countries became receiving countries for immigration and they have since become particularly prone to illegal immigration from the Middle East and from North Africa.

Despite restrictive legislation, immigration into Europe continued because of family reunions, the rise of illegal immigration and the increase in asylum seekers. Public opposition to immigration and government restrictive policies proved largely ineffective. It is this paradox that has raised again the debate concerning the power of the nation-state in today's increasingly globalized world. Governments in Europe are unable to police their borders as effectively as in the past.

In the United States, the pace of immigration quickened but with most of the new immigrants coming from Asia and Latin America rather than from Europe as was the case in the past. Thus while during 1951–60, European immigrants totalled 53 per cent of all immigrants, the corresponding proportion for 1995 was 18 per cent (Castles and Miller, 2000, p. 84). Both Canada and Australia experienced the same trend as the US – a rise of immigration from Asia and a sharp decline of European immigrants. Unlike the European countries, legal immigration either continued to rise or remained constant.

This period also saw the rise of emigration to the oil-rich countries of the Arab world, as well as Nigeria and Venezuela. These were immigrants not only from neighbouring countries but also from Asia and Europe – another sign of the global nature of contemporary migration movements.

Feminists have rightly complained that women have been kept 'hidden from history'. Until recently, women had been seen as those left behind or joining their husbands in the case of migration. This had always been a half-truth but totally incorrect during this period of modern migration. Demand for women's work in the catering, caring, entertainment and sex industry was high during the last quarter of the twentieth century and hundreds of thousands of young women from the Philippines, Sri Lanka, Bangladesh and the former Soviet republics entered the AICs mostly legally but many illegally. While their normal intention is to return to their countries after a few years, many of them will stay on much longer and some will inter-marry to become part of their local communities. Bearing in mind the fact that this period saw the migration of wives to join their husbands in large numbers, what has been happening lends support to the claim of the feminization of migration for many countries in recent years.

Illegal immigration increased and became more transnational during this period partly because of the restrictions on legal immigration, the strict interpretation of the definition of political asylum, the rapid population growth in developing societies, better organization of illegal migration and several other reasons associated with globalization that we will discuss below. Illegal migration usually causes public resentment but it also reveals the conflicting pressures within the receiving countries themselves on this issue. Employers welcome, or at least tolerate, illegal immigration because it helps to depress wage and other labour costs, trade unions see it as another force that undermines the living standards of their members, and many sections of the general public see it as just another piece of evidence that their country has been taken over by foreigners.

The migration of illegal Mexican workers into the US, particularly for agricultural work, is a good example of this conflict of interests. As Schuck points out, Americans are hostile to illegal immigration but they have also 'become both more dependent on illegal workers and more aware of this dependence' (Schuck, 1998, p. 197). Many of them work 'in sweetshops, as farm workers and in the service industries, sometimes for as little as $3 an hour. They are unable to complain for fear of being deported' (Campbell, 2000, p. 17). The same can be said of illegal immigrants to all advanced industrial societies.

The collapse of the Soviet regimes at the beginning of the 1990s created a new situation that was bound to result in greater immigration to the advanced industrial countries. Germans living in Russia were allowed to return to Germany; Jews to Israel; and Greeks to Greece. Many others asked for political asylum or managed to enter EU member countries legally or illegally despite all efforts to keep them out.

Refugees and Asylum Seekers

The multiplicity of new nations created as a result of the break up of colonial empires in the 1950s, as well as the disintegration of the Soviet Block in the early 1990s and of Yugoslavia in the late 1990s, provided the political background for a huge upsurge in refugees and asylum seekers. This has been a period of nation building in Africa and Asia and it has been accompanied by internal conflicts and border wars reminiscent of the process in Europe during the sixteenth and seventeenth centuries.

If the twentieth century has produced 'the greatest number of refugees in history' (Loescher, 1992, p. 9), it has also seen the establishment of the first international body supposedly to deal with the problems of refugees. The creation of the United Nations High Commissioner for Refugees (UNHCR) and the enactment of the Geneva Convention for Refugees in 1951 were products of the cold war designed to deal with refugees from the East to the West. As a result the definition of a political refugee was couched in individualistic terms – someone who left his/her country because of a clear risk of persecution on account of political or religious beliefs. In practice, few managed to escape from Soviet East Europe to claim refugee status during the 1950s, '60s and '70s and practically all those who did were almost automatically granted political asylum and were used by the West as evidence of the superiority of its political and economic system.

The definition did not fit at all well the situations that arose later when thousands of people fled their country en masse for fear of persecution rather than as isolated individuals. Numerous civil wars in Africa, Asia, and the Middle East have led to the creation of millions of refugees. Most of them are looked after in the adjoining countries in the third world. Of the 22 million refugees and others of concern to the UNHCR at the end of 1999, 32.7 per cent were in Europe and 5.6 per cent in North America. The remaining 61.7 per cent were mostly in Africa and Asia. This does not take into account the number of internally displaced persons which runs into millions – these are not officially considered as refugees.

The response of European countries to the growing numbers of refugees has been largely exclusionary. Every attempt has been made to keep as many out as possible; the living conditions of those admitted have been made worse to act as a deterrent; and the expulsion efforts have been intensified. The interpretation of the legal definition of refugee status is largely discretionary and political depending on the country's needs for migrants. Harding illustrates this very well with the following figures:

'In 1996, Canada deemed that 76 per cent of applicants from the former Zaire, 81 per cent from Somalia and 82 per cent from Sri Lanka qualified for Convention status. In the same year in Britain, only 1 per cent of applicants from Zaire, 0.4 per cent from Somalia and 0.2 per cent from Sri Lanka were considered eligible' (Harding, 2000, p. 44).

Applications for political asylum raise, in a very stark way, the dual responsibility of the nation-state: to protect what it sees as the interests of its citizens and at the same time to observe international conventions on human rights that attempt to safeguard the welfare of immigrants. With the hostile state of public opinion on refugees, nation-states in Europe have veered heavily in favour of their first duty, irrespective of the political character of the government. Comparing the policies towards refugees in seven EU member countries, Schuster concludes that 'the change in governments in these countries has not led to sharp changes in policy in general and asylum policy in particular' (Schuster, 2000, p. 125). This discrepancy between the European and the North American attitude toward asylum seekers may not be as wide as it first appears because many of the rejected asylum applicants still stay on in both Europe and North America as a result of the practical and legal difficulties involved in repatriating them. International conventions on human rights make it difficult for governments in democratic countries to ride roughshod over the rights of asylum seekers.

The UNHCR has the unenviable task of protecting the rights of refugees world-wide. Its resources are limited and its powers depend very much on the willingness of national governments to be helpful. The number of persons of

Table 6.1   'Persons of concern' to UNHR on 1 January 2000.

Region	Refugees	Asylum seekers	Returned refugees	IDP's-and others	Total
Africa	3,523,250	61,110	933,890	1,732,290	6,250,540
Asia	4,781,750	24,750	617,620	1,884,740	7,308,860
Europe	2,608,308	473,060	952,060	3,252,300	7,285,800
LatinAmerica and Caribbean	61,200	1,510	6,260	21,200	90,170
North America	636,300	605,630	–	–	1,241,930
Oceania	64,500	15,540	–	–	80,040
Total	11,675,380	1,181,600	2,509,830	6,890,530	22,257,340

Source: UNHCR web site: www.unhcr.ch/consulted in July 2001.
IDPs = Internally displaced persons.

concern to the UNHR rose from 10 million in the 1970s to 15 million in 1990, 27 million in 1995 and then declined to 22 million in 2000. Table 6.1 above shows the different categories of 'persons of concern'. They are all estimates but it is generally accepted that the category of 'Internally Displaced Person' is a gross underestimate. It refers to all who are displaced in their own countries as a result of civil wars, natural disasters or industrial development projects such as deforestation or the building of dams.

Globalization and Pressures for Increased Migration

Every strand of globalization creates pressures for an increase in migration. Nation-states have an extremely difficult task in their attempts to hold back the force of these pressures. As a result, it is more than likely that the volume and the reach of migration will increase in the future despite government attempts in Europe to reduce it. Indeed, Europe is haltingly coming to accept that the future welfare of its citizens will benefit from certain types of immigration.

First, there are the obvious technological and transportation changes which on one hand facilitate both legal and illegal migration and on the other make it that much more difficult for the state fully to control its borders. It is easier, quicker and cheaper to travel from one part of the world to another than it was in the past. Until the mid-1950s travel from Europe to Australia, the Caribbean and so on was mostly by ship that took days or even weeks. Now it is a matter of hours.

Modern means of communication have also made the organization of illegal migration easier. This is particularly true of illegal migration that is often organized by profiteering gangs across the globe. As a result, it is that much more difficult and costly for governments to fully resist such pressures, particularly when sectional interests within the country make conflicting demands on the state. National borders are more porous than they were a couple of decades ago.

Second, economic globalization almost inevitably leads to more migration. To begin with, MNCs have in practice the right to move their staff from one country to another. Economic globalization also raises the demand for professional and for highly skilled personnel, for example in the information technology field. Since there are acute shortages of such staff in AICs, governments have recently been trying to recruit them from IDCs. The US increased the number of visas for skilled foreign workers from 115,000 to 195,000 a year in 2000 in order to deal with the shortage of computer experts. The UK and German governments are both actively seeking to attract more foreign workers of this type and they are both looking to India to provide them (Steele, 2000, p. 17). Thus while advanced industrial countries are hostile to unskilled migrants they are more than prepared to try to attract the skilled and the techno-numerate – the very staff that IDCs desperately need for their own development.

Economic globalization leads to increased migration pressures in another important way. When the weak economies of IDCs are exposed to strong commercial pressures from outside or from the internal growth of agrobusinesses, 'the agricultural sector can collapse, leading to rural exodus, which will swell the population of cities and increase pressure to emigrate' (Hollifield, 2000, p. 151). This has taken place in Asia, Africa, South as well as Central America and the migration from Mexico to the US is a vivid example of this process. Similarly, the IMF austerity measures in IDCs in the 1980s, as well as some of the decisions of the World Trade Organization, resulted in increased rural migration to the cities with similar results. The cities of the IDCs have grown at a pace that is much faster than the rate of job creation with the inevitable result that some of the surplus labour will seek a livelihood by emigrating to other countries – legally or illegally.

Third, there are increasingly strong cultural pressures for emigration from the IDCs to the AICs. Current media presentations of life in AICs may not reflect reality but they increase feelings of deprivation among audiences in IDCs. In contrast to the slog and dreariness of daily life in developing countries, everything appears rosy and exciting in the welfare garden of the affluent countries. Such pictures exert a strong influence not so much on the destitute but on the ambitious and the upwardly mobile in IDCs. The pull and push factors associated with voluntary economic migration movements have always been more influential with this group of the population than with the utterly impoverished.

Fourth, strong social reasons at the transnational level have been boosting migration movements. Modern means of communication have shortened the social distance between the sending and the receiving countries and they have enabled immigrant communities to maintain close contacts with their home country, with the relatives and friends they left behind. Vice-versa, immigrant communities act as enablers for new immigration of both the legal and the illegal kind. There is, in other words, a constant line of communication and exchange between immigrant communities in the receiving countries and their countries of origin that makes immigration not such a final act as it used to be. The world is no longer such a closed system divided between countries that send and countries that receive immigrants. This is what has come to be known as the thesis of transnationalism in migration. 'From a transnational perspective,' says Brettell, 'migrants are no longer uprooted, but rather move freely back and forth across international borders and between different cultures and social systems' (Brettell, 2000, p. 104).

It is a matter of opinion as to what proportion of immigrants fly back and forth let alone how many of them feel at ease with different cultures. In the UK, for example, 60 per cent of the Chinese and the Pakistani as well as almost 50 per cent of Indian migrants made a trip to their country of origin during the five years prior to the survey in 1994 (Office for National Statistics (ONS), 1996, Chart 1.9, p. 15). The others did not, which suggests that contacts through visits are not so frequent as implied by the thesis. They may, of course, have maintained contacts with their home country in other ways.

It is also the case that immigrant communities not only encourage further immigration but they also promote further the globalization of the world in the sense that they encourage economic, social and cultural networks between different countries. In this sense, migration is both a response to and a stimulus to the globalization process.

Fifth, there is a growing body of opinion claiming that the post-war period has seen the emergence of postnational forms of citizenship rights which encourage migration despite the wishes of the nation-state. Until recently, the notion of citizenship was associated with the concept of the nation-state. Legal nationals of a country enjoyed certain legal, political and social rights. Experience, however, has shown that during the post-war period immigrants have been able increasingly to enjoy these rights irrespective of the fact that they were not naturalized citizens of the country. This is best illustrated in some countries where refugees who are stateless persons, or immigrants who have not been granted nationality status nevertheless qualify for benefits from, and the protection of, the nation-state in whose jurisdiction they live. In this way 'individual rights, historically defined on the basis of nationality, are increasingly codified into a different scheme that emphasizes universal personhood' (Soysal, 1994, p. 136).

Postnational citizenship derives its moral and legal legitimacy from the growth of both an international legal discourse of human rights and the increase in the number of international and regional bodies advocating as well as protecting the inviolability of these human rights. It has come to be accepted that human beings have certain basic rights that the nation-state should meet irrespective of such considerations as a person's legal nationality, religion, race or gender. These rights have assumed an international character with the agreement of the nation-states and have now gained a force of their own which cannot easily be repudiated by democratically elected governments of AICs.

This suggests that whether immigrants entered a country legally or illegally is largely immaterial to their entitlement to basic human rights. It also means that mass deportation of even illegal immigrants is not a feasible policy. Each immigrant has a legal right for his or her case to be heard and legally defended as well as a right of appeal before being deported. In all these ways, the authority of the nation-state is diminished and hence its ability to control immigration has also suffered. In brief, the extension of human rights to foreigners has acted as a spur for further immigration.

Three main objections to the thesis of postnational rights have been voiced. First, there are those who acknowledge the accretion of rights to foreigners but who argue that these rights 'still derive primarily from the laws and institutions of the liberal state' and hence can be rescinded by the nation-state even though with considerable difficulty (Hollifield, 2000, p. 149). Thus in recent years all EU member countries have reduced the generosity of their provisions for refugees in terms of housing, health and social security benefits. But, significantly, they did not go as far as to do away completely with these provisions. Second, there is evidence that illegal immigrants and refugees do not always possess exactly the same social rights as full citizens. A recent examination of the social security arrangements for migrants in 15 EU member countries concluded that 'there are numerous disentitlements and disqualifications which exclude groups of migrants from benefits' (Roberts and Bolderson, 1999, p. 218). Third, the thesis applies to the handful of AICs and not to other countries. During the 1990s, for example, there were mass expulsions of migrant workers from Saudi Arabia, Kuwait, Malaysia, Thailand, South Korea, Nigeria and many other countries for both economic and political reasons.

On balance, the central argument of the postnational rights thesis is correct – the emergence of such rights has made it more difficult for the nation-state to control immigration. Moreover, these rights are not so transient that they can easily be revoked by democratically elected governments. The weakness of the thesis lies in its exaggerated claims.

Whether or not the growth of postnational rights has created a new environment for migration in which the nation-state has irrevocably lost its ability to fully police its borders is a matter of opinion. As Sassen, one of the advocates of this approach, conceded: it is too early to be certain on this. 'These are transformations in the making as we speak. My reading is that they matter. It is easy to argue the opposite: that the state is absolute and nothing much has changed. But it may well be the case that these developments signal the beginning of a new era' (Sassen, 1998, p. 73).

Despite the increased effect of globalization on migration, the fact remains that the nation-state still possesses substantial powers in this area. For this reason the migration of people between countries is much more restricted than the movement of goods, capital, news and images. The wishes of the nation-state and the pressures of globalization will continue to confront each other in the area of migration for as far as one can see in the future even though there is increasing recognition that current demographic trends in AICs have strengthened the case for increased migration. As public expenditure on the retired increases, governments are faced with difficult options: they can raise the age of retirement; they can strive to increase productivity; they can increase social security contributions; they can reduce the level of benefits; they can privatise benefit systems; or they can accept young immigrants into their countries. These are hard decisions for governments and compromises are inevitable. It is estimated that to maintain the current ratio between the working age population (15–64) and the retired (aged 65 and over) until 2050, Britain would need a net immigration total of over one million immigrants, Germany more than three and a half million and the EU as a whole a total of thirteen and a half million (Steele, 2000, p. 17).

It is a moot point whether a new approach to migration will gradually emerge that considers migration not in adversarial terms but as a process with costs and benefits to both the sending and the receiving societies. Much has been said about the balance sheet of gains and losses to the receiving societies. Far less has been said about the costs and benefits to the sending societies: on the one hand they lose many of the young, energetic and sometimes better educated members; on the other hand they gain from the massive monetary remittances of immigrants, from the reduction in unemployment and from possible investment ventures from economically successful immigrants who return after a few years.

An open acknowledgement of this balance sheet of gains and losses will make it more possible to plan both the migration movements themselves as well as the settlement of immigrants in their new countries. Such an approach will view immigrants in a positive light that is essential to their chances of satisfactory settlement and to the maximization of the benefit to their country of migration.

To sum up, globalization factors both increase the pressures for migration and facilitate the actual process of migration. Economic and cultural factors increase the pressures for migration while technological and social forces as well as transnational rights make the process of migration more possible. There is, however, a relationship between the two: an intending migrant is more likely to embark on a journey if he or she feels that the chances of reaching the receiving society are reasonable. Apart from the individual hardships involved in most migrations, there are also heavy financial costs particularly in the case of illegal migration where large sums of money are paid to the organizers – often criminal gangs.

Exhibit 6.1

Globalization, migration and ethnicity

- Globalization has both encouraged and facilitated global migration movements.

- Globalization has created multi-ethnic communities in all AICs.

- Globalization forces will encourage even more migration movements in the future.

Ethnic Divisions in Society

Globalization encourages migration in a variety of ways. Migration, in turn, creates new social divisions in the receiving societies and different types of ethnic adaptation patterns. At least four general factors can affect the nature of such divisions and the kind of adaptation that immigrants are likely to make in the receiving society.

The first of these is the very nature of the migratory process itself. It is possible to distinguish three types of migratory processes: illegal, guestworker migration and citizenship migration. Illegal immigrants are likely to find employment in low-paid, insecure employment, to reside in undesirable accommodation, perhaps change addresses often to avoid the police and not to enjoy the political, social and economic rights of the country. Their adaptation to the receiving society will be precarious until governments declare an amnesty for existing illegal immigrants – something that governments are loath to do too frequently. 'Guestworkers' are recruited for specific jobs, they cannot change their employment until the period of their contract expires, they often have to reside in government accommodation, they are denied political rights and their families cannot join them for several years. The expectation is that they will return to their home country when their labour is no longer needed. These conditions exert an adverse influence on the kind of relationships established between them and the native population. Other things being equal, the best prospects for good relations between immigrants and the receiving society are to be found in the migratory process that shows adequate appreciation of the value of immigrants as both workers and citizens. Such an approach involves no conditions on the kind of job, residence or length of stay and grants immigrants citizenship rights from the start. The receiving society is encouraged to consider immigrants as useful members – economically and socially.

Second, the ethnicity of the immigrant group as perceived by the receiving society is important. Ethnicity is not some objective and unchanging criterion but rather a socially constructed image that changes over time and through which one group perceives and is perceived by another. The image of Jews as an ethnic group as perceived in the UK has changed over the years; the same applies to the image of the Irish. What is considered desirable or acceptable can change over time, even though rather slowly. If the receiving society perceives an immigrant group as desirable because it performs a specific useful function then the ethnicity of the immigrant group will be accepted. If, however, an immigrant group is perceived as a threat to society, then the ethnicity of the group will be seen in negative terms and will be a hindrance to successful social adaptation. A number of rational and irrational reasons are involved in the public perception of an ethnic group as desirable or undesirable – economic, social, cultural and colour factors all play their part individually and jointly. As Cornell and Hartmann put it, 'There is little inherently good or bad about ethnicity or race. They are categories invented by human beings, and in this they are of little distinctive importance. What makes them significant is what human beings do with them' (Cornell and Hartmann, 1998, p. 252)

The third factor that influences ethnic divisions and the nature of the relationships between immigrants and the receiving society is the attitudes displayed, and the type of policies adopted, by the government. These policies can range from the discriminatory to the promotional and to the laissez-faire type. Discriminatory policies were clearly found in the 'guestworker' type of immigration at least in the early stages of settlement. The promotional policies include anti-discrimination legislation on grounds of gender, race, religion or other such characteristics, language courses for immigrants, training facilities and assistance to immigrants in relation to housing as part of the housing policy for low-income groups in society. A laissez-faire approach will let immigrants sink or swim on their own irrespective of the degree of discrimination against them in society. The policies of governments in the AICs during the post-war period have involved elements of all these three approaches though over the years there has been a general convergence towards a modified version of the promotional approach.

Fourth, the state of the economy of the receiving society is of paramount importance for the process of adaptation. However helpful the migratory process may be or however welcoming the attitude of the receiving society to an ethnic group, and however promotional the nature of government policies, they will achieve little if the state of the economy is not also helpful at the time of arrival and later. The provision of jobs, regular wages and prospects of upward social mobility and the absence of a threat to the economic aspirations of members of the receiving society are key factors to the whole process of adaptation. It is not unexpected that ethnic discrimination and violence rise at times of protracted high unemployment. Seen in this light, government attempts to reduce immigration at times of economic crisis are justifiable for all concerned. Such a policy would receive greater legitimacy, however, had it been arrived at in consultation with the sending societies – another indication of the need for a new approach to immigration policy.

The limited space available in this chapter allows for only the briefest of sketches of the socio-economic divisions between immigrants on one hand and the native population on the other as well as between the various ethnic groups themselves.

The Labour Market, Earnings and Poverty

There is substantial evidence that first generation immigrants are more likely than the native population to be in low-paid jobs and to suffer more from unemployment for a variety of reasons. On one hand, they may possess skills that may not be much in demand in their new society, they may not be able to speak the language, they may be unfamiliar with many of the labour market practices, and so on. On the other hand, employers may be more likely to discriminate against immigrants in both the employment recruitment situation and decisions regarding job losses.

What is crucial for long-term social adjustment is whether government policies enable first, and particularly second generation, immigrants to move up the social ladder according to their qualifications and experience. First generation immigrants 'may not mind being at the bottom of the economic ladder' but their children will resent it and they will show their resentment, sometimes in violent ways (Martin, 1997, p. 24). Without government policies, labour market disadvantage can become inter-generational, immigrants' economic potential can be wasted and the resulting sense of grievance can threaten the social stability of society. Second generation frustration erupting into social unrest has been commonplace in all AICs in recent years. The violence witnessed in several towns and cities in the UK in mid 2001 was born out of frustration and discrimination suffered by Indian, Pakistani and Bangladeshi youth born and brought up in the UK who considered themselves British.

The evidence of the US, which has the longest history of modern immigration as well as the most adequate set of statistics, supports both a pessimistic and an optimistic interpretation of labour market trends, even after controlling for education. Black men with high school education earned 39 per cent of the equivalent earnings of white men in 1960, 77 per cent in 1980 and 77 per cent in 1998. The earnings of black male college graduates amounted to 76 per cent of those of white male graduates in 1980 and 69 per cent in 1998; and the earnings of black MA graduates totalled 80 per cent of those of the equivalent whites in 1980 and 71 per cent in 1998 (US Census Bureau, 1999, Table 266, p. 170). Education raises the earnings of all ethnic groups but does not always close the ethnic gap in earnings. Women's earnings were lower than those of men at all education levels for both black and white workers though white women earned only slightly more than black women.

Evidence from the UK corroborates this picture. In 1995, only 41 per cent of Pakistani and Bangladeshi men were working full-time compared to 65 per cent of the Indian and 72 per cent of the native population. The corresponding proportions of women were 12 per cent, 36 per cent and 38 per cent (Office for National Statistics, 1996, tables 4.2 and 4.3, p. 40). In addition to differences in rates of economic activity, the various groups also differed on the hourly rates of pay reflecting both discriminatory practices and the types of jobs they had. Women's rates of hourly pay were lower than those of men even though white women were better off than any of the groups of immigrant women. Pakistani and Bangladeshi men and women earned less than any of the other groups (ibid., Table 4.17, p. 47).

Seifert's work in Germany shows that the earnings of immigrant workers in the early 1990s were lower than those of the German workers and that most of this difference was attributable to their different employment patterns. The decline in unskilled and semi-skilled jobs in the late 1980s hit immigrants harder than Germans and inevitably widened their differences in unemployment patterns (Seifert, 1996). Faist's study shows that labour market differences between second generation immigrants and German youths remain wide. While two-thirds of the latter had completed, or were completing, apprenticeships, the corresponding proportion for Turkish youth was a mere one-third and even this was in the less well-paid sectors of the economy (Faist, 1993).

Unemployment rates for immigrant groups tend to be higher than those of the rest of the population particularly at times of economic recession. All the evidence from the EU shows that unemployment rates of immigrants were not only very high during the 1980s and the early 1990s but also above those of other workers. More recent evidence from the UK supports this but it also shows the differences between the various immigrant groups. The rate of unemployment in 1995 was at its highest for Pakistani and Bangladeshi workers – 27 per cent, compared with 12 per cent for the Indian and only 8 per cent for the native workforce (Office for National Statistics, 1996, Chart 4.14, p. 46). The evidence from the US points to the same conclusions: black workers have the highest unemployment rates followed by the Hispanic and then the white workers. Moreover, this picture has persisted over several decades now with only minor fluctuations (US Census Bureau, 1999, Table 680, p. 430). Indeed, black youths with no educational qualifications are almost excluded from the regular labour market.

There is a general tendency for some immigrant groups to have high rates of self-employment in shops and restaurants. This is in many ways a sign of the vitality of immigrant communities but it is also a partial reflection of their inferior position in the labour market. It is for this reason that the Pakistani and Bangladeshi rate of self-employment in the UK was the highest – 22 per cent of all Pakistani workers were self-employed, double the figure of either the Indian or the native workforce (Office for National Statistics, 1996, Chart 4.12, p. 45). This type of self-employment can create a few wealthy individuals but it also has its downside – it involves long hours of work for the whole family and exploitation of employees, some of whom may be illegal immigrants.

It is not unexpected that the risk of poverty is higher among ethnic groups than in the white population. In the US, 10.2 per cent of all whites, 21.8 per cent of all Hispanic persons and 32.5 per cent of all black people had incomes below the American poverty line in 1980; the corresponding proportions in 1997 were 11.0 per cent, 27.1 per cent and 26.5 per cent respectively (US Census Bureau, 1999, Table 760, p. 483). These ethnic differences are reflected in the poverty rates of both children and of retired persons.

Housing Conditions

Residential concentration is a common feature of immigrant communities though the degree of segregation varies both between countries and between immigrant groups. There are no ghettoes in the European countries comparable to those in the US. The reasons for such concentration are obvious enough. On the one hand, immigrants prefer to be among their own people for economic and social support particularly during the early years of their settlement. On the other hand, their low wages and the discrimination they face in the housing market force them to congregate in low cost housing districts. A study of asylum seekers in the UK showed that finding somewhere to live was seen as the second most serious problem, after unemployment. Many stayed with relatives and friends and moved around a lot 'in order to shift the burden from one household to another' (Home Office, 1995, p. xi).

Housing conditions for immigrants are inferior to those of the native population in all AICs. The evidence from recent censuses in the UK 'showed very clearly not only that levels of unfitness and disrepair were much higher for the "non-white" groups but also that the situation did not appear to be improving' (Ratcliffe, 1999, pp. 6–7). As in the case of employment, there were variations among the various ethnic groups, with the Pakistani and the Bangladeshi groups suffering the worst housing conditions.

The types of immigration encouraged by globalization – continual, diverse and illegal – coupled with the recent retreat of the welfare state from the housing field does not augur well for the housing conditions of immigrants in the future. Much will depend on how effective anti-racist policies are in reducing the severity of individual and institutional discrimination against immigrants in the field of housing – and the prospects do not appear very encouraging for 'anti-discrimination measures are to a large extent ineffectual' in EU member countries not only in relation to housing but employment as well (Iganski and Jacobs, 1997, p. 159).

In general, residential ethnic segregation is almost inevitable during the early days of settlement. The extent and depth of ethnic concentration encourage the persistence of ethnic identity with implications for the future development of the relationships with the receiving society, as we shall be discussing below. To the extent that immigrants and their descendants find it difficult to break out of this segregation, there is the likelihood that a hostile or at least unhelpful social climate for fostering good relationships with the receiving society will develop. This is particularly the case when residential segregation is coupled with employment segregation or with high rates of long-term unemployment.

Educational Inequalities

Education has always been acknowledged as essential for the economic advancement of both the individual and of society as a whole. In an increasingly globalized world, the value of education will become even more apparent. Most of the immigrants who were attracted to Europe in the 1960s and 1970s to boost the economic development of European countries by filling low-paid manual jobs had educational standards that were below those of the receiving societies. What is, therefore, important is to examine the educational standards of their children *vis-à-vis* those of the rest of the population.

We know from the experience of the US, that the education gap between white and black has been bridged to some extent in recent decades. In 1960, 2.8 per cent of black men completed four years of college or more compared to 10.3 per cent of white men. In 1998, the corresponding figures were 13.9 per cent and 27.3 per cent respectively showing not only a rise in years of education for all but a closing of the gap between black and white. The gap also narrowed in the case of women: the figures for 1960 were 3.3 per cent of black women and 6.0 per cent of white women completing four or more years of college; for 1998, the figures were 13.9 per cent and 22.8 per cent respectively (US Census Bureau, 1999, Table 264, p. 169). The gap narrowed even further in the case of the younger age groups.

The same process seems to be happening in the UK even though the data is not as robust. The proportion of West Indian and Indian children that went to university in 1978 was 1 per cent and 3 per cent respectively compared with 5 per cent of children from all state schools (George and Wilding, 1984, Table 3.5, p. 75) By the mid-1990s, not only had the proportion of young people staying on at school after compulsory school age or studying for degrees increased for everyone but the figures for ethnic groups surpassed that for the white population. Thus the lowest percentage of 18 year-olds at school in 1994 was that of the white population – 38 per cent – compared to 50 per cent for black children, 65 per cent for the Indian and 72 per cent for the Chinese (Office for National Statistics, 1996, Table 3.2, p. 34). Similarly, the proportion of young people studying for a degree in 1995 was lower among the white population than among most immigrant groups: while 30 per cent of the young Indian and Chinese were studying for a degree, the corresponding proportion for the native group was only 12 per cent – a figure that was similar to that of the Pakistani and the Black young people (ibid., Chart 3.6, p. 37).

Despite the many qualifications that can be made to these figures from the US and the UK, they are encouraging for the future education of ethnic groups. They also show, however, that improvements in education do not fully counteract the discrimination that immigrant groups suffer in the labour market in terms of both jobs and wages. As has been said so many times in the case of class inequalities, education does not fully compensate for society. The same comment applies to inequalities based on gender or ethnicity.

Violence Against Ethnic Groups

Violence is endemic in contemporary societies – violence of one citizen against another, violence against women and violence against ethnic groups. Ethnic or racial violence ranges from verbal insults to physical attacks and to murders. All these manifestations of racial violence are commonplace in all societies with immigrant communities today. What varies from one society to another is the ethnicity of the victims, the range of violence as well as its frequency and severity. In Germany, it has been the Turkish community that has been the most abused including 'several arson fires that resulted in the deaths of Turkish children born in Germany' (Martin, 1997, p. 22). In France, it has been North African immigrants, while in the UK it has been the Pakistani and the Bangladeshi communities that have been the most common victims.

Clearly any statistics on racial violence underestimate the severity of the problem. To begin with, many such attacks are not reported to the police and, according to one government study in the UK, 'not all – and possibly a minority – of racially motivated incidents reported to the police are being recorded as such' (FitzGerald and Hale, 1996, p. 60). What we are seeing from the statistics is merely the tip of a large iceberg.

Though reported racial violence appears to increase during periods of high unemployment, its causes go beyond the prevailing socio-economic conditions in society. They are embedded in the history and the culture of western societies that are fundamentally racist, largely as a result of their recent colonial history. Racism has to be understood as a multidimensional process with its roots deep in the history of a country. It has 'to be located within economic, political and ideological relations' that have developed over recent centuries in AICs (Anthias and Yuval-Davis, 1993, p. 1).

It is for this reason that we speak not simply of individual acts of racism but also of institutional racism – a less obvious but equally destructive form of violence pursued in the policies of the various institutions of society in a conscious and unconscious manner. Not surprisingly, institutional racism is to be found in education, housing, the police, the courts, the work of insurance societies and so on. Anti-racist policies, if they are to be effective, have to be strong and multifaceted – they 'must seek both fundamental, structural change and gradualist, piecemeal changes within institutions' (Ginsburg, 1992, p. 130).

Cumulative Disadvantage

Disadvantage is often cumulative. The low-paid tend to be in insecure employment, to be inadequately housed, to live in run-down environments, to have low educational achievement and so on. This applies to ethnic minorities perhaps more than to others because ethnicity is often a disadvantage in itself. It is a situation that creates a 'chronic cumulation of disadvantages which triggers malign circuits and leads to social exclusion or the formation of an underclass' (Mingione, 1996, p. 33). It is usually found in the large cities where most ethnic groups tend to live.

Exhibit 6.2

Globalization, migration and disadvantage

- The living standards of ethnic communities in AICs are lower than those of the receiving society.

Exhibit 6.2 *(cont'd)*

- Only in education can one perceive clear progress for second generation immigrants.
- Ethnic violence is a major problem in all AICs.
- Racism is endemic in all AICs.
- The influence of globalization in this area has been mixed: it has helped to strengthen as well as to undermine those forces making for improvement in the living standards of ethnic communities.

The Future of Immigrant Communities

Globalization has set in motion two contradictory processes in ethnic relations in recent years. On the one hand, it has encouraged the flow of goods, capital, people and cultural images across the world at a pace unknown before. It has brought people and ethnicities closer together in physical terms. As a result, it has aroused the expectation of a more united world, a more cosmopolitan world, where ethnicity does not matter that much. On the other hand, it has boosted the confidence and the ability of ethnic groups to campaign and fight for what they consider the fulfilment of their economic, cultural and political rights. It has given birth to a multiplicity of new nation-states based on ethnicity with many others in the making.

Ethnic identity has been a source of both unity and separation; of ethnic conflicts as well as of national achievements. It has spawned both cosmopolitanism and localism. It has been a force for both convergence and divergence. The recent ethnic struggles in Yugoslavia capture both faces of this process. Whether for good or ill 'at century's end ethnic and racial identities have emerged as among the most potent forces in contemporary societies' (Cornell and Hartmann, 1998, p. 4).

Over the years of the last century, globalization has spawned three main types of ethnic adaptation reflecting the convergence and the divergence trend. When globalization was at its low ebb in the 1920s and the 1930s, it encouraged the view of assimilation stressing convergence; later in the 1970s when globalization gained momentum it stressed a divergent view of adaptation – multiculturalism; and more recently, the idea of ethnic diasporas. We examine each of these three separately though in real life they coexist.

Assimilation

The convergence view was the first to appear in the writings of Park in the 1920s (Park and Burgess, 1921) and of many others later, particularly Gordon in the 1960s with their theories of acculturation and assimilation of immigrants (Gordon, 1964). Acculturation was seen as a one-way process through which immigrants acquired the customs, practices and values of the receiving society. It was a necessary, but not a sufficient condition for assimilation for the latter was considered a two-way process that could not take place without the consent of the receiving society. Assimilation was also a much longer process that spanned several generations and had to go through a number of stages before it was fully completed. Assimilated immigrants not only incorporated the culture of their new society but they were also accepted as full participants not only in the formal but also in the informal institutions of society, for example, social clubs, churches and the family. The extent of intermarriage between the ethnic group and the native society was one of the clearest indices of assimilation. A great deal of evidence supports the view that intermarriage across the ethnic divide undermines ethnic solidarity while ethnic endogamy has the opposite effect (Alba, 1990).

The assimilation thesis has come under criticism from three quarters. First, those who object to it on ideological grounds because at best it implies the disappearance of ethnic identities and at worst it calls forth government measures to achieve this goal. This criticism only stands if assimilation is perceived in normative terms calling for government measures to bring it about rather than in analytical terms as the result of everyday human interaction. Second, the thesis has been criticized on the grounds that there is no dominant way of life in the receiving society to which immigrants are supposed to acculturate and assimilate. Rather, there are several dominant ways of life in contemporary advanced industrial societies. While there is some truth in this criticism in relation to the US, it is not so valid in the case of European societies with long cultural traditions and with only recent arrivals of immigrants. Third, the empirical evidence shows that even after generations of immigration in the US, assimilation has not taken place, as evidenced by the discrimination against the black community in the US, the growth of black ghettoes and the widespread race riots of recent years. This is a far more valid criticism and it raises serious doubts about the usefulness of the assimilation thesis in relation to certain ethnic groups in certain countries. It is for this reason that more recent statements of assimilation incorporate the thesis of segmented assimilation, that is a process that affects differently different ethnic groups.

In analytical terms, assimilation has a place in the analysis of ethnic adjustment with receiving societies. Thus Alba and Nee conclude their survey of the assimilation debate in the US with the judgement that none of the arguments made so far is 'sufficiently compelling to rule out *a priori* the possibility of assimilation as a widespread outcome for some, or even most, contemporary immigrant groups' in the US (Alba and Nee, 1997, p. 849). Historically, the evidence supports the conclusion that assimilation is a possible outcome of social interaction for some immigrant groups in the very long run but not for others. The Huguenots have been assimilated into British society, the black Africans have not in American society while the British and the French in Canada have maintained a fair social distance from each other.

Multiculturalism

The problems faced by the assimilation thesis became more obvious as globalization gained strength from the 1970s onwards. This gave rise to several pluralist or multicultural models of adjustment between immigrant groups and the receiving society. The adherents of multiculturalism insist that many ethnic groups will not be assimilated but they will reach some form of accommodation, a *modus vivendi*, with the receiving society whereby the ethnic group 'while retaining its own culture and religion, adapts itself to and is accepted as a permanent member of the majority society in all the external aspects of association' (Rose *et al.*, 1969, p. 24). In the UK, this view was first given government support in 1966 when Roy Jenkins, the Home Secretary, announced that the government's policy on the future of immigrant communities was integration which he defined as 'not a flattening process of assimilation but as equal opportunity accompanied by cultural diversity, in an atmosphere of mutual tolerance' (quoted in Rose *et al.*, 1969, p. 25).

The perennial difficulty with multiculturalism is to decide on the details of this truce between the ethnic and the national culture – where to draw the dividing line between the acceptable and the unacceptable features of the ethnic culture in the eyes of the dominant society. Certain values and practices of an ethnic group may be in such a sharp conflict with the values of the dominant society that they may cause conflict or may not be tolerated. It may also be that they are incompatible with the legal system of the country. In such situations individuals may well come under direct and indirect pressure either to modify their ethnic culture or not to act in accordance with it. The Rushdie affair in the UK during the 1990s illustrates the problems that flow from the clash of cultures and the steps that a government will take to protect the norms of its native culture.

As a social process, multiculturalism is natural, inevitable and beneficial during the early stages of the life of an immigrant community. In the long run, however, multiculturalism as a social process is just as likely to gradually change into assimilation for some ethnic groups as to lead to hybrid cultures for other ethnic groups depending on the particular situation. Total separation between the culture of an ethnic group and of the receiving society is impossible today in the multi-ethnic, television dominated societies of AICs. Ethnic youth cultures will absorb values from their own ethnic community from that of the receiving society, from other ethnic cultures in the area as well as from the growing global culture. For some second generation immigrants, 'such choices can be a source of stress and conflict (e.g., with more traditional parents), but for others – and for society in general – they can be a source of enrichment' (Castles and Davidson, 2000, pp. 139–40).

If multiculturalism is seen in normative terms, i.e. the state should provide policy support to the idea that immigrants have a right to maintain their own culture, it again has to take cognisance of the fact that there are limits beyond which ethnic cultures may not be allowed to operate. Very few countries have taken the step of either recognizing or actively encouraging ethnic cultural rights but the few that have done so clearly marked the rights and limits of multiculturalism. Australia's official document on multiculturalism in 1989 was one of the first of its kind. It clearly stated that immigrants have a right to maintain their culture and that the state should enable them to do so. At the same time, however, it set out the boundaries within which multiculturalism could be practised as follows:

> Multicultural policies require all Australians to accept the basic structures and principles of Australian society – the Constitution and the rule of law, tolerance and equality, freedom of speech and religion, English as a national language and equality of the sexes. (Office of Multicultural Affairs, 1989, p. viii, cited in Castles and Davidson, 2000, p. 166)

The implication of this is that there is a core of the Australian culture that should be observed by all, including members of ethnic groups. As citizens, they have the right to try and change the situation either through the democratic process or through the courts. In both cases their chances of success are obviously limited for the cards are stacked against them – they may not get enough political support for their proposals and the judges, by and large, reflect the values of the dominant society. In brief, multiculturalism, either as a social process or as a normative statement, has much to commend it, but it can only operate within certain boundaries in most situations. Only where the ethnic group is as large and geographically separate, as the French Canadians are, can it hope to survive culturally.

Diasporas

In both the assimilation and the multicultural model, individuals perceive their identities in relation to the nation-state and/or the home country. The recent expansion in the scope and the intensity of globalization, however, has meant that many members of the same ethnic group who are spread in different countries of the world as immigrants are able to perceive themselves as members of their ethnic group, their home country and their different receiving societies. The Jews, the Chinese, the Greeks and other ethnic groups have formed diasporas, sometimes on their own accord and sometimes with the support of their home country governments. Members of diasporas are, in Kotkin's words, members of global tribes (Kotkin, 1992). 'Diasporas form', says Soysal, 'when populations disperse from their homeland to foreign lands, engage in movements between the country of origin and destination, and carry out bi-directional transactions – economic, political and cultural' (Soysal, 2000, p. 3).

Diasporas may well attract the most educated, the most entrepreneurial, or the most cosmopolitan members of immigrant communities who can perceive and enjoy the advantages of their ethnic background as well as of the twin countries that they belong to. Many of them may be bilingual and may have dual citizenship. They will see themselves as persons with double identities and be happy and proud about that. Nation-states may well be opposed to such diasporic identities among their citizenry, but 'they are increasingly spitting in the wind' in the face of the strong globalizing forces (Cohen and Kennedy, 2000, p. 253).

There is another aspect of the diaspora that is crucial to the identities of some immigrant groups. Black populations in different countries – the US, UK, France, Canada, Latin America, the Caribbean, Australia and so on – have their roots in Africa though they have tried or have been forced to adapt to the cultures of different countries. Now, thanks to the compression of time and space as a result of globalization, they can begin to share in a common cultural background though adapted to the local situation and to learn from each other's experience. Gilroy expresses this as follows in relation to the Black British:

> Black Britain defines itself crucially as part of a diaspora. Its unique cultures draw inspiration from those developed by black populations elsewhere. In particular, the culture and politics of Black America and the Caribbean have become raw materials for creative processes which redefine what it means to be black, adapting it to distinctively British experience and meanings. (Gilroy, 1987, p. 154)

Yet, care must be taken not to exaggerate the idea of a unified black community for at times there are divisions within it signifying the existence of several black communities which can discriminate against each other. Racism is not simply a black versus white notion. It can also involve white against white as well as black against black (Mac an Ghaill, 1999).

Finally, members of diasporas in different countries may well rally to the support of their homeland when the need arises. This can take a variety of forms – financial, social and political. As members of the same 'global tribe' they re-enforce their identity with their homeland without jeopardizing their membership of their new society.

In brief, globalization has, on the one hand, encouraged assimilation through its effects on the gradual emergence of a global culture of sorts but, on the other, it has boosted the forces making for multiculturalism and diasporas. In the days before the last World War, contacts between immigrants and their homelands 'often lay mainly in the imagination rather than in regular concrete interactions' (Scholte, 2000, p. 171) because of financial and practical problems. Such circumstances encouraged the processes of acculturation and assimilation. Nowadays, with the growth of media communications and the cheapness of travel, contacts between immigrant communities, their homeland and other co-ethnics in other countries are far easier, giving support to both multiculturalism and diasporas.

In the final analysis, different immigrant groups will make different adjustments to their receiving societies depending on a host of economic, social, cultural and political factors. Moreover, different groups of individuals of the same immigrant group will arrive at different adjustments for the process involves both structural as well as individual features. Whichever of these three types of adjustment is arrived at in the long run, the crucial issue is whether ethnic groups are able to compete with members of the receiving society on an equal footing in education, housing, the labour market, and so on for this will decide the level of their welfare in society.

Exhibit 6.3

Globalization and ethnicity

Globalization has encouraged both ethnic pride and cosmopolitanism.

Globalization has given support to different forms of adjustment between ethnic groups and receiving societies: assimilation in the early days, multiculturalism in the 1970s and ethnic diasporas in more recent years.

Different ethnic groups as well as different individuals will make different adjustments with the receiving society depending on a host of factors.

The challenge facing AICs is how to accept difference as a source of strength rather than a source of conflict.

Conclusion

The vast majority of people never leave their country of birth for another country – their village is their world. For a small minority, however, the world is their village – they are prepared to emigrate to better their lives, to avoid economic deprivation and to escape religious or political persecution. The most common estimate is that immigrants total about two per cent of the world's population. Bearing in mind the depth and spread of deprivation in IDCs relative to the affluence in advanced industrial societies, the question to be asked, is not 'why immigration' but rather 'why not much more immigration' (Hammar, 1995, p. 176).

Globalization has had a marked effect on the nature of migration. Contemporary migration movements are different from previous ones in three significant ways. First, their global nature: almost every country is either a receiving country or a sending country or both. Second, migration is not such a final act today as it used to be. Immigrants can keep in touch with their home countries far more easily than before, many of them retain dual nationalities and some move back and forth several times. Third, so much of recent migration has been directed at Europe with the result that in a period of less than forty years all European societies have become multi-ethnic.

Globalization has not only affected the nature of the migratory process but also the nature of the adjustment between immigrant communities and the receiving societies. It has helped to extend the legal rights of immigrants and has given them more choice as to whether to assimilate or not in the receiving society. It has made multiculturalism an accepted notion and has made possible the growth of ethnic diasporas.

It is difficult to be certain whether the effects of globalization on the living standards of immigrants and of their children have been, on balance, positive or negative. On one hand, recent globalization trends in the labour market and in rates of pay, have widened inequalities in society and immigrants are the most likely losers of this process. On the other hand, globalization has encouraged the growth of human rights and anti-discrimination policies which must have had some positive effect on immigrants' standard of living even though it remains inferior to that of the native populations.

Three main interrelated challenges face AICs today in this area:

● First, how to go beyond the current adversarial nature of migration in order to create a new pattern of migration which takes account of the needs of both the sending and the receiving societies. Demographic trends point to a greater demand for immigrants in the affluent countries. Moreover, bearing in mind 'the ineffectiveness of much immigration policy and given the undesirability of policy methods to control immigration, how much can be lost by innovating in immigration policy?' (Sassen, 2000, p. 75). Such a change of policy, however, has to be counterbalanced by the ability of the receiving society to accept more newcomers that are bound to influence not only the economic but the political and cultural life of the country. How to strike a balance between these two seemingly conflicting processes is a major dilemma for governments in AICs.

- The second challenge is how to change the current mind-set that sees social solidarity as only possible when everyone conforms to the same values and practices in a society. Agreement on core values is necessary for social cohesion but this need not apply to many aspects of the national culture. After all, with or without more immigrants, advanced industrial societies are becoming increasingly pluralistic in all aspects of life. The challenge is how 'to use difference as a resource rather than fear it as a threat' (Bulmer and Solomos, 1998, p. 834).

- The third challenge revolves around the nature of government policies that are necessary to abolish racism in society. Governments have a duty to ensure that all citizens – and non-citizen residents – are treated fairly irrespective of gender, ethnicity, religion or other such group criteria in all walks of public life. As globalization continues to make AICs more multi-ethnic, this task will become both more pressing and more difficult. Government responses to these challenges, which are constantly intensified by globalization, will vary according to the country's social values and institutional structures.

Further Reading

Brettell, C.B. and Hollifeld, J.F. (eds) (2000) *Migration Theory* (London, Routledge).

Castles, S. and Miller, M.J. (2000) *The Age of Migration*, 2nd edn (Basingstoke, Macmillan).

Mac an Ghaill, M. (1999) *Contemporary Racisms and Ethnicities* (Buckingham, Open University Press).

7

Global Social Policy Today

One of the most important insights which gathered support in the 1990s was that markets need states and states need markets, that unless capitalism is regulated, supported and civilized by public policies it will not survive. This was first accepted at the national level and more recently has begun to be asserted and accepted at the international level – a striking contrast to the dominance of neo liberal ideology in the 1980s. Deacon, for example, writes of 'the socialisation of global politics' (Deacon, 1995, p. 56). Shaw argues that 'The development of global society requires a new politics of global responsibility' (Shaw, 1994, p. 187). The *Human Development Report 1999* warns that 'Globalization offers great opportunities for human advances – but only with stronger governance' (UNDP, 1999, p. 1). The World Bank view is that 'Actions at the global level are...crucial complements to country level action' (World Bank, 2000, p. 179). Globalization, it is being realised, is too important to be left to the play of market forces. To achieve the universal economic gains which it promises, to avoid the damaging emergence of 'core' and 'marginalized' states and to ensure the social and political stability on which its success depends, it needs to be 'managed'.

Deacon argues that there is now a global social policy made up of 'transnational redistribution, supranational regulation and supranational and global provision' (Deacon *et al.*, 1997, p. 22). This may be a little optimistic but there are certainly signposts and prefiguring elements – in the policies emerging from international bodies in particular fields – for example, labour and the environment, in the influence which international bodies exert on the policies of national states and in the emerging models of supranational social policies – most obviously in developments in the EU.

But what has developed so far is essentially reactive, piecemeal and ad hoc. There has not been any kind of global social strategy or even much discussion of the kind of social policies 'required' in a more global economy. There are some tentative and embryonic models which could be built on but the essentially national nature of traditional social policy makes it of limited value as a guide to the global project.

Global social policy will have to be very different from national social policy in its approach, strategy and aims, flexible enough to accommodate states at very different levels of economic and social development, more focused on regulation than on social provision, more concerned with minimum standards and safety net type provision than with the pursuit of equality, acutely sensitive to the risk of conflict with national policy goals. To achieve even limited goals it must involve significant redistribution of resources from rich AICs to poor IDCs. The development of global social policy will also be dependent on the parallel development of policies for managing the global economy. Social policy cannot sensibly be considered in isolation from economic policy.

This chapter explores three questions –

● why is there a need for global social policy?

● what already exists by way of global social policy?

● how far does what exists meet the need for such policies?

Why is There a Need for a Global Social Policy?

We summarize the case under ten headings.

Greater Global Interdependence

Globalization compresses time and space and creates a keener sense of the world as one and so of interdependence. Scholte, for example, writes of 'a continued growth of global consciousness' since the 1960s (Scholte, 2000, p. 85) and of a mind set encouraging supra territoriality. The Commission on Global Governance called its report 'Our Global Neighbourhood' (Oxford University Press, 1998). Giddens argues that 'humankind in some respects becomes a "we" facing problems and opportunities where there are no "others"' (quoted in Scholte, 2000, p. 179).

Globalization fosters a more global discourse about welfare fed by reports from, for example, the World Bank on old age (World Bank, 1994), the OECD on the future of welfare provision (OECD, 1999a) and the EU on the possibilities of European social policy (EU, 1994). An emerging global consciousness creates a sense of problems as global – for example the concept of 'the global commons' – which is both fed by, and feeds, the growth of global networks of, for example, environmental organizations. This, in turn, strengthens the sense of global consciousness and momentum for an attempt at global solutions.

The conceptualization of issues as global depends to a large degree on a sense of global consciousness emerging to complement a sense of national belonging, a sense of the world as one that feeds and legitimates the search for global solutions to problems redefined as global.

Global Social Problems

A global approach is needed to deal with problems which are global in character. In 1997 the OECD spoke of 'a growing internationalisation of many policy issues which were previously more domestic in nature' (OECD, 1997a, p. 36). More and more issues are global in their impact and implications and they can be solved only by concerted international action – as, for example, was the eradication of smallpox or in current efforts to safeguard the ozone layer.

Crime and drugs have become genuinely global problems in their scale, nature and impact. Weiner writes of 'the growing global crisis in international population movements' (Weiner, 1995, p. 155). Water supply and use is rapidly emerging as a major global issue. World consumption of fresh water quadrupled between the 1950s and the 1990s and continues to increase rapidly. Elliott reports over eighty countries, with 49 per cent of the world's population, facing water shortages with twenty six countries officially designated as water scarce (Elliott, 1998, p. 2). The problem is global in its scale and in its implications and in the fact that global solutions are needed to complement national efforts.

AIDS is another example of a global problem only amenable to containment or solution on a global scale. As the World Health Organization Global Programme on AIDS put it 'AIDS cannot be stopped in any single country unless it is stopped in all countries' (quoted in Johnson and Soderholm, 1996, p. 122). In October 1987, AIDS was discussed by the UN General Assembly, the first time a specific disease had ever been discussed in the Assembly – an illustration of the global acceptance of its global nature and of the perceived limitations of the nation state in AIDS policy-making.

The emergence and acceptance of a range of social problems as genuinely global stimulates pressures for the development of global social policies.

Mitigation of the Effects of Global Competition

Global action in social policy is required to prevent a race to the neoliberal bottom. The neoliberal ideology of globalization puts pressure on national welfare states in the way it fuels demands for cuts in public expenditure, reductions in social welfare provision and the easing of labour and environmental regulation. These pressures grow out of particular notions of how economic efficiency and global competitiveness are to be achieved.

There is nothing new about competition. What is new, however, is its intensity, the overriding importance given to it by governments and the dominance of neoliberal notions of how it can best be promoted. The impact of these changes on states is highly significant. Cerny suggests that such pressures problematize the capacity of the state to embody communal solidarity so threatening its legitimacy and so reducing its capacity under globalization's pressures (Cerny, 2000, p. 118). This is why there is a need for action at the global level.

Mishra suggests one answer to these down-driving pressures on nation state welfare – that standards of social protection must not become part of a competitive game but must be part of the rules of the game. That, he argues, requires a global social policy to compensate for the limitations which globalization imposes on national welfare states and to sustain the levels of social provision seen as necessary for civilised life at the national – and by extension – at the global level. The only way to head off pressure for a race to the bottom is for states to stand together and collaborate with supranational bodies to develop a raft of global social policies (Mishra, 1998, p. 490).

Support for the Idea of Global Human Rights

Global social policy is an appropriate expression of emerging ideas of global citizenship and global human rights. One aspect of the development of global consciousness is the evolution of the concept of global citizenship and global civil society. Such ideas lead to a tentative extension of national aspirations to the global level. They foster ideas of global justice, of global minimum standards in health, education and income, of a concept of human rights at a global level. McCarthy sees the most successful transnational concept-building effort in recent years as the creation of a global concept of human rights (McCarthy, 1997, p. 245). The concept is developed and promoted by several UN bodies, NGOs and international social movements.

The UNDP argues that the potential benefits of globalization will only be realised via stronger governance based on a principled globalization which is guided and governed by respect for human rights, a concern for equity, an emphasis on inclusion, a commitment to reduction of poverty and insecurity, a concern for a sustainable future (UNDP, 1999, p. 2). What UNDP is arguing for, essentially, is globalization based on ideas of global citizenship. The World Bank's *World Development Report 2000–2001* argues along similar lines (World Bank, 2000).

The huge expansion in the number, size, resources and prominence of international NGOs and global social movements is both an expression of an emerging global citizenship and a force for its further development. At the Rio Earth Summit in 1992, for example, there were 20,000 participants from 9,000 NGOs from 171 countries. There have been similar manifestations of a new notion of global citizenship in other areas. O'Brien *et al.*, for example, speak of the four UN Conferences on Women in 1975, 1980, 1985 and 1995 as having acted 'as great catalysts to the development of women's organisations and movements nationally and internationally' and of a global consciousness of gender rights and issues. (O'Brien *et al.*, 2000, p. 34).

Complementing Global Economic Policy

Global social policy is a corollary of a global(izing) economy. The symbiotic relationship between economic and social policy and between trade and social policy is now part of conventional wisdom. Globalization is partially economically driven but that does not mean it can sensibly be seen simply in economic terms. As *Our Global Neighbourhood* put it, 'Stability requires a carefully crafted balance between the freedom of markets and the provision of public goods' (Oxford University Press, 1998, p. 135). If stability requires the provision of public goods, so too does economic integration if it is to be sustained (Leibfried and Pierson, 1994, p. 43).

Development today is seen as meaning more than simply economic growth. It must be sustainable in the sense of not mortgaging the future for the sake of the present. It must raise all boats not just Olympic racing craft. The quest for sustainability raises major questions about the distribution of wealth, power and opportunity between rich and poor countries and within nation states. These questions suggest an important role for social policy – in UNDP's words 'to make globalization work for human development' (UNDP, 1999, p. 9) or as the World Bank puts it 'global forces need to be harnessed for poor people' in a wide ranging set of strategies (World Bank, 2000, p. 12).

Social policy has also become a more significant element in the globalization process as confidence in fundamentalist free market liberalism has ebbed. Informed opinion has moved away from a faith in unregulated markets to a belief in a socially regulated, socially embedded capitalism – and that means a global capitalism smoothed, sanded and sustained by social policies. Efficiency and competitiveness are important but so too are safety nets and human welfare.

The interdependence of economic and social policies is nicely illustrated by the way in which the World Bank and the IMF have come to give much more attention to social policy and the social dimensions of economic policy – and the pressure on the WTO to move towards 'conditional trade policies' – using trade agreements as a way to bring pressure to bear on countries to adopt desired policies in relation, for example, to core labour standards and environmental protection.

This is not to say that social democracy rules the hearts and minds of the big beasts of global economic policy-making. Rather it is to argue that social policy has now edged back into the frame of reference of economic policy-makers after two decades in the wilderness. Traditional economic thinking still dominates, but there is some acceptance of the need to develop social policies as a corollary of global economic development.

Strategy for a Global Social Policy

A strategy for a global social policy would formalize existing trends and developments. Deacon boldly asserts that 'There is now a global social policy' made up of global redistribution mechanisms, global regulatory mechanisms, elements of global social policy provision and a global discourse about the future of national social policy (Deacon *et al.*, 1997, p. 213). Certainly there is a patina of incremental social policy superimposed on the globalizing economic system. The World Bank and the IMF have both come to take the social implications of globalization more seriouly (Deacon, 2001, pp. 60–63). There is the varied pattern of activity of the UN's social policy divisions – WHO, UNICEF, ILO, UNHCR, for example – and the work of a wide range of specialist elements ranging from the Commission on Sustainable Development to the Global Programme on AIDS and the Global Environmental Facility. The WTO is constantly being pressed to add a concern for labour and environmental policy to its brief.

What exists is a plethora of very different organizations nibbling at a social policy agenda but in an essentially ad hoc and reactive fashion. There is – perhaps inevitably at this stage of development – no overall social policy strategy to match the grand liberalizing economic project which has been the primary, and uniting, preoccupation of the big economic players.

What is clearly needed is some rationalization of what is happening, some standing back from the here and now, some consideration of aims and objectives, strategies and choices and some attempt to coordinate the rather ragged looking rag tag and bobtail of policies which has emerged from such a disparate set of bodies.. There need to be discussions about the overall shape, possibilities and limitations of global social policy – and a move on from what is essentially and hopefully a pre-figurative stage of development.

To Avoid a Backlash Against Globalization

Global social policy is essential to avoid a backlash against globalization. Globalization may be a powerful force for economic development but it is increasingly recognized that it has social costs. There is strong evidence that globalization – as it has developed in the past thirty years – has increased inequality, injustice and insecurity in some countries and has fragmented societies (e.g., Scholte, 2000, chs 9 and 10). As the *Human Development Report 1999* put it 'Globalization is creating new threats to human security – in rich countries and poor' (UNDP, 1999, p. 3). 'The volatility of markets', the Report concluded, 'is creating new vulnerabilities' (ibid., p. 84). Globalization also increases knowledge of the nature and scale of deprivation and inequality and of the impact of disasters connected to the decline of market confidence and the resulting capital flight and of trends such as global warming.

The more perceptive analysts of globalization, Rodrik for example, see the need for policies designed to secure popular acceptance of globalization (Rodrik, 1997). That means policies to compensate losers, moderate inequalities and redress the more provocative inequities. If such pre-emptive measures are not put in place, there is the very real risk of a backlash as was first expressed to all the world in the television coverage of the demonstrations at WTO meetings in Seattle in November 1999 and at subsequent meetings of the WTO and the G8 – most notably in Genoa in July 2001.

On its own, the national state cannot guarantee to provide what is needed – because of the pressures of the new competitiveness and because of the nature of the problems which are at issue. What is needed, is action at a regional and a global level to protect and preserve the achievements of national welfare states and to display an acceptable face of globalization. The case can be made on grounds of economic and political rationality as well as justice because high rates of inequality, whether national or global, do not promote economic growth or political stability.

Expectations Created by Globalization

Globalization makes a global social policy (more) possible. Globalization creates the possibility of a global social policy. It helps create the economic resources which are a necessary, if not a sufficient, condition of global action. It stimulates aspirations on both sides as the poor see how the rich live and the rich are vividly confronted with the stark realities of abject poverty and unmet basic human needs. It creates a fragile consensus that some things should not be, for example high infant mortality rates, because they do not need to be. There is an emerging consensus about some issues of human rights – of workers, of women, of ethnic minorities and of children – and a feeling that basic human rights should be universally guaranteed. These elements are necessary preconditions of social policy development at the global level.

Crucial, too, has been the development of global networks of NGOs – most obviously in relation to the environment but also in relation to human rights. Globalization has been the midwife of that development and the emergence of a global network has transformed the debate in these areas. It has made it impossible for national governments to ignore environmental concerns and it has pushed them towards globally coordinated action because this is the way in which NGOs have successfully framed the debate.

There has also been the necessary institutional development. Supranational institutions have matured and consolidated their position and come to a broader view of their role and responsibilities, for example, the ILO, the WHO, the World Bank and the IMF. There has been a huge proliferation of treaties, committees, commissions, programmes and protocols. Globalization has also fostered the development of an issue-based social politics which transcends state boundaries and erodes the position of the state as the pre-eminent site of social policy making. If key issues are global – the rights of women, the rights of poor people, the rights of ethnic minorities, the protection of the biosphere – then the focus and canvas for social policy making must be global too.

Neoliberal Ideology is not Necessary

A global social policy is a corollary of the sense that the future is (at least partially) open. The development of a global social policy depends on the conviction that the outcomes of the particular model of globalization – neoliberal globalization – which has been dominant for the last thirty years do not simply have to be accepted as inevitable. As Michie put it, 'the fact that the economy is becoming internationalised does not dictate the form that this process is taking' (Michie, 1999, p. 6). The process and the outcomes are open. There is scope for Scholte's 'ambitious reformism' (Scholte, 2000. p. 39), Deacon's 'socialisation of global politics' (Deacon, 1995, p. 56) or Radice's 'progressive internationalism' (Radice, 2000, p. 16). This belief in possibilities is crucial to any attempt at social engineering. The decline of confidence in neoliberalism has opened the door to the reconsideration of the possibilities and potential of governance at a global level. Recent World Development Reports from the World Bank are edging towards this position.

States Need Global Social Policy

State social policies need the complementary and parallel support of global social policies because of the key role which social policy plays in securing and maintaining state authority and legitimacy. Social policy has been central to the maintenance of the legitimacy of the modern state – as has state legitimacy to the development of social policy. The modern state cannot be seen to be failing in what have come to be defined as among its central responsibilities without suffering serious damage. Globalization makes it more difficult for the national state, acting on its own, successfully to fulfil these responsibilities. The development of policies at a global level to protect the environment, to combat AIDS, crime and drug trafficking, to secure core labour rights, to reduce unemployment, for example, can help bolster state legitimacy which is essential both to successful economic globalization and to securing the welfare of citizens.

What Already Exists By Way of Global Social Policy?

Few people talk or write about 'global social policy'. There is a considerable literature on specific policy areas such as environmental protection, employment, AIDS and crime but little about the wider possibilities of a global approach to social policy. Essentially, that is for three reasons. First, the ideology underpinning recent and current globalization has been neoliberalism which historically has been hostile to state action and state social policy. Second, social policy has always been strongly national in its focus, something done by nation-states. Third, establishing global social policies is obviously a very complex task threatening a potential loss of authority for national-states, tricky issues of harmonization, acute problems of implementation and monitoring and divisive debates on the balance of funding responsibilities.

Nevertheless, if we look closely, there is actually a considerable amount of what might reasonably be defined as global social policy but, in line with national traditions, it is an agglomeration of the ad hoc, a tesselated pavement of seemingly unconnected initiatives underpinned by no common philosophy or strategy. It is reactive and piecemeal but nevertheless significant.

A wide range of supranational bodies is involved. For some, particular social policy issues are their primary concern – for example the ILO or the WHO. For others, for example the OECD, the World Bank or the WTO, social policy concerns are a rather uneasy add-on. Then there is the huge range of organizations, loosely connected to the UN with a finger in the social policy pie – coordinating information, developing policy, drafting treaties and protocols and promoting policy implementation on issues such as the rights of children and of people with disabilities, educational development or the improvement of aspects of health services. There are also the international courts – the Court of Human Rights, the International Court of Justice.

There have been attempts to coordinate policies, for example to get the WTO to take on environmental and labour issues when it is negotiating trade agreements, or the World Bank's efforts to stress the importance of the links between economic and social policy and the broad approach needed to tackle the problem of poverty. At this stage, however, policies are essentially conceived and considered in specific and functional terms rather than as particular but interconnected elements in a strategy of global social development.

Human Rights

A clear framework for human rights was set out in the Universal Declaration of Human Rights in 1948, the Covenant on Civil and Political Rights (1966), the Covenant on Economic, Social and Cultural Rights (1966), the Convention on the Elimination of Discrimination Against Women (1979), the Convention on the Rights of the Child (1989). These were complemented by the creation of the UN Commission on Human Rights to police abuses. In 1998 the process for establishing an International Criminal Court was completed. The Court will deal with war crimes, genocide and crimes against humanity.

Governments have accepted – in theory at least – that there are rights which transcend national sovereignty, which people can claim as rights which are theirs as human beings whatever the nature of the government under which they happen to live. The main human rights covenants have been ratified by over 140 governments out of 190 (Held *et al.*, 1999, p. 67). The main problem with these UN Covenants is that, as Mishra puts it when commenting on the International Covenant on Economic, Social and Cultural Rights, the various caveats 'turn the Covenant largely into a statement of principles and objectives ... rather than a set of standards to be developed within a specified time frame' (Mishra, 1999, p. 125).

The growth of NGOs concerned with human rights issues has increased dramatically since the 1970s. They have secured a high profile on many issues and can bring strong pressure to bear on national governments deemed to be in breach of human rights or laggardly in implementing conventions to which they have subscribed. Falk describes the overall record of achievement as impressive (Falk, 1999, p. 175) but a gap between promise and performance remains starkly obvious. Enforcement in most parts of the world rests on states – and states continue to abuse fundamental rights.

The crucial step forward to make rights talk real is first, the acceptance of the right of citizens to appeal to supranational bodies which have the responsibility to pronounce on the legality of national state policy and actions and, second, the state's acceptance of the binding nature of such pronouncements. At present, acceptance of the judgements of such supranational bodies is variable in AICs and limited in IDCs where they tend to be ignored. European citizens now have the right, in certain circumstances, to take legal action against their own government on the basis of government abuses of human rights. Individual citizens do not, however, have direct access to the International Court of Justice at the Hague. The *Human Development Report 1999* aptly sums up the situation – the international legal framework for human rights is a great achievement but 'the lack of mechanisms for enforcement is glaring' (UNDP, 1999, p. 39).

Environment

The most publicised area of global social policy is probably environmental protection. There has been a rapid and important development of both law and institutions. The UN Conference on the Human Environment in Stockholm in 1972 was the first major UN conference on environmental issues. It agreed twenty-six key principles and approved an Action Plan with 109 recommendations. Its significance lay in the way in which some of the principles have shaped subsequent policy, in the way it led to improved environmental monitoring systems which stimulated further action, in the creation of the UN Environment Programme which followed, and in the way in which it stimulated national governments to create ministries for the environment or other national environmental agencies (Greene, 1997, p. 317). In turn, UNEP was a force for further development in the way it placed the link between environment and development firmly on the international political agenda (Garner, 1996, p. 111).

If we look back on what has been achieved in environmental policy in the past twenty years or so there are some major achievements – the institutionalization of control of marine pollution in a series of international and regional agreements, international agreements to govern the movement of toxic and hazardous waste, developments to safeguard a range of endangered species, the protection of fishing stocks and the control of commercial whaling, measures to control trans boundary air pollution and acid rain. The Global Environmental Facility was established to support environmental protection projects in poorer countries. Agreements were signed to postpone development of the natural resources of the Antarctic. Agenda 21 at the 1992 Rio Earth Summit was accepted as a blueprint for sustainable development. The 1992 Conventions on Climate Change and Biodiversity were promulgated and in 1993 the UN Commission on Sustainable Development was established. Perhaps most significant of all, were agreements to control the use of CFCs which were diagnosed as the primary element in the destruction of the ozone layer.

There has been massive activity. There has been a proliferation of laws, conventions and regulations. There has been a gradual, if delayed, move from regulation to prevention. Inevitably, less has been achieved than the environmentalists hoped for. Of the five key agreements signed at Rio in 1992, only two are legally binding, the agreements on biodiversity and on climate change, and these involve few specific commitments. Key tensions remain unresolved – the conflict between state sovereignty and global stewardship, the reluctance and/or inability of national states to implement international agreements, the conflicts between rich and poor nations over responsibilities, priorities and who pays, the problems of reconciling environmental concerns and economic development, and the perennial problem of balancing the strong claims of the present against the inevitably weaker anticipated needs of the future. But many of the basic building blocks of a global environmental protection policy are in place.

Employment and Social Security

The ILO has been working to establish common standards of employment practice since 1919 in relation to the right to join a trade union, hours of work, equal pay for men and women for equal work, the outlawing of child labour, rights for migrant workers and social security provision. There are now some 200 conventions covering this wide range of activities providing the basis for a well regulated international employment system.

The way the ILO works, however, imposes inevitable limitations on its achievements. It frames conventions and then works to persuade governments to ratify them and once ratified, to observe them. Inevitably there is a significant ratification gap – in 1996 the OECD reported that only 62 countries had ratified all ILO conventions on core labour standards. The ILO does seem, however, to have exerted a progressive influence on laggard welfare states in the industrial world nudging some along the labour protection road and fighting to protect earnings related social security systems against the threats of privatization and residualization. In recent years, the ILO has developed new conventions such as the 1996 Convention on Home Work which aims to protect the working conditions and rates of pay of home workers.

In relation to a possible or potential role as advocate of social security development at the international level or the international encouragement of national developments, the ILO suffers from the fact that its brief is essentially limited to employment related social security provision rather than the development of social security systems generally.

The revival of neoliberal ideology in the 1980s put the ILO firmly on the defensive as it was associated with precisely those characteristics of western employment and social protection systems which were diagnosed as rendering western capitalism uncompetitive. Scholte points out that the ILO has been significantly less vigorous in its pursuit of global rights than the WTO and the IMF have been in pursuing policies of trade and financial liberalization (Scholte, 2000, p. 225). Over the years, while it has clearly been a force for the protection of labour, it has not been strong enough to combat the erosion of security at work and the chipping away at systems of social protection which has been one of the significant side effects of globalization.

Health

The World Health Organization is a long established body but it figures relatively little in discussions of globalization or global social policy. For example, it gets only one reference in the index to Scholte's *Globalization* (2000) and in Deacon *et al.*'s *Global Social Policy* (1997). It does not appear in the index to Mishra's *Globalization and the Welfare State* (1999) nor in the index to *Globalization in Question* (Hirst and Thompson, 1999). In contrast, the WTO and the World Bank figure prominently.

The WHO certainly has achievements to its credit but they are relatively limited. It can claim a share of the credit, along for example, with UNICEF, for the massive increase in child immunizations in IDCs in the 1980s, from around 15 per cent to around 80 per cent of children, saving an estimated twelve million lives. It has worked hard, and with some success, to combat malaria. Another area of comparative success was the promotion of health as 'everybody's business' and as a strand which should run through all social policies and permeate the preoccupations of institutions such as schools, workplaces and trade unions. Another more controversial area in which WHO was involved was population control policies 'one of the earliest examples of global social policy' (Yeates, 2001, p. 121). By the early 1990s, over 120 IDCs had adopted such policies.

The WHO was also active in the development of global AIDS prevention strategies from 1987. It won lots of support initially, and seemed to be working from a strong global consensus about what needed to be done, but international efforts were, in Soderholm's view, 'accompanied by conflict, resistance, doubts and contention' (Soderholm, 1999, p. 266). WHO did not manage to secure effective coordination between national and international activity.

When the Global Programme on AIDS was launched, WHO never managed to create an effective global policy network. The programme never achieved the standing which would have enabled WHO to act as the coordinating link between different elements of the UN system concerned with AIDS, a point which ties in with Berlinguer's argument that in the 1980s and the 1990s, WHO lost its political leadership in health policy to the World Bank and to the IMF (Berlinguer, 1999, p. 584) primarily because of the extra resources they could command.

Education

There is no body with the task of pressing the claims of basic education in the corridors of global power with even the limited capacity of the WHO. UNESCO's brief is broader and more general rather than focusing on basic education. A decade ago the world's governments promised 'education for all' by the year 2000. It has not happened. When, in 1995, the goal was seen as unattainable it was prudently rescheduled for 2015!

In April 2000 the world summit on education met in Dakar. Evidence it received showed clearly that although standards had risen in some countries since 1990, they had deteriorated in others and inequalities had increased. The educationally rich had got richer. The Global Campaign for Education, a coalition of the big charities, development groups and teachers' unions, set out nine key commitments with the support of the World Bank and a small number of countries in an effort to kick-start progress.

There was strong opposition to a global plan of development from a number of AICs on the basis that country-by-country initiatives were a better approach, that the key problem was mismanagement of funds rather than inadequate funds, that education should not be separated from other aspects of social development. In the end, world leaders oozed goodwill and promised a global initiative and more money but without specifying how much or how it might be distributed (*The Guardian*, 26 April, 28 April, 29 April 2000). When the chips were down, there was a lack of the commitment needed to assess the precise nature of the problem, to develop a strategy and to raise the funds required.

Crime and Drugs

International crime has flourished on the back of globalization. It has become a multi billion dollar global business which is far more sophisticated than the prevention-enforcement agencies which have been developed to combat it. Laws are passed, for example, to control migration, drug trafficking and trafficking in women and children, but the capacity for effective cooperative action at the level of prevention or apprehension of offenders remains limited.

Interpol was set up as long ago as 1923 and has become global in its membership. In recent years it has extended its areas of concern to trafficking in women and children, pornography and environmental crimes but at the end of the day it remains a relatively small organization. In 1995, the EU set up Europol to try to tackle transborder crime in the EU. In the same year the G8 established an Expert Group on transnational crime. There have also been specific initiatives to combat particular problems, such as money laundering.

Gordon and Williams conclude that the major problem is that the development of organizations to combat international crime has been ad hoc and haphazard. What is needed is 'a single comprehensive and coherent strategy to combat organised crime developed by a guiding authority' (Gordon and Williams, 1998, p. 74). The response to global crime must be global.

Social Development and Anti-Poverty Policies

In the Foreword to the *World Development Report 2000–2001*, the President of the World Bank proclaimed that, 'We at the Bank have made it our mission to fight poverty with passion and professionalism, putting it at the center of all the work we do' (World Bank, 2000, p. v). The Bank's position is interesting for two reasons. First, because of the priority given to fighting poverty something which would have been way out of line with the Bank's orientation only a few years before. Second, there is the very broad definition of poverty which is adopted encompassing dimensions such as powerlessness, lack of 'voice', vulnerability and fear.

The Bank has a three pronged strategy for poverty reduction – the promotion of opportunity, the facilitation of empowerment, enhancing security (World Bank, 2000, pp. 6–7) and it goes on to try to turn strategy into policy. It defines four key areas of international action for poverty reduction. The first is expanding market access to high income countries for IDC goods by the reduction of tariffs which 'can place significant constraints on poor countries efforts to grow'(ibid., p. 180). The second is working to reduce the risk of economic crises, for example, by controls on capital flows. Third is the encouragement of the global provision of public goods which are particularly beneficial to the poor, for example control of infectious diseases. The fourth is ensuring a voice for the poor in global forums such as the WTO where decisions crucial to the development and well-being of IDCs are taken (World Bank, 2000, Ch. 10). These areas represent aspiration rather than actual policy but they are important representations of how one of the world's premier financial institutions has come to see the centrality of social development and poverty reduction to economic development.

In the 1990s, the World Bank and the IMF both got involved in debates about future pension policies in both AICs and IDCs, cutting across the traditional role of the ILO in this area and arguing strongly for the centrality of private provision and a merely residual role for the state in pension provision.

Does What Exists Provide What is Needed?

What exists is a rather messy patchwork of policies. Certainly, there have been specific initiatives in particular areas but it is the broad overview which has been lacking. There has been no real attempt to explore in depth what might be required by way of social policy development in a more global economy.

Between the varied initiatives there is overlap and duplication and there are many gaps. There are unresolved – and seemingly almost unresolvable

tensions – for example, between national sovereignty and global responsibility, between those who see the market as the great problem solver and
those who put their faith in public policy, between longer and shorter term
goals, about cost sharing between nations, between the conflicting claims and
needs of AICs and IDCs.

There is a lack, too, of the institutions required to make effective global
social policies – and to make such policies effective. A range of organizations,
whose primary responsibilities lie elsewhere, dabble in social policy concerns.
The IMF advises countries on the design of new social security systems. The
World Bank has pronounced on a wide range of social policy issues. Inevitably
there are differences of view between different international bodies. The ILO
has traditionally been a supporter of state social security and of the earnings-
related principle – both of which principles are questioned by the World Bank
and the IMF. The WTO is in a position to make a potentially powerful impact
on social policy but has been reluctant to link trade with labour standards or
with environmental protection.

In the first section of this chapter, ten reasons are set out as to why there is
a need for global social policy. They can usefully be consolidated into four
questions for brief evaluation.

First, do the global social policies which have developed adequately reflect
the emerging sense of one world, global citizenship and global human rights?

The answer has to be 'At best, only partially'. The nation state rather than
the world, or the region, is still for most policy makers and people the central
frame of reference.

There are policies which very clearly reflect an emerging global understanding but it is national concerns and interests which dominate discussion rather
than the needs of the planet as a whole. There is little clear sense of an awareness of a great, emergent transformation. Social policy at the global level is
seen as an add on. 'States still rule OK' remains the dominant motif. The
national still waits to be transcended or even adequately supplemented or
complemented. The sense of global citizenship remains largely an academic
fiction except at moments of crisis.

Second, do global social policies represent an adequate response to the
evolving understanding of certain problems as global and only to be adequately dealt with by action at the global level?

Here the answer is clearly – and understandably – in the negative. Thirty
years of global environmental policy have some important achievements to
their credit but what has been achieved in no way matches the scale or
urgency of the problem. The agreements made to try to halt global warming
are important but patently inadequate – as the latest scientific forecasts show
with terrifying clarity (*The Guardian*, 23 January 2001). There is even less sense
of the urgency of working towards a policy on global water conservation and
use. Migration issues are still seen as essentially questions for the nation-state

even though the problem is manifestly global in its nature and scale as Chapter 6 shows.

Third, are global social policy developments adequate to spread the costs and gains of global economic development in an equitable manner and secure the redistribution needed to achieve crucial policy goals?

In Chapters 3 and 4 it is shown how globalization has exacerbated poverty and inequalities in many countries while stimulating global economic growth. The backlash against globalization has recently become more manifest on the streets. The evidence suggests that fears of a race to an unpleasant neoliberal bottom of very residual social policies may have been exaggerated but the evidence on restrictions on social security provision is very clear even if not catastrophic. Perhaps the most significant failure of imagination, and so of policy, is the failure of the AICs to grasp, and proclaim, that there can be no hope of effective environmental policies at a global level without massive resource redistribution from rich nations to IDCs because of the direct costs which such policies will impose on all participants including those least able to bear them.

Fourth, do the policies required to realise the social possibilities which exist in a more global world actually exist?

The answer again has to be 'No'. There have been flashes of inspiration in global social policy, for example the notion of sustainable development, but in general policy has been gloomily pragmatic, focusing on the immediate and the short term. It has been about problems rather than possibilities. The vision which underpinned the development of national welfare states has generally been absent as has the vision which led to the creation of the key supranational institutions after the Second World War.

Six key factors have inhibited, and seem likely to inhibit, the development of global social policy. In a sense the lack of development is unsurprising even though the need is clear and urgent. It is useful to draw out the key difficulties.

First, there is resistance by national states to loss of policy autonomy to supranational bodies. National governments do not like to cede power and will almost always defend traditional areas of state responsibility however much they are committed in principle to internationalism.

Second, public opinion in most countries is not yet ready to support major initiatives in global social policy. The national state is still the primary focus of concern, aspiration and action. There is little sense that the nation-state's ability to deliver on its key social policy aspirations is today frequently limited by its very nature and that supranational institutions and policies are a vital complement to national action. Existing supranational bodies lack the legitimacy which they need to secure public support. They operate with a damaging lack of transparency, a worrying absence of clear lines of accountability and a wounding democratic deficit.

Third, the way social policy responsibilities are fragmented between supranational bodies is an obstacle to the development of any kind of overall global strategy. There are bodies with very clear responsibilities for key social policy areas, for example, WHO and health policy, the ILO for labour policy. But there are also other bodies which have assumed abutting or even potentially conflicting roles, for example the World Bank's commitment to a broad anti-poverty strategy involving issues of trade and health.

What is needed for the development of effective global social policies is a reform and rationalization of existing institutions, organizations and respons-ibilities and the creation of new organizations – for example an overarching Council for Social Development, a World Environmental Organization and an International Migration Organization.

Fourth, the still dominant, even if ebbing tide of neoliberal ideology, has created a residual atmosphere of scepticism and pessimism about the possib-ilities of public policies. There may have been helpful talk about bringing the state back in, and an acceptance by key bodies such as the World Bank that markets need states, but many of the supranational bodies are still strongly influenced, if not actually dominated, by pro-market doubts about the value and legitimacy of extending the supply of public goods. O'Brien *et al.*, can still describe the IMF, the World Bank and the WTO as 'the iron triangle of liberalism' (O'Brien *et al.*, 2000, p. 233)

Fifth, there is the very practical problem that a global social policy cannot be uninhibitedly global in the sense of one size fits all global policies. There has to be great flexibility, for example, in terms of the application of global labour standards or the drawing of poverty lines. Global social policy has to take account of different national histories, different national priorities, different patterns of economic activity, hugely diverse levels of economic development, different levels of administrative capacity. This need for flexibility is clearly an added problem in the design of effective and acceptable global social policies.

Sixth, there is as yet no strong or compelling consensus that a sustainable future depends on the development of an overall global social policy. There is at best a rather reluctant acceptance that the future – or at least the well-being – of the globe may well depend on tackling certain specific problems such as the increase in international crime, depletion of the ozone layer, the spread of AIDS or global warming. But there is relatively little sense of any kind of com-pelling conviction that there is a need for an overall global social strategy to match the drive for economic liberalization and economic growth.

Conclusion

There are powerful arguments to be made for the development of global level social policies. In our view, such policies are needed for the very future sur-vival of the world not merely for its cosy well being. There are promising developments in terms of attitudes, policies and institutions but the progress made falls well short of what is, and will be, needed for a sustainable global future. In the final chapter, we set out the range and nature of the global social policies required for a just and sustainable future.

Further Reading

Deacon, B. (1995) 'The Globalisation of Social Policy and the Socialisation of Global Politics', in J. Baldcock and M. May (eds) *Social Policy Review 7* (Canterbury, Social Policy Association).

Mishra, R. (1998) 'Beyond the Nation State: Social Policy in an Age of Globalization', *Social Policy and Administration*, **32** (5), 481–500.

World Bank (2000) *World Development Report 2000–2001: Attacking Poverty* (New York, Oxford University Press).

8

The Future of Global
Social Policy

This chapter discusses the nature of the social policies required 'to make globalization work for human development' (UNDP, 1999, p. 9) and to secure a sustainable global future. Running through the discussion is a fundamental issue – the inherently political and contested nature of social policy. In a world sharply divided by differences in levels of economic development and so in interests between AICs and IDCs, social policy cannot be seen simply as a neutral instrument of rational actors concerned solely with the general good. It has to be seen as a site and instrument of conflict in the historic struggle between haves, have nots and have not yets. Social policy can be an instrument for the general promotion of human welfare. But it can also be used by those in positions of power to bolster their own position and maintain an inequitable status quo. The WTO, for example, is dominated by the world's richest nations. Only 34 of the 134 members are from the world's poorest countries and around half of them have no representatives in Geneva to defend their interests. In contrast, the USA has around 250 negotiators based there permanently.

Our approach is based on four premises, first that certain basic needs and human rights are universal in nature and demand satisfaction in an affluent world; second, that the world today suffers from 'an under-provision of global public goods' (Kaul *et al.*, 1999, p. 450); third that it is possible to sketch the broad outline of a global social policy while bearing in mind the hugely different circumstances and often conflicting aspirations and interests of different countries; fourth that, as Soros one of the leading actors on the stage of financial globalization has put it, 'Our global open society lacks the institutions and mechanisms necessary for its preservation' (quoted in Arrighi, 1998, p. 64).

What Role for Global Social Policy?

We begin with a general discussion of the role of global social policy and how it relates to the social policies of nation states, the traditional context for social policy making. Seven major roles for social policy at a global level can be identified.

First, global social policy is concerned with the promotion and establishment of basic human rights at an international level – the rights of a range of exposed, discriminated against and marginalized groups such as the poor, women, workers, ethnic minorities, people with disabilities, children, those at odds with the government under which they happen to live. Such rights can range from the level of principle, for example, freedom of speech, to rights which require a strong supporting infrastructure of laws, services and institutions – laws about equal treatment, services to 'normalize' the lives of those with disabilities, mechanisms to ensure the satisfaction of such basic needs as income, health care, education and housing.

There are obvious problems with trying to proclaim and provide for such rights on a global level. For example, in most AICs, allowing young children to work in paid employment would be seen as an abuse of human rights. In many IDCs, in contrast, restrictions on children's employment could increase family and child poverty which is an erosion of the fundamental right to an adequate income. Again, AIC concern to universalize workers' rights is seen in many IDCs as an attempt to weaken their competitive advantage and protect AIC home industries. The promotion of human rights has to be tackled sensitively with an eye to the national and cultural context. But it is clearly a central strand in the development of a global social policy.

Second, global social policy is needed to supplement and complement national level social policy. The emergence of issues which clearly and obviously transcend both national state boundaries and the capacity of the nation-state to devise and implement effective solutions means that, in the words of Kaul, Grunberg and Stern, 'we have entered a new era of public policy' (Kaul *et al.*, 1999, p. xxv). Policies at the national level have a limited capacity to deal with an expanding range of social problems. There is an increasing number of issues which individual states cannot tackle satisfactorily when acting on their own. State policy and capacity need supplementation with, and, by global initiatives.

For example, every national government needs its own policies to deal with AIDS, crime, drug abuse, migration and environmental problems. No state, however, can hope to tackle these problems effectively in isolation because of the very nature of the problems in a more global world. National policies can only make a limited impact. They will fail unless complemented and underpinned by parallel policies at the global level. When national welfare states came into being and flourished in the 1940s, 1950s and 1960s there were few social problems which had ramifications beyond the reach of individual nation-states. States could be sovereign in their social policies. Half a century later, national self-sufficiency in social policy is no longer a realistic option. In an increasing number of areas, action at the national level has to be complemented and supplemented by action at a supranational level.

Third, global policies are required to create a level international playing field. The ILO, said Polanyi, was set up 'partly in order to equalise conditions of competition among the nations so that trade might be liberated without danger to standards of living' (Polanyi, 1957, p. 26). Free trade can have very painful side effects if states do not accept basic ground rules of competition. Only an international body and international rules could, for example, safeguard standards of labour protection which all states might want to maintain but fear to fight for in the face of non-observance by their competitors. The ILO was, of course, thinking primarily of industrial nations at comparable levels of economic development.

Increased international competition can create outcomes which no one really wants because it puts pressure on states to be ever more competitive. Competition can induce a race to the bottom in social policy provision, both generally and in specific areas deemed to push up labour costs, as states seek to gain or retain a competitive position in global markets. Initiatives at the global level can work to harmonize and sustain policies so they become a given in competitive relations rather than a site of competition and an unintended casualty of a more global world.

The problem with this line of approach is the very different interests of AICs and IDCs in some areas, for example, in relation to core labour standards. Whatever the motives, the AIC concern with standards of labour protection in IDCs looks, from the IDC perspective, like an AIC attempt to protect their own workers and markets and undermine a key element in IDC competitive advantage.

Fourth, global social policy is concerned with raising standards internationally by action at the global level. The aim is to raise standards of social provision and human welfare through global action when action by individual nation states is unlikely to raise standards across the global board – for example, to institute policies more likely to safeguard the future of the global environment by strengthening rules and regulations, to apply pressure on states to accept, enforce and raise core labour standards, to promulgate universal human rights and to advance the standing and protect the position of women, children and ethnic minorities.

Global social policy has a potential vanguard role in relation to improving levels of provision in key policy areas, for example education and health, and in setting international minimum standards of provision in others. It can do this by IGOs promulgating acceptable levels of practice and provision and engaging in 'policy dialogue' with national states (Yeates, 2001, pp. 116–18). Absolutely crucial, too, as a precondition of securing the funding necessary for any kind of progress, are policies of redistribution from AICs to IDCs. Such policies are an essential precondition of the raising of standards in IDCs. To guarantee basic standards of education for all children, or to set clear targets for the reduction of infant death rates in IDCs, is well within the resources and capacity of global action but it depends on redistribution of resources.

Fifth, the aim must be to reduce poverty and inequalities and to provide a safety net for global capitalism because 'Inequality in a globalised world is a cause of migration, environmental degradation, disease transmission and political instability' (Jolly, 2000, p. 79). Poverty is also at the heart of IDC opposition to the development of core labour standards and the extension of environmental policy.

Globalization unleashes creative – and uncreative – gales of destruction and reconstruction. There will always be winners and losers. Looking at the issues purely pragmatically, if social stability is to be maintained there has to be a safety net and schemes of compensation for the losers – for example, for those who lose their jobs to workers in other countries where labour is cheaper, for those whose wages are driven below a level of adequacy by global competition. Losers in one country may threaten the whole forward march of globalization and so the gains of others or even of the majority. For reasons of pragmatism – as well as justice – there has to be a safety cushion – or else there will be no soft landing for the losers or the winners. The bumpy course of economic change has to be smoothed or else the losers may turn out to be the new giants barring the road to global reconstruction.

Working out what such a safety net would mean in countries at very different stages of economic development is obviously complex but it is important to proclaim the principle. Globalization can bring overall gains in terms of the growth of world GDP but it can at the same time impose huge costs, for example the East Asian financial crisis or the spread of AIDS. The costs which the gains of the better off impose on the poorest cannot simply be allowed to lie where they fall.

Sixth, global social policy is needed to provide the services which global capitalism needs to survive and prosper. Global social policy is concerned with the support, regulation and servicing of capitalism at the global level as well as with modifying its distributional outcomes. It is concerned with establishing environmental laws which will restrain, or hopefully outlaw, environmental destruction in the cause of economic growth and international competition, with regulating the conditions of employment to avoid a race to the bottom in the terms and conditions of work, with the provision of the health services required to improve health and prevent the spread of infectious diseases. Global social policy is also concerned with the servicing of global capital in the sense of providing education and training for workers, regulating the migration of the numbers and types of workers required to keep the wheels of production and reproduction, both economic and social, turning smoothly.

Nation-states have found that collective provision of services can be functional to capital in terms of promoting efficiency, encouraging economic and social stability, improving the quality of human capital and reducing the costs of preventable disease. The arguments can be extended to the global level.

Seventh, global social policy is about promoting a sense of one inextricably linked global world. Global social policy is both a response to a new under-standing of life and human need in a globalizing world and a force for creating a new international order. In the latter role, it exists to express and promote a sense of the new one world which is coming into being and the emergent ideas of global citizenship and global responsibility, to prefigure a new global civil society and a new international social, as well as economic and political, order. Global social policy is, at the same time, both a response to the emerging sense of problems transcending the reach and grasp of the national state and a force for the further development of a greater global consciousness. Global social policy can provide stepping stones in, and to, that new world both by the process of incremental development, of which it is expression and catalyst, as well as by the guarantees of global justice which it can, and should, offer.

Global social policy is both similar to national social policy and different. It is similar in its essentially political nature, in the values and concerns driving it – for example, the broad concern with human rights, societal sustainability and human flourishing. It is different in that its primary focus is going to be declaration, policy promotion, subsidization and regulation rather than actual service provision at the global level. It is also different in that its funding depends on an international redistribution of resources from rich to poor countries.

What Policies are Needed?

What the nature of global social policy should be is obviously a crucial and contested question for the future development of globalization. Here we can do no more than sketch desirable lines of development. How such policies should be organized and implemented is obviously closely linked to what the policies should be, but those issues are dealt with separately in the next section.

This section has three parts. First it sets out a number of assumptions which underpin the proposals which follow, assumptions about developments in other fields which are nevertheless central to the proposals for global social policy. Second, it explores the general aims and principles which, in our view, should govern global social policy. Third, it sets out the broad lines of the global social policy which is needed.

Assumptions

Seven assumptions underpin our proposals for global social policy.

First, there are core – albeit flexible – supranational rights or social standards (Mishra, 1999, pp. 119–21) which, in the rich world of the twenty-first century, can and therefore should be available to all – the right to a basic income, the right to health care, the right to basic education, the right to clean water, the right to basic liberties, etc. They can, and should, be financed from the general growth dividend of globalization or from specific taxes such as the Tobin tax on foreign exchange transactions. In a global economy, individual nation states may be unable, or unwilling, to provide them because of fears of damage to national competitiveness. Securing the provision of these becomes, therefore, an issue of global social policy.

Second, it is clear that 'Globalization is too important to be left as unmanaged as it is at present because it has the capacity to do extraordinary harm as well as good' (UNDP, 1999, p. v) as was argued in Chapters 3, 4, 5 and 6. A key assumption underlying this position, of course, is the belief that globalization not only should, but can, be managed.

Third, in a globalizing world, global social policy is a necessary complement and supplement to national social policy. It is needed to ensure the achievement of national social policy goals, to civilize the process of globalization and to secure the just distribution of its fruits. To gain the political support which globalization needs, the case for global social policy must be argued not in terms of surrendering national social policy space but rather in terms of logical policy development, filling gaps and creating something which has been lacking hitherto. Global social policy opens up the possibility of dealing with those disruptive problems which are beyond the reach of the national state. Clearly, it is important to work out the relationship between global, national and regional policy but there can be a positive sum outcome.

Fourth, national governments have not the reach or the power to contain or control MNCs who set out to put themselves beyond the reach of the nation-state. A global code for the effective governance of MNCs is crucial to a responsible globalization. It is needed to ensure that they accept their economic and social responsibilities, for example, their observance of workers' rights, that they pay appropriate taxation, that they pay due regard to environmental protection and that they do not establish antisocial monopolies. It is in no one's interests, apart from the MNCs themselves and their shareholders, and that only in the short term, that the current situation continues. Only action at the global level can enforce a modicum of social and economic discipline on these unruly giants.

Fifth, there has to be a system for the international management and coordination of FDI. FDI has grown dramatically in recent years and is a crucial factor shaping the future of the international economy and in particular the economic and social prospects of IDCs. It is far too important simply to be left to market forces. As Hirst and Thompson put it, after some specific proposals as to how regulation might be managed, 'This is an area where strengthening the international public policy regime is most pressing' (Hirst and Thompson, 1999, p. 214).

Sixth, the movement of finance capital must be regulated and restrained. This is accepted by many of the giants of global finance (e.g., Soros, 1998). We saw in Chapter 2 how the amount of capital circulating in global financial markets and concerned solely for quick profits is a dangerously destabilizing force. As the *Human Development Report 1999* put it, 'financial crises are now recognised as systemic features of global capital markets. No single country can withstand their whims' (UNDP, 1999, p. 4). The World Bank has pinpointed control of capital flows as central to policies to reduce the risk of economic crises which, in turn, is a key element in the Bank's strategy for international action to reduce poverty (World Bank, 2000, p. 180). The need is for some kind of global financial and monetary authority such as an enhanced, and humanized, IMF (Scholte, 2000, p. 294).

Seventh, global social policy cannot be comprehensively global because the world is so varied a place. The kind of policy measures we suggest must be tempered to national levels of economic and social development and national interests. IDCs, for example, cannot be expected to implement the same standards of labour protection or guarantee similar levels of basic income as would be properly and reasonably expected in AICs. Equally, in IDCs there may have to be a different trade-off – in the short term at least – between pursuing economic growth and protecting the environment from what would be acceptable in AICs. A sensitive flexibility is vital while keeping firm hold of essential principles.

Aims for Global Social Policy

There are two related aims for global social policy. First, 'to achieve globalization with a human face' (UNDP, 1999, p. v). This approach is pragmatic but firmly rooted in the conviction that just as national markets need state action to sustain them so too do global markets. They need global public policies to counter the insecurities, injustices and dis-welfares which are the inevitable outcomes of markets unaccompanied by appropriate public policies. Second, the aim is to create a more sustainable world order by redistributing wealth from rich to the poor nations. Global economic, social, political and environmental stability can be achieved only when abject poverty and gross inequalities are eradicated in IDCs. Very few, if any, of the ambitions of global social policy can be achieved without such a redistribution.

The global social policy required to achieve this will be multi dimensional – a mix of regulation, redistribution, provision of services and guaranteeing of basic rights. It will be both radical and incremental. Scholte's 'ambitious reformism' (Scholte, 2000, p. 39) admirably captures the ethos of this approach – ambitious in intent but incremental in strategy and concerned wherever possible to build on existing institutions rather than to get involved in complex and time and energy absorbing restructuring.

Income

The most basic of all rights is, perhaps, the right to an income adequate to buy the basic necessities. Few would question that. But how to embody such a right in global social policy is very difficult both because of the huge variations in national wealth and income and because of the practical problems of instituting any kind of global basic income. But it is clearly a basic right underpinning all other rights. It is also absolutely central to remedying the injustices and inequalities which seem inherent in neoliberal globalization illustrated most sharply in the shocking statistics that, while there were improvements in many countries, 60 countries have been getting steadily poorer since 1980 (UNDP, 1999, p. v). There are 1.2 billion people still living on less than $1 per day – the World Bank's poverty line; 2.8 billion people, nearly half the world's population, live on less than $2 per day (World Bank, 2000, p. 3).

A basic income for all is clearly affordable in the global economy of the twenty-first century assuming 'basic income' means the income needed to maintain simple physical efficiency. Kapstein urges a debate on the creation of an international social minimum. Each country should define what would constitute a decent standard of living for its citizens in terms of access to health care and education as well as wages and rights to social protection. Some suitable international body – perhaps the World Bank or the United Nations Development Programme – should then be charged with the responsibility of producing an annual audit of progress in achieving such a social minimum (Kapstein, 1999, p. 104). What is required to achieve such a goal, is an imaginative and creative exercise in global income redistribution which would also be an exercise for global justice and sustainability.

Green suggests a system to be financed by contributions related to national GDP per capita and settles on a low level average of 0.25 per cent of the paying country's GDP because he sees the current 0.75 per cent aid target as unrealistic and therefore ignored (Green, 1995, pp. 43–6). Other sources of funds might be a tax to be levied on MNCs or a Tobin type tax to be levied on foreign exchange transactions. The use of such funds would have to be accompanied by tight conditions and would need to be monitored by a cadre of independent experts accountable to an appropriate global body.

A complementary line of approach, strongly advocated by the World Bank, is the opening up of international markets to IDCs. The Bank emphasizes that all countries which have achieved major reductions in poverty have done so partly, at least, through increasing international trade (World Bank, 2000, p. 8). The Bank reckons that tariffs facing IDC exports to high income countries are, on average, four times those facing AIC exports to IDCs (ibid., p. 180). By opening up their markets to agricultural products, labour intensive manufactured goods and services, AICs could offer a major hand-up to IDCs. The World Bank quotes estimates that OECD tariffs and subsidies cost IDCs some $20 billion per year – equivalent in 1998 to about 40 per cent of aid (ibid., p. 11).

As the *World Development Report 1999* put it, 'trade is the primary vehicle for realising the benefits of globalization' (World Bank, 1999, p. 4).

Deacon's view is that 'It is not fanciful to suggest that some decades hence either the right to social assistance or the right to a minimum income could be enshrined as one of the global citizenship entitlements that the reformed UN system would expect its member states to uphold' (Deacon *et al.*, 1997, p. 211). AICs recognized many years ago that poverty and deprivation were economically and socially destructive. That is equally true in a shrinking global world and has to become the basis for new global initiatives.

Health

In health, the global policy level is of growing importance as a result of increasing movement of people and so of infections and as globalization opens up new possibilities. There is the need for global policies to deal with problems which are clearly global – AIDS is the most obvious example. Climate change is also creating conditions and situations, for example the northwards march of malaria, which require global rather than simply national initiatives. There is also the need for global action to make available core health rights to all – vaccination, immunization, the right of access to primary health care and essential hospital care, the right of access to clean air and clean water. A global health policy will have to have at least three dimensions.

First, it must include clear targets for improving global health, for example, reductions in infant mortality rates, in death rates of children under the age of five and in rates of malnutrition.

Second, it requires a global body to take clear charge of such a policy. The obvious candidate is a reinvigorated WHO with a clear concept of itself as the key organization for improving and achieving global health standards working with national governments to achieve key aims as suggested in *Our Global Neighbourhood* (Oxford University Press, 1998, p. 269).

It must become the protagonist and advocate for health concerns and standards in global policy-making arenas. It must be the body driving forward the cause of core health standards in WTO negotiations, World Bank development plans and in all discussions about economic and social development. The WHO's historic, if now somewhat tarnished, commitment to 'Health for All' needs to be dusted off and adopted as the key guiding policy commitment. On some issues, health policy has to be global if the aims willed by nation-states and their citizens are to be achieved. On other issues, global support and resources are required if national aims, which would have global approval, are to be realized.

Third, such a policy needs resources and this means redistribution from AICs to IDCs to fund such initiatives. The WHO estimates that only some 10 per cent of the $50–60 billion spent world wide every year on health research goes on those diseases which affect 90 per cent of the world's people. Only 13 of the 1,233 new medicines patented between 1975 and 1997 were for tropical diseases (World Bank, 2000, p. 183). The reason for this misdirection of research is obvious. Research follows money and purchasing power. The necessary purchasing power for new drugs does not exist in IDCs. For the multi-national drug companies there is little point in developing expensive new drugs for which there will not be profitable markets. There must, therefore, be subsidies to IDC-oriented research and to ensure that there are markets for products which meet the health needs of IDCs.

Globalization creates new health problems. But it also opens up new possibilities for improving standards of health and health care as new drugs become (in theory at least) globally available and as the wealth and infrastructure are created to make global initiatives possible.

Education

Education is both global and intensely local. The higher education market has become increasingly global with more and more students spending part of their course in a country other than their own or pursuing whole programmes, generally postgraduate, overseas. However, basic education remains essentially local. That means the absence of some core rights in IDCs, for example, universal access to free primary and secondary education, a trained teaching profession, provision of basic books and equipment – the infrastructure required to achieve fundamental aims and aspirations.

These are not issues only for nation-states. They are global issues, for three reasons. First, lack of education helps to perpetuate poverty and underdevelopment. Improving educational opportunities for girls, for example, is a key factor in achieving the lower fertility rates which are central to sustainable development. Second, the problem can only be tackled through a global programme of advice, and assistance financed through global redistribution. The poorest countries cannot, today, finance their own educational advance. Third, education is increasingly seen as a global right, a right which should be available to all.

Historically, education has been seen as essentially a matter for the nation-state. It has never really been seen as a global issues. True, there has been UNESCO but it has always been primarily concerned with rather more esoteric issues – higher education, research, cultural exchanges – than issues of basic provision. UNICEF has been active in promoting education in IDCs, although education has only been one of its many concerns. We have had a WHO since the 1940s but no World Education Organization. Now, in a more global world, there is increased pressure to see education as a global issue and access to it as a core social right. What is described in Chapter 4 is a very mixed picture, but it is clear that in a significant number of countries education expenditure actually fell in the 1980s and the 1990s.

At the World Summit on Education in April 2000, representatives of over 180 countries – nearly a full world representation – gathered to discuss future policy towards IDCs. There were also 400 major NGOs represented there, concerned to promote the education of the poorest, along with the World Bank now the largest international provider of education aid (*The Guardian*, 28 April 2000). There was, however, no consensus on the precise nature of the problems which had to be overcome – was it shortage of resources or misuse of resources? – or on the best way forward. The issues – and the rights which are at stake – have, however, to be seen as global if progress is to be made and rights turned into realities.

Employment

Conditions of employment have become an issue in global debates for two main reasons – increasing public awareness of exploitative labour conditions and concern about loss of jobs in AICs supposedly as a result of the import of cheap manufactured goods from IDCs (Lee, 1997, p. 176).

Core labour standards are an essential strand in global social policy to avoid a race to the bottom in the search for national competitive advantage and to guarantee basic human rights. They are also 'a core site of global social politics' (Yeates, 2001, p. 112). Enforcing such standards without sensitivity to national differences creates serious problems. As O'Brien *et al.*, comment, while most states will discuss the environment, many refuse even to embark on a dialogue about labour issues (O'Brien *et al.*, 2000, p. 99). They are seen as too economically and politically sensitive. IDCs see AIC attempts to promote core labour standards globally as an attempt to reduce a key source of their competitive advantage and protect the position of rich countries. AICs see IDCs gaining an unfair advantge from labour market practices which would not be allowed in AICs. Some AICs, too, are anxious about any supranational regulation which might restrict their own freedom to seek enhanced competitiveness through 'more flexible' employment policies.

The notion of core labour standards was conceived in a world in which competitive trade relations were less dominant than they are today. Mechanisms are needed now to protect existing standards, to extend them progressively and flexibly in line with current thinking and to ensure that they do not become elements in international trade competition. There are two broad approaches to the problem.

The first is to develop the ILO, which has been the key relevant international body for many years. The ILO operates by establishing labour standards and then working to secure their ratification by its member states. The ILO's conventions about core labour standards cover freedom of association, the right to collective bargaining, the outlawing of discrimination in employment, the establishment of a minimum age for employment and the abolition of forced labour. Mishra draws out three key weaknesses of the ILO approach. First, ratification of conventions is voluntary. Second, compliance with conventions, once ratified, remains substantially voluntary. Third, the ILO has not managed to link the extension of core labour standards with levels of economic development (Mishra, 1999, p. 126). The general consensus on the ILO is neatly summarised by O'Brien *et al.*, in the judgement that 'the ILO has not been a tremendously effective organisation' (O'Brien *et al.*, 2000, p. 103). What it has lacked is the support from governments which would have allowed it to monitor and enforce compliance with its conventions. But the ILO has the experience, the skills and the capacity to take a more proactive role in promoting core labour standards if there was the national and international will to move forward. It could be re-engineered on these lines without undue difficulty.

The second approach is to work through the WTO and to link trade agreements with the extension of core labour standards. Coupling labour standards with trade agreements has potential as a force for progress but there has been a great deal of argument about the desirability of this route (e.g., Krueger, 1998; Lee, 1997). The WTO has never wanted to assume any kind of social policy role, arguing that it should stick to trade issues and the ILO should deal with labour matters. *Our Global Neighbourhood* endorsed this division of labour (Oxford University Press, 1998, p. 170). The ILO has also been anxious about sanctions-based social clauses as going against its model of progress through voluntary agreement (Yeates, 2001, pp. 115–16). At the end of the day, however, the WTO is in a position of great power and influence – Blackhurst speaks of its 'emerging role as the pre-eminent international economic organisation' (Blackhurst, 1997, p. 533). Trade is central to the well being of a global world and this gives the WTO immense policy leverage. It cannot reasonably and properly ignore the centrality of core labour standards to human well being or the role it could play in raising such standards.

Our preference would be for a twin-track approach. The ILO should be encouraged to adopt a new more proactive stance and should be given new powers to monitor the implementation of conventions and to enforce compliance. At the same time, the WTO should be given a parallel role in the promotion of core labour standards in trade agreements while being sensitive to the concerns of IDCs.

Environmental issues

There is now a huge corpus of international environmental law designed to protect the global commons and promote sustainable development. It covers the major areas of contemporary concern such as climate change, the destruction of the ozone layer, deforestation, loss of biodiversity, the processing of hazardous waste. Obviously there are gaps, but environmental protection is, in many ways, the most developed area of global social policy because the issues affect AICs as much as IDCs.

There are, however, significant issues which have not been adequately addressed and which need to be addressed. Three stand out. First, effective environmental protection has to be conceived on a global scale and this means redistribution of resources from rich to poorer nations as is pointed out in Chapter 4. It is only right that those costs should fall primarily on the broader shoulders of those who have gained prosperity by way of what we now see to be processes involving environmental abuse. Poorer nations cannot be expected to, and will not, trade off economic growth in favour of environmental protection. That trade-off only becomes politically realistic, or economically and socially acceptable, at levels of affluence above those attained by IDCs. Effective environmental policy, therefore, requires as a prerequisite, policies of redistribution and cost sharing. Otherwise what needs to be done will simply not get done.

Second, environmental policy needs a global lead body to parallel the ILO, the WTO or the WHO. As Esty puts it, the current management of international environmental affairs 'is marked by policy gaps, confusion, duplication and incoherence' (Esty, 1994, p. 290). There is no one organisation with the authority or the organizational capacity to serve as the coordinator of international efforts and to drive forward global environmental policy. There is no shortage of bodies doing their bit – UNEP, the UN Commission on Sustainable Development, the Global Environmental Facility – but their briefs are narrow, their resources are limited and they lack the standing and voice which a World Environmental Organization (WEO) would bring to the cause and which is so clearly needed.

Third, there are major problems of enforcement. The corpus of international environmental law is impressive but, just as with labour law, many countries have not ratified crucial conventions and distance themselves from major initiatives. Such problems are inevitable in a world where nation states are the primary implementation units, but failure to ratify and enforce international agreements has to be contested. The lack of a WEO-type organization means that there is no body in a position to do the moving and the shaking. A WEO does not mean that enforcement problems will melt away – the history of the ILO is painful evidence of that – but it is a right and necessary beginning.

Human Rights

Globalization has helped to generate and spread a broad sense of core human rights. Global social policy must build on that sense and develop policies to give expression to it. The issues are general, but are most usefully considered in relation to particular groups, for example, migrants, women, ethnic minorities, people with disabilities and children.

There is widespread agreement on the need to develop more comprehensive, institutionalized global cooperation in relation to international migration and to codify the rights of migrants and the issues are explored in some detail in Chapter 6. Today, more than 100 million people are working outside their countries of birth. Migration on this scale clearly needs regulation at the global level.

At the moment a range of bodies has a finger in the pie – the UNHCR, the International Organization for Migration, the ILO, the WTO, the UN Population Fund. The development of policies to govern international migration is complex and tricky because of the way such development touches the raw nerve of sovereignty and because of the sharp economic, social and political issues raised by immigration. But the need for a global policy is urgent and calls for a policy response at three levels. First, there is a need for policies to control and manage migration between countries. Second, there is a need for global policies laying down the rights of migrants of all types from refugees to economic migrants. Third, there is the need for international bodies to check that global policies are observed.

In the 1980s and the 1990s, a range of gender issues have been globalized – violence towards women and children, access to methods of fertility control, inequality of opportunity in education, health and employment. The issues have been globalized and politicized through research, national and international campaigns and mega events like the International Women's Conference in Beijing in 1995. A sense of the inequity of unequal opportunities has grown, fostered by a number of reports from the United Nations Development Programme – for example, the 1999 report which showed that women had equal opportunities in none of the 130 countries surveyed (UNDP, 1999, p. 251), Policies are needed to promote equality of opportunity in employment, to secure equal pay, to guarantee reproductive rights. What globalization has done is to promote a global sense of women's rights, to quicken a sense of the unacceptable nature of continuing inequalities, and to feed and foster claims for equality.

The Commission on Global Governance proposed the appointment of a Senior Adviser for Women's Issues to work in the office of the Secretary-General of the United Nations and to be the principal advocate of women's interests within the UN system. Similar posts were proposed for the executive bodies of specialized agencies and institutions (Oxford University Press, 1998,

p. 285). Such posts can be useful catalysts but they need to be institutionalized and empowered by global social policies which provide a legal framework for assertive and affirmative action.

In 1989, the UN General Assembly adopted the Convention on the Rights of the Child and it was quickly ratified in more than 190 countries. It had three obvious limitations, however. It was supported with only limited resources, enforcement has been weak, it was not able effectively to press the issue of the rights of children in other areas of global policy-making.

The rights which children should have will readily attract high levels of agreement – access to appropriate health care, access to education, freedom from poverty, protection from damaging childhood employment, protection from physical and sexual abuse. Once the principles are accepted, two manifest problems nevertheless remain – adapting these rights sensitively to different societies and enforcing them. The focus has to be on basic rights which are achievable by way of practicable levels of resource redistribution on an international scale – for example, so many years of education, access to basic vaccinations, immunizations and clean water. The essential task for global social policy is the establishment of basic rights on the assumption that rights once established have a powerful and benevolent tendency to grow.

There has to be careful thought not only about the development of rights based policies but also about the implementation and enforcement of rights when proclaimed in policy. Change has to be achieved by a sensitive combination of inspection, negotiation and pressure by global bodies on governments, MNCs, etc.

How Can Global Social Policy be Developed?

'How?' questions have historically been a neglected aspect of social policy. The sunny uplands of grand theory or bold policy proposals have always had higher status than grubby ground level work on organisations and policy implementation. The importance of these questions in relation to national policy initiatives has, however, been increasingly accepted in recent years – how aspirations are to be turned into policies, how policies are to be implemented, how success or failure are best evaluated. In relation to global social policy, the issues are even more important – and difficult, As Scholte puts it 'the struggle to reform globalization is in good part a struggle to supply the means to effect change' (Scholte, 2000, p. 310).

There are several crucial 'how' issues that are central to making progress in the development of global social policy. The difficulty of separating what and how questions was clear in the previous section but there are advantages in dealing with them separately for analysis even if in the real world they are inextricable connected.

First, it is vital to work to overcome the problem indictaed by Bloom *et al.*, in the statement that 'we live in a global economy but with little global vision' (Bloom *et al.*, 2000, p. 29). Vision and imagination are absolutely central to the creation of a global social policy – a vision of possibilities and of a new future.

Second, a sense of the profound impact and implications of globalization for the framework and scope of social policy has to be promoted. Globalization does limit the capacity of the nation-state to achieve central social policy goals. States on their own can no longer easily achieve some of the traditional responsibilities of the nation state such as full employment, the reduction of insecurity, the protection of the environment, the establishment and maintenance of core labour standards. States have to accept their own limitations in a globalizing world and set these alongside the new opportunities which globalization brings with it. They have to accept new relationships with supranational bodies as the price for achieving national economic and social goals.

The effect on social policy derives essentially from the impact globalization has on national sovereignty as both concept and as reality. Sovereignty has become more complex. We must cease to think of the state as the sole legitimate source of public policy because it is not and in our world it cannot be. We have to see sovereignty as multi-layered and multifaceted and face the complexity which that brings (Cerny, 1999b). Sovereignty becomes shared, cooperative, complementary and bounded. In a sense, these qualifications conflict with the very notion of sovereignty as traditionally understood, but this is the nature of the impact of globalization, to modify our abstract and our working notions of sovereignty. Unless that is accepted, with all its implications, there can be no progress in relation to key domestic social issues or in relation to issues which transcend the now bounded capacities of the nation state. The new situation, and the new relationships it brings with it, are not simply negative – a loss of power, authority and autonomy. They are also positive in the possibilities they offer for enhanced capacity to deal with problems which transcend national boundaries.

Kaul *et al.*, capture what is perhaps the essence of the change which globalization brings – the need to transform international cooperation from its traditional place as 'external affairs' into an activity relevant to most, if not all, domestic issue areas. This will require the development of new concepts and instruments to overcome the problems of collective action (Kaul *et al.*, 1999, p. xxv).

Third, state support for global social policy has to be secured and an effective partnership has to be forged between supranational and regional bodies and national states. Interdependence has to be accepted and managed. Without the support of the nation-state there is little hope for global social policy. At the end of the day, international organizations are, in fact, intergovernmental in the sense that ultimately they can do little more than express the shared aspirations of their member states. In most policy areas, too, the nation-state

will retain the vital task of policy implementation. Unless the state is supportive of global initiatives, global social policies will simply not be implemented.
This means that nation-states have to accept the legitimacy and appropriate-
ness of social policy initiatives at the global level and of working with supranational and regional bodies. These relationships will vary between policy areas.
In relation to health and education policy, for example, relationships will be
cooperative and complementary. In relation to areas where global social
policy is essentially regulatory, for example environmental policy and the
establishment of core labour standards, global bodies will have to have a more
coercive enforcement type role.

Achieving a productive relationship between supranational bodies and
the nation-state will be crucial to the success of global social policy. It will
not be easy because domestic policy-making and international cooperation
are still seen as separate spheres of action (Kaul *et al.*, 1999, pp. 466–7). But
the only solution to many of the most pressing global problems is, as Hardin
put it, 'mutual coercion, mutually agreed upon' (quoted in Wagner, 1996,
pp. 28–9). That is far from easy to achieve or accept. Such a relationship,
however, has to be forged, and domestic and international policy-making
have to be systematically integrated. Kaul *et al.*, suggest that one way to
establish clear national responsibility for global public goods might be for
sectoral ministries to maintain two budgets, one for domestic expenditure
and one for meeting the financial implications of international cooperation
(Kaul *et al.*, 1999, p. 497).

Fourth, existing supranational organizations will have to be reformed.
If they are to be the agents and instruments of an effective global social policy, they will have to change in line with the changes which accompany
globalization.

There need to be organizations with clear responsibilities for key policy
areas. The growth of supranational bodies has been evolutionary and ad hoc
and therefore incoherent. For example, there is no one body with clearly
defined overall responsibility in relation to education or environmental policy
or to migration. There is no organization responsible for the governance of
MNCs or for the supervision of FDI. The creation of bodies and regulations to
fill these gaps is vital to the future development of global social policy but the
point can be broadened to embrace other policy areas where there is this same
lack of a single body to provide necessary leadership and coordination.

There needs to be a rationalization of responsibilities. Too many bodies, for
example, are involved with environmental policy for there to be any hope of a
coherent policy. There may well be a case for functional bodies dealing with
particular aspects of environmental issues but coordination of the total environmental enterprise is crucial.

Supranational bodies have to sell themselves as engaged in a collective
enterprise rather than as building and managing unrelated private empires.

'To date', says Scholte, 'relations between many trans-world bodies have known more turf battles than co-operation' (Scholte, 2000, p. 310). Inevitably, different organizations will have different stances on issues – the ILO is concerned with core labour rights, the WTO is preoccupied with promoting trade liberalization. There is no legal provision to encourage cooperation. Tension is inevitable and it has to be managed collectively and creatively.

Responsibilities need to be clarified. The IMF was set up to take an overview of the international monetary system and to try to ensure that the economic policies of major countries were not damaging to the rest of the world economy. In recent years, its role has broadened to impinge significantly on social policy. The World Bank suffers from similar uncertainties as to its role. Over the years it has become much more deeply involved in development issues but without a formal redefinition of its role and responsibilities. Deacon suggests the Bank's role be extended to encompass environmental issues, poverty alleviation and responsibility for refugees and disaster relief (Deacon, 1999, pp. 241–2). This seems to threaten all the problems which always afflict super ministries but the proposal illustrates just how far the Bank has strayed into global social policy territory.

The key issue for most supranational organizations is their relationship to national states as the primary social policy units. The ILO epitomizes the traditional role of change through persuasion, education and argument from comparative example. Environmental policy has proceeded along similar lines. No state, of course, wants to surrender sovereign rights to supranational bodies, but all states want other states to observe international conventions from which all stand to gain even if only some states observe them. The dilemma is inherent in supranational action – when and to what extent will nation-states accept the potentially coercive power of majority voting on, say, environmental protection policy? All states would prefer not to, because they may become victims of policies of which they disapprove, but non-compliance and progress at the rate of the slowest is, as becomes ever more apparent, a recipe for eventual – or even early – disaster.

The development of global social policy depends on a more proactive type of approach by supranational bodies to policy development in key fields, in monitoring and enforcing agreed policies and in linking issues. This depends in turn on the development of an overarching global social policy and of a single body to give appropriate overall direction in each field. Supranational bodies need both to be able to locate their particular policy area in a broader context and to be very clear about the nature and extent of their particular role and responsibilities.

The *World Development Report 1997: the State in a Changing World* (World Bank, 1997) makes an interesting proposal for organizational reform to facilitate more vigorous international collective action. It suggests a linked structure of groups – functional groups to deal with specific issues such as macroeconomic policies, environmental protection, labour standards, regional groups such as NAFTA, the EU and APEC to deal with across the board issues relevant to neighbouring countries, and coordinating groups to link the regional and functional bodies, for example the OECD (World Bank, 1997, p. 132). What the proposal conspicuously fails to do, however, is to create a body to take a broad overview – an Economic/Social Development Council – something which is surely vital to the development of a necessarily more proactive role for supranational bodies.

Fifth, work has to be done to remedy the current legitimacy deficits of supranational organizations. Supranational organizations lack the legitimacy which they need if they are to be effective. O'Brien *et al.*, for example, write of 'the legitimacy deficits of the IMF and the WTO', two of the most powerful supranational bodies (O'Brien *et al.*, 2000, p. 232). These supranational bodies face various legitimacy problems. First, they are seen as threatening national sovereignty. Second, they are not subject to democratic control. 'Only in the most attenuated way', says Keohane, 'is democratic control exercised over major international organisations' (Keohane, 1998, p. 92). Third, there is little independent monitoring of their work. Fourth, they operate in ways which are far from transparent.

The situation is problematic on two counts. First, these supranational organizations are bodies of immense power and influence. They make decisions which have a major impact on the lives of millions of people and on the way the world develops. They *should* be more democratically accountable in a world moving towards more democratic ways. Second, their legitimacy deficits damage their effectiveness. They need legitimacy to command support and approval and that means clearer accountability, perhaps to the UN General Assembly or to some sort of representative council elected from the Assembly. Wilkinson and Hughes take the view, in relation to the WTO, the IMF and the World Bank, that they 'increasingly realise it takes public support to sustain the liberalisation policies they prescribe' (Wilkinson and Hughes, 2000, p. 273). That is clearly true and these bodies will not be able successfully to assume the larger role which we are proposing for them unless they are able to overcome this damaging legitimacy/democratic deficit.

The closer relationship which global organizations such as the IMF, the World Bank and the WTO have begun to develop with NGOs in recent years has brought them into contact with well informed and critical groups which have questioned and challenged both their ideologies and their policies. Supranational organizations have had to become more transparent, more prepared to justify and defend their policies as they have become more exposed to criticism and lobbying. This is a beginning but no more. NGOs are useful sources of ideas and criticism but they themselves are not always models of democratic representative governance.

As long as these global giants moved only in the shadows, their legitimacy deficits were hardly noticed and did not really matter. Now that they have come out of the closet and are taking a much more prominent role in economic and social development such deficits take on increased significance. A vigorous and more wide ranging global social policy cannot be developed and sustained by unaccountable and undemocratic bodies and at the same time secure the public support which is a prerequisite of success.

There is no obvious way in which these supranational bodies can be made subject to traditional forms of democratic control by elected representatives of the people. It is necessary, therefore, to look at other varied and non-traditional approaches which will improve transparency and accountability and so increase legitimacy. There are several possibilities. Kapstein, for example, urged the development of mechanisms to secure labour representation at the IMF and the World Bank as one way of giving workers a voice in international institutions (Kapstein, 1999, p. 104). *Our Global Neighbourhood* proposed an Assembly of Parliamentarians made up of representatives of existing legislators as a way in which the democratic input to supranational institutions could fairly easily be increased pending the establishment of a world assembly through direct elections. The same study also proposed an annual Forum of Civil Society to draw on the expertise of the growing body of non-governmental organizations and global social movements (Oxford University Press, 1998, pp. 257–8).

Scholte suggests various ways in which globalization could be democratized – direct consultation exercises on global policy issues, making globalization issues a matter of debate and discussion at general elections, national referenda on specific issues, assemblies of stakeholders, directly elected assemblies, ad hoc consultations with grass roots organizations, more debate on key issues of global policy in national legislatures (Scholte, 2000, pp. 303–4).

There is no dispute that the democratic record of existing supranational bodies has been poor. There are a range of ways in which that democratic deficit could be reduced even if direct democratic control may not be a realistic option in the short term.

Sixth, the creation of new supranational bodies is necessary. In addition to reforming existing institutions and increasing their political and administrative capacity there is a strong priority case for creating at least three new organizations.

Priority needs to be given to the establishment of a Council for Social Development to lead and oversee the development of the key areas of global social policy. At the moment, there is no effective overarching body. The World Bank has moved towards this role but it is not part of its formal brief, it must be doubtful whether it has the required skills and experience and such an add-on responsibility could easily lose priority in a change of personnel at the top. At present, there is no effective way in which social and environmental issues can be looked at in the round, let alone related to economic development. This is a serious weakness.

The Commission on Global Governance proposed an Economic Security Council to keep the overall state of the world economy continuously under review, to provide a framework for sustainable development, to secure consistency between the goals and policies of the major international organizations and to work to build consensus between national governments about the development of the international economic system (Oxford University Press, 1998, p. 156). Our proposed Council for Social Development would have parallel and complementary responsibilities – to monitor and review social development, to provide a framework for the development of global social policy, to secure coherence between the policies of different supranational bodies, to promote dialogue and consensus between national governments on the direction of future social development. A strategy for the development of global social policy, on the lines we propose, requires a body which can take an overall view, provide incisive leadership and coordinate policy development.

The second new organization which is needed is a World Environmental Organization to sit alongside the WHO and the WTO. Several individuals and committees have endorsed such an idea, for example, the Commission on Global Governance (Oxford University Press, 1998, p. 216), the *Human Development Report 1999* (UNDP, 1999, p. 113), Scholte (Scholte, 2000, p. 293). The proposals obviously vary in detail but all point up the fragmented nature of the current situation and argue that such fragmentation prevents the development and implementation of an effective raft of coherent global environmental policies.

The idea does not, however, have universal approval. Hurrell and Kingsbury argue strongly against such a proposal on the basis of the continuing strength and capacity of the nation-state, the huge opportunity costs involved in the creation of a new body of this kind, and the belief that if there was a real commitment to move beyond the existing state dominated system then that itself would ensure a level of inter-state cooperation which would make the creation of a new overarching body unnecessary. (Hurrell and Kingsbury, 1992, pp. 7–8). These points have force, but Hurrell and Kingsbury do not, perhaps, give adequate weight to the point that a WEO is not going to replace or displace the nation state but rather supplement and complement it. If action on a global level and scale is necessary for adequate environmental protection then there must be a single body of some kind to lead and manage. Coherence will not be achieved by a division of responsibility which owes everything to history and nothing to reason.

Third, a new supranational body is required to coordinate policy and planning in relation to migration – an International Migration Organization. Such a body, Hirst and Thompson argue, is needed to develop common standards and procedures for migrants, to deal with illegal immigration, family and refugee movements and to create appropriate disputes procedures (Hirst and Thompson, 1999, p. 216). Migration issues, of course, raise major political difficulties. Movement from national to supranational policy will be slow, but uncoordinated national responses to migration – legal and illegal – on its current scale are doomed to be unsatisfactory and are likely to neglect important human rights issues as is pointed out in Chapter 6.

Seventh, it is essential to secure an independent source of revenue for supranational social policy bodies. Supranational bodies need a carefully crafted measure of independence of national states or else they can simply become their poodles or be starved to death. Crucial to this is a measure of financial independence which, in turn, rests on securing a source of revenue other than annual grants from national governments.

Various possibilities have been mooted. The Commission on Global Governance, for example, suggests six possible sources of revenue ranging from a surcharge on international air tickets to fees for various uses of the ocean and parking fees for space satellites (Oxford University Press, 1998, pp. 220–1). The Commission's main concern here was with raising revenue from environmentally threatening activities but the ideas could be extended. There are also potentially bigger yielding measures such as a carbon tax or the sale of permits for carbon emissions.

Probably the oldest, and certainly the most discussed, proposal is the so called Tobin tax, a proposal made by the economist James Tobin in the 1970s for a tax on foreign exchange transactions for macroeconomic purposes rather than to raise revenue. Obviously, its introduction would produce massive opposition from the powerful world of international finance but such a tax could have two popular and beneficent purposes. It would help to reduce the volume of speculative financial transactions, something which is widely seen as desirable, and it would raise revenue. Clearly the revenue raised would depend on the level at which the tax was levied but the sums collected could be considerable. The revenue raised – up to US$250 billion per year from a 0.5 per cent tax (a high rate) (Arestis and Sawyer, 1999, p. 158) – could fund a major increase in supranational global social policy activities. And there is a pleasing logic about funding global public goods through levies on global activities such as foreign exchange dealings (Kaul and Langmore, 1999, p. 256).

If global social policy is to develop it has to be funded. It could be funded by taxes levied on individual countries according to GDP per capita or some comparable formula. But countries can always withhold their contributions as many have done in the past. What would be preferable would be a source of revenue which, once the formula has been agreed as in the Tobin tax, would be automatic and independent of changes of national political mood.

Conclusion

Globalization remains a vigorously contested concept and, as suggested in Chapter 1, there is a range of possible interpretations of its origins, nature, effects and likely future. The position, both of those who argue that a border-less world is now the reality, and of those who insist that the world is not in essence very different from how it was in the 1960s and the 1970s, is not sup-ported by the economic, political and social evidence. We argue that highly significant changes have taken place – in the increased mobility of finance capital, in increased FDI, in the growth in number and size of MNCs and in the increase in world trade, as well as in the speed and ease of communication and in popular frames of reference and perceptions. The world has become smaller. Certain aspects of western culture have become global. These changes have affected the reach, grasp and standing of the nation-state and so have affected states' capacity to promote human welfare. The changes have had both positive and negative implications.

On the negative side, in AICs globalization has constrained the nation-state's welfare role even if in varied ways and to varying degrees. State spending is constrained by beliefs and experience of what markets will regard as acceptable and unacceptable levels of expenditure. The neoliberal ideology of contempor-ary globalization encourages a negative approach to public expenditure and public service provision. In addition, welfare spending is limited by the heavier emphasis on competitiveness. The rise of the competition state has constrained and eroded the welfare state.

Globalization also both exacerbates, and makes more visible, a range of social problems – environmental degradation, drug trafficking, legal and illegal immigration. AIDS, unemployment, social dislocation. And it exposes the limitations of the nation-state as a solver of social problems.

More positively, globalization has clearly contributed to an improved qual-ity of life for many people. It has contributed to world economic growth by increasing the volume of world trade, by stimulating demand and by opening up new markets. It has increased consumer choice as products from all over the world become readily available in AICs. It has contributed to less expens-ive travel and so to greater geographical mobility. It has been a factor in the spread of democracy and has helped to spread an increased sensitivity to a wide range of human rights issues. Globalization has also encouraged the development of new, liberating and life enhancing frames of reference. At the political and policy making level it has fostered the development of global policy networks and the global sharing of ideas about national developments in public policy.

Globalization has had some similar impacts on IDCs. Countries have been constrained to pursue particular economic and social policies to secure FDI and to attract MNCs. They have also been encouraged to borrow money to secure quick-start development. In many cases, they have ended up with crush-ing debts, the interest on which often exceeds their expenditure on health and education. Their debts put them in a dangerous and debilitating position of dependence on the IMF and its Structural Adjustment Programmes or their seemingly more benevolent successors – Poverty Reduction Strategy Papers. The increase in world trade has benefited some IDCs but essentially they still lack the tariff free access to AIC markets for agricultural and manufactured products which could be a major stimulus to economic and employment growth.

In many IDCs, incomes have grown in the years since 1975 but in the poorest countries they have fallen. The aggregate income gap between AICs and IDCs has scarcely changed. Though the proportion of people in IDCs who are in poverty has declined slightly in recent years, the actual numbers in poverty have increased. In health, the picture is mixed, with some improvements due, for example, to the spread of vaccination and immunization but with a disastrous decline in some IDCs because of the spread of AIDS and the inability of IDCs to afford the life extending drugs now available to AIDS patients in AICs. In education, there have been advances and expansion in provision but there is still a huge shortfall in basic provision as is made clear in chapters 4 and 5. The most significant failure of globalization in IDCs is the failure to achieve substantial reductions in poverty. The fruits of globalization have not been spread equitably or used to benefit the worst off.

Our analysis of the mixed impact of globalization on human welfare in AICs and IDCs poses the central question of how human welfare can best be safeguarded and advanced in a more global world. For a generation in AICs, the nation-state was seen as the key and most promising instrument for the promotion of human well-being. In IDCs, the issue was one of national self help, with some crumbs of aid from the AICs and a hopefully beneficent fallout from the operation of MNCs.

What has become plain is that the strategies of the past are, at best, of limited value in a global world. In AICs, what the nation-state does can still make a major difference to the quality of life of its citizens through the services it provides (or does not provide), through its responsiveness (or not) to a changing global economy. In IDCs, we clearly need radically different strategies if those countries are ever to break out of the cycle of poverty, bad health, illiteracy, environmental degradation, inadequate infrastructure, etc. The only answer is to think again about the nature, role, potential, focus and sphere of social policy in a more global world.

Our argument is that economic globalization requires a matching global social policy. The basis of the argument is national experience. Capitalism is the most successful economic system known to humankind in terms of its ability to tap energy and generate wealth. But capitalism does provide its own grave-diggers unless it is accompanied, complemented and civilized by appropriate public policies. The national experience is transparently clear. National capitalism was saved from self-destruction by just such civilizing policies in most AICs after the Second World War. What is required now is a similar civilizing project at the global level – to secure the survival of global capitalism which is ultimately the best hope for combating poverty in IDCs and promoting human welfare. In this chapter we spell out a range of reasons for the development of global social policy but the basis of the case is very simple – markets, whether national or international, need state action to secure their just and efficient functioning. Capitalism must be complemented by civilizing and redistributive public policies if it is to survive and prosper.

If this broad argument is accepted – that a globalizing economy needs global social policies – then there are clear implications. First, there is a need for clear, hard and creative thinking about the nature of such a radically new approach to global governance. Second, there is a need to develop flexible new policies at a global level – complementing, supplementing and supporting national policies. Third, there is a need for new institutions to develop the policies, to promote their acceptance in global forums, to secure their implementation with the necessary sensitivity and flexibility, and to monitor their working and outcomes. The policies and institutions already exist, although sometimes in no more than in embryonic form, sometimes in a state of promising infancy and sometimes in a state of troubled adolescence.

The difficulties of such a project are all too clear. It requires the transcending of the pessimism about human creativity and the potential of government which it has been a central aim of neoliberalism to foster. It depends on big and bold thinking. Historically, social policy has always been essentially national in its frame of reference and approach. In today's world there is need for a new and broader kind of thinking, a new kind of global and national welfare pluralism, a new pattern of strategic global partnerships has to be developed. It will need fundamental changes in already existing supranational institutions. They have to become much more transparent, more accountable, more democratic and more proactive. They have to work productively both with global economic institutions, because economic and social policy are part of a seamless web of action to promote human welfare, and with national governments. It also requires a humble acceptance by nation-states that in an increasing number of areas the potential of national social policy to secure its goals is limited unless it is supplemented and complemented by global social policies.

Such an initiative depends on accepting and countering the suspicions of IDCs that proposals for extending labour and environmental legislation are essentially directed at blunting their competitive advantage. It depends crucially too on the redistribution of global resources. Global social policy has to be financed and to achieve its aims it will have to be significantly redistributive. To safeguard the forward march of globalization, as well as to promote global justice, the funding will have to come from AICs – directly or indirectly – because clearly IDCs cannot pay. Redistribution from AICs to IDCs is the only practical and fair option.

Alongside the difficulties can be set forces which will help to take forward the global social policy project – the ebbing of the tide of neoliberalism, the increasing sense of many economic and social issues as global, the development of global reference points and global social policy networks, the increasing sense that resolving certain historic problems really is in the interests of the whole global community not just of the sufferers – for example the World Bank's attitude to poverty in IDCs in its most recent reports. It would be overly optimistic to say that the way is clear for 'ambitious reformism' or for 'progressive international-ism'. But there is a cranny of opportunity opening up. Neoliberalism has reached a stage when its inherently problematic nature is becoming more accepted. At the same time, there is a clearer range of options for a global social policy.

Developing global social policies is a daunting task but it is not a question of starting from scratch. There is half a century of experience of success and fail-ure in national social policy-making. There is a valuable infrastructure of inter-national bodies which have built up a rich resource of data and have had many years experience of embryonic supranational social policy. What is needed now is imaginative building on those promising foundations. Clearly it will not all be straightforward. It is, though, crucial to human welfare in the new cen-tury. Unmanaged globalization will not deliver its benefits justly or equitably. It will not, on its own, abolish poverty or hunger or disease but it does help create the resources which make possible the abolition of those historic ills.

In our view, globalization is both fact and opportunity. The opportunity exists today to promote human welfare on a global level and scale. That oppor-tunity cannot responsibly be allowed to pass. We can – if we so wish – make globalization work for human welfare. As Beveridge said, in a similar but very different context, 'A revolutionary moment in the world's history is a time for revolutions, not for patching' (HMSO, 1942, para. 7).

Further Reading

Deacon, B. (1999) 'Social Policy in a Global Context', in A. Hurrell and N. Woods (eds) *Inequality, Globalization and World Politics* (Oxford, Oxford University Press).
Scholte, J. A. (2000) *Globalization*, Part III (Basingstoke, Macmillan).
Yeates, N. (2001) *Globalization and Social Policy* (London, Sage).

Appendix 1

Globalization and the Events of 11 September 2001

1. The events of 11 September were truly global in the horror they evoked, in the media coverage given to them and in their economic and political implications. What light can our analysis of the nature and processes of globalization throw on these events?

2. On the 11 September 2001, two hijacked planes were flown into the twin towers of the World Trade Centre in New York. The two towers collapsed with a massive loss of life of people of many different nationalities working for the global firms housed in the Centre. A third plane did serious damage to the Pentagon and caused further significant casualties. The moments when the planes hit and destroyed the World Trade Centre were relayed round the world by television and seen again and again by horrified audiences of many millions. The perpetrators were thought to be members of the global Al-Qaida terrorist network funded and directed by Osama bin Laden from Afghanistan.

3. The attack on the USA was fuelled by many forces. On the cultural level, it was fuelled by strong feelings of hatred towards the globalization of American culture and the way it was thought to be undermining traditional Islamic culture – evidence of how deep the cultural chasm still is between tradition and modernity, between Islamic fundamentalism and western/American culture. Any claim that globalization has led to the globalization and westernization of world culture and the creation of a new global cultural synthesis is patently unsustainable.

4. These events showed the importance of globalized modern technology in the planning and execution of the attack. Communication between members of the terrorist group was clearly vital and the globalization of information technology played an important part in this. The actual instruments used – jumbo jets – are symbolic of the globalization of trade and travel and the destruction of time and space – which are central aspects of globalization.

5. The attack shows the increasingly exposed nature of individual countries and their citizens in a more globalized world. There is no longer any such simple, straightforward thing as national security even for the most powerful nation on earth. The only security has to be global.

6. The easy and covert way in which large sums of money can be moved across the world's banking systems was essential to the sustaining of the necessary networks and to the planning and financing of the attack. This would have

been a far more difficult task in the past before the globalization of financial markets. What was done provides a small example of the way in which financial systems are now truly global.

7. The response of the USA was to set out to build a global coalition to destroy what was defined as global terrorism. The USA clearly felt a political, as well as a strategic, need for a network of global support. The ability of the USA to enlist the initial support of the governments of most Islamic countries shows the dominance of one country in today's increasingly globalized world, its ability to build on global revulsion, to coordinate an ethical-political coalition against terrorism and, in addition, to offer the promise of tangible rewards for support in terms of aid, arms, trade concessions or a blind eye turned to particular issues. A global super power had much to offer in return for the global support it needed to legitimate its actions.

8. The events of 11 September illustrate very vividly the global nature of the contemporary economy – and the global nature of its fragility. The events seemed to threaten the global economic future. Stock markets all over the world went into free fall or, at best, had very bad attacks of the jitters. Some sectors of the economy – air travel and tourism, for example – suffered massive losses in the weeks which followed with prestige airlines poised on the verge of collapse because of the drop in North Atlantic air travel.

9. The importance of global television coverage was clear in the way the events were seen by so many millions and the way they affected ordinary people. It was used, too, as an instrument in the creation of the global coalition and as a medium for influencing public opinion. It also functioned as a mechanism of restraint in that civilian casualties of the bombing of Afghanistan could be seen world wide and casualties deemed excessive would clearly quickly undermine the fragile support for a global coalition. The potential of television to mobilize opinion was also recognized by bin Laden in his use of televised video messages to Islamic countries. Wars have to be fought with global public opinion in mind in today's global world.

10. The decision by a few young British Moslems to travel to Afghanistan and fight with the Taliban against British troops shows both the powerful global influence of Islamic fundamentalism and the depth of alienation which some young Moslems experience in the country in which they were brought up or born. Globalization has not led to their assimilation or acculturation to British culture. It is not even multiculturalism which emerges from this coexistence but rather the continuance of two very separate and very different cultures existing side by side with each other, often in harmony but often also in latent or open conflict.

11. Television images from Afghanistan illustrate all too clearly the vivid and growing disparities in living standards and opportunities in what is supposed to be one world. Globalization, as we have pointed out throughout this book, has had widely disparate effects on the lives of people in different countries.

References

Afshar, H. and Agarwal, B. (eds) (1989) *Women, Poverty and Ideology in Asia* (Basingstoke, Macmillan).

Agarwal, B. (1994) *A Field of One's Own – Gender and Land Rights in South Asia* (Cambridge, Cambridge University Press).

Alba, R.D. (1990) *Ethnic Identity: The Transformation of White America* (New Haven CT, Yale University Press).

Alba, R.D. and Nee, V. (1997) 'Rethinking Assimilation: Theory for a New Era of Immigration', *International Migration Review*, 31 (4), 826–74.

Alber, J. and Standing, G. (2000) 'Social dumping, catch up or convergence? Europe in a comparative global context', *Journal of European Social Policy*, 10 (2), 99–119.

Albrow, M. (1996) *The Global Age* (Cambridge, Polity Press).

Anderson, B. and Brenton, P. (1998) 'Did Outsourcing to Low Wage Countries Hurt Less Skilled workers in the UK?', in P. Brenton and J. Pelkmans (eds) *Global Trade and European Workers* (Basingstoke, Macmillan).

Anthias, F. and Yuval-Davis, N. (1993) *Racialized Boundaries* (Basingstoke, Macmillan).

Arestis, P. and Sawyer, M. (1999) 'What role for the Tobin Tax in World Economic Governance?', in J. Michie and J. Grieve Smith (eds) *Global Instability* (London, Routledge).

Arrighi, G. (1998) 'Globalization and the Rise of East Asia', *International Sociology*, 13 (1), 59–77.

Ashworth, J. (1999) 'Reebok reveals hazards faced by Asian workers', *The Times*, 18 October, p. 17.

Axford, B. (1995) *The Global System: Economics, Politics and Culture* (Cambridge, Polity Press).

Baker, D., Epstein, G. and Pollin, R. (eds) *Globalization and Progressive Economic Policy* (Cambridge, Cambridge University Press).

Baker, D., Epstein, G. and Pollin, R. (1998) 'Introduction', in D. Baker, G. Epstein and R. Pollin, ibid.

Ball, S.J. (1998) 'Big Policies/Small World: an introduction to international perspectives in education policy', *Comparative Education*, 34 (2), 119–30.

Barber, B.R. (2000) 'Can Democracy Survive Globalization?', *Government and Opposition*, 35 (3), 275–301.

Barnet, R.J. and Cavanagh, J. (1994) *Global Dreams* (New York, Simon & Schuster).

Bauer, P.T. (1971) *Dissent on Development* (London, Weidenfeld & Nicolson).

Bayne, N. (2000) 'Why did Seattle Fail? Globalization and the Politics of Trade', *Government and Opposition*, 35 (2), 131–52.

Beck, U. (1992) *Risk Society* (London, Sage).

Beck, U. (1997) *The Reinvention of Politics* (Cambridge, Polity Press).

Bellamy, C. (1999) *The State of the World's Children, 1998* (New York, UNICEF).

Beneria, L. (1999) 'The enduring debate over unpaid labour', *International Labour Review*, 138 (3), 287–309.

Berlinguer, B. (1999) 'Globalization and Global Health', *International Journal of Health Services*, 29 (3), 579–95.

Beyer, P.F. (1990) 'Privatization and the Public Influence of Religion in Global Society', in M. Featherstone (ed.) *Global Culture: Nationalism, Globalization and Modernity* (London, Sage).

Biggs, S. (1998) 'The Biodiversity Convention and global sustainable development', in R. Kiely and P. Marfleet (eds) *Globalization and the Third World* (London, Routledge).

Blackhurst, R. (1997) 'The WTO and the World Economy', *World Economy*, 20 (5), 527–44.

Bloom, D.E. and River Path Asdociates (2000) 'Social Capitalism and Human Diversity', in OECD, *The Creative Society of the 21st Century* (Paris, OECD).

Bonoli, G. and Pahier, B. (1998) 'Changing the Politics of Social Programmes: Innovative Change in British and French Welfare Reforms', *Journal of European Social Policy*, 8 (4), 317–30.

Bonoli, G., George, V. and Taylor-Gooby, P. (2000) *European Welfare Futures: Towards a Theory of Retrenchment* (Cambridge, Polity Press).

Bouget, D. (1998) 'The Juppe Plan and the Future of the French Social Welfare System', *Journal of European Social Policy*, **8** (2), 155–172.

Boyer, R. and Drache, D. (1996) 'Introduction', in R. Boyer and D. Drache (eds) *States Against Markets* (London, Routledge).

Brettell, C.B. (2000) 'Theorizing Migration in Anthropology', in C.B. Brettell and J.F. Hollifield (eds) (2000) *Migration Theory* (London, Routledge).

Broad, D. (1995) 'Globalization Versus Labor', *Monthly Review*, **47** (7), 20–31.

Bulmer, M. and Solomos, J. (1998) 'Introduction: Rethinking Ethnic and Racial Studies', *Ethnic and Racial Studies*, **21** (5), 819–838.

Bureau of Industry and Economics (1993) '*Multinationals and Governments: Issues and Implications for Australia*', Research Report 49 (Canberra, Australian Government Publishing Service).

Buttel, F.H. (2000) 'Ending Hunger in Developing Countries', *Contemporary Sociology*, **29** (1), 13–27.

Campbell, D. (2000) 'High Fliers get First-class Welcome but Unskilled Stay Grounded', *The Guardian*, 30 October.

Carnoy, M. (1999) 'The family, flexible work and social cohesion at risk', *International Labour Review*, **138** (4), 411–29.

Carter, M.R. and May, J. (1999) 'Poverty, Livelihood and Class in Rural South Africa', *World Development*, **27** (1), 1–20.

Casper, L. and McLanahan, S. (1994) 'The Gender Poverty Gap: What we can Learn from Other Countries', *American Sociological Review*, **59** (4), 594–605.

Cassen, R. and associates (1986) *Does Aid Work?* (Oxford, Oxford University Press).

Castles, S. and Davidson, A. (2000) *Citizenship and Migration* (Basingstoke, Macmillan).

Castles, S. and Miller, M.J. (2000) *The Age of Migration*, 2nd edn (Basingstoke, Macmillan).

Cerny, P. (1996) 'What next for the State?', in E. Kofman and G. Youngs (eds) *Globalization: Theory and Practice* (London, Pinter).

Cerny, P. (1997) 'Paradoxes of the Competition State: The Dynamics of Political Globalization', *Government and Opposition*, **32** (2), 251–74.

Cerny, P. (1999a) 'Globalising the Political and Politicising the Global: Concluding Reflections on International Political Economy as a Vocation', *New Political Economy*, **4** (1), 147–62.

Cerny, P. (1999b) 'Globalization, Governance and Complexity', in A. Prakash and J.A. Hart (eds) *Globalization and Governance* (London, Routledge).

Cerny, P.G. (2000) 'Restructuring the Political Arena: Globalization and the Paradoxes of the Competition State', in R.D. Germain (ed.) *Globalization and its Critics* (Basingstoke, Macmillan).

Chang, H.J. (1998) 'Globalization, transnational corporations and economic development; can the developing countries pursue strategic industrial policy in a globalizing world?', in D. Baker, G. Epstein, and R. Pollin (eds) *Globalization and Progressive Economic Policy* (Cambridge, Cambridge University Press).

Chen, M., Sebstad, J. and O'Connell, L. (1999) 'Counting the Invisible Workforce: The Case of Homebased Workers', *World Development*, **27** (3), 603–10.

Chinkin, C. (1999) 'Gender Inequality and International Human Rights Law', in A. Hurrell and N. Woods (eds) *Inequality, Globalization and World Politics* (Oxford, Oxford University Press).

Chung, C. and Gillespie, B. (1998) 'Globalisation and the Environment: New Challenges for the Public and Private Sectors' in *Globalisation and the Environment* (Paris, OECD).

Cohen, B.J. (1996) 'Phoenix Risen: the Resurrection of Global Finance', *World Politics*, **48**, 268–96.

Cohen, R. and Kennedy, P. (2000) *Global Sociology* (Basingstoke, Macmillan).

Colclough, C. and Lwein, K. (1993) *Educating All the Children: Strategies for Primary schooling in the South* (Oxford, Clarendon Press).

Connelly, M.P. (1999) 'Gender matters: Global Restructuring and Adjustment', *Social Politics*, **3** (1), 12–32.

Cooper, R.N. (1995) 'Commenting', in P. Krugman 'Growing World Trade: Causes and Consequences', *Brookings Papers on Economic Activity*, pp. 327–77.

Cornell, S. and Hartmann, D. (1998) *Ethnicity and Race* (London, Pine Forge Press).

Cox, R.W. (1997a) 'A Perspective on Globalization', in J.H. Mittelman (ed.) (1996) *Globalization: Critical Reflections* (London, Lynne Rienner Publishers).

Cox, R.W. (1997b) *Production, Powers and World Order* (New York, Columbia University Press).

Crotty, J., Epstein, G. and Kelly, P. (1998) 'Multinational Corporations in the Neo Liberal regime', in D. Baker, G. Epstein, and R. Pollin (eds) *Globalization and Progressive Economic Policy* (Cambridge, Cambridge University Press).

Daly, M. (1997) 'Welfare States Under Pressure', *Journal of European Social Policy*, 7 (2), 129–46.

Daly, M. (2001) 'Globalization and the Bismarckian Welfare States', in R. Sykes, B. Palier and P.M. Prior (eds) *Globalization and European Welfare States* (Basingstoke, Macmillan).

Davies, S. and Guppy, N. (1997) 'Globalization and Educational Reforms in Anglo American Democracies', *Comparative Education Review*, 41 (4), 435–59.

de Benoist, A. (1996) 'Confronting Globalization', *Telos*, 108, 117–37.

Deacon, B. (1995) 'The Globalisation of Social Policy and the Socialisation of Global Politics', in J. Baldock and M. May (eds) *Social Policy Review 7* (Canterbury, Social Policy Association).

Deacon, B. (1999) 'Social Policy in a Global Context', in A. Hurrell and N. Woods (eds) *Inequality, Globalization and World Politics* (Oxford, Oxford University Press).

Deacon, B. (2001) 'International Organizations, the EU and Global Social Policy' in R. Sykes, B. Palier and P.M. Prior (eds) *Globalization and European Welfare States*, (Basingstoke, Palgrave).

Deacon, B. with Hulse, M. and Stubbs, P. (1997) *Global Social Policy*, (London, Sage).

Dicken, P. (1998) *Global Shift*, 3rd edn (London, Paul Chapman).

Doyal, L. (1996) 'The Politics of Women's Health: Setting a Global Agenda', *International Journal of Health Services*, 26 (1) 47–65.

Drache, D. (1996) 'From Keynes to K. Mart', in R. Boyer and D. Drache (eds) *States Against Markets* (London, Routledge).

Duffus, G. and Gooding, P. (1997) 'Globalization: scope, issues and statistics', *Economic Trends*, 528, 28–45.

Dunleavy, P. (1994) 'The Globalization of Public Services Production: Can Government be "Best in World"?', *Public Policy and Administration*, 9 (2), 36–64.

Elder, S. and Johnson, L.J. (1999) 'Sex-specific labour market indicators: What they Show', *International Labour Review*, 138 (4), 447–64.

Elliott, L. (1998) *The Global Politics of the Environment* (Basingstoke, Macmillan).

Elliott, L. (1999) 'The battle over trade', *The Guardian*, 26 November.

Elson, D. (1999) 'Labor Markets as Gendered Institutions', *World Development*, 27 (3), 611–27.

Esping-Andersen, G. (1999) *Social Foundations of Postindustrial Economies* (Oxford, Oxford University Press).

Esty, D. (1994) 'The Case for a Global Environmental Organisation', in P.B. Kenen (ed.) *Managing the World Economy: Fifty years after Bretton Woods* (Washington, Institute for International Economics).

European Commission (1997) *The State of Women's Health in the European Community* (Luxembourg, EC).

European Commission (1998) *Social Protection in Europe 1997* (Luxembourg EC).

European Commission (1999) *Employment in Europe* (Luxembourg, EC).

European Union (1994) *European Social Policy – A Way Forward for the Union, A White Paper* (Brussels, Commission of the European Communities).

Euzeby, C. (1998) 'Social Security for the Twenty-First Century', *International Social Security Review*, 51 (2), 3–16.

Faist, T. (1993) 'From School to Work: public policy and underclass formation among young Turks in Germany during the 1980s', *International Migration Review*, 27 (2), 306–31.

Fajth, G. and Foy, J.E. (1999) 'Women in Transition: A Summary', in *After the Fall: The Human Impact of Ten Years of Transition* (Florence, UNICEF).

Falk, R. (1999) *Predatory Globalization* (Cambridge, Polity Press).

Falk, R.A. (1994) 'Democratizing, Internationalizing and Globalizing' in Y. Sakamoto (ed.) *Global Transformation: Challenges to the State System*, (Tokyo, United Nations University Press).

Fieldhouse, D.K. (1999) *The West and the Third World* (Oxford, Blackwell).

FitzGerald, M. and Hale, C. (1996) *Ethnic Minorities: Victimisation and Racial Harassment* (London, Home Office).

Flemming, J. and Micklewright, J. (1999) *Income Distribution, Economic Systems and Transition* (Florence, UNICEF).

Flynn, N. and Strehl, F. (1996) *Public Sector Management in Europe* (London, Prentice-Hall).

Foo, G. and Lim, L. (1989) 'Poverty, Ideology, and Women Export Factory Workers in South-East Asia', in H. Afshar and B. Agarwal (eds) (1989) *Women, Poverty and Ideology in Asia* (Basingstoke, Macmillan).

Food and Agricultural Organization (FAO) (1996) *The State of Food and Agriculture, 1996* (Rome, FAO).

Food and Agricultural Organization (FAO) (1997) *The State of Food and Agriculture, 1997* (Rome, FAO).

Food and Agricultural Organization (FAO) (1998) *The State of Food and Agriculture, 1998* (Rome, FAO).

Fox Piven, F. (1995) 'Is it Global Economics or Neo Laissez Faire?', *New Left Review*, **213**, 107–15.

Freeman, R. (2000) *The Politics of Health in Europe* (Manchester, Manchester University Press).

Friedman, T.L. (1999) *The Lexus and the Olive Tree* (New York, Farrar, Straus & Giroux).

Fukuyama, F. (1992) *The End of History and the Last Man* (London, Hamish Hamilton).

Garner, R. (1996) *Environmental Politics* (London, Prentice-Hall/Harvester Wheatsheaf).

Garrett, G. (1998a) 'Global Markets and National Politics: Collision Course or Virtuous Circle?', *International Organisation*, **52** (4), 787–824.

Garrett, G. (1998b) *Partisan Politics in the Global Economy* (Cambridge, Cambridge University Press).

George, S. (1988) *A Fate Worse than Debt* (Harmondsworth, Penguin).

George, V. and Wilding, P. (1984) *The Impact of Social Policy* (London, Routledge).

George, V. and Wilding, P. (1999) *British Society and Social Welfare* (Basingstoke, Macmillan).

German, T. and Randel, J. (2000) 'Trends towards the new millennium', in J. Randel, T. German and D. Ewing (eds) *The Reality of Aid, 2000* (London, Earthscan).

Giddens, A. (1990) *The Consequences of Modernity* (Cambridge, Polity Press).

Giddens, A. (1998) *The Third Way* (Cambridge, Polity Press).

Gilroy, P. (1987) *There ain't no Black in the Union Jack* (Oxford, Blackwell).

Ginsburg, N. (1992) 'Racism and Housing in Britain', in P. Braham, A. Rattansi and R. Skellington (eds) *Race and Anti-Racism* (Buckingham, Open University Press).

Goodstein, E. (1998) 'Globalization and the Environment', in D. Baker, G. Epstein and R. Pollin (eds) *Globalization and Progressive Economic Policy* (Cambridge, Cambridge University Press).

Gordon, D.M. (1987) 'The global economy: new edifice or crumbling foundations', *New Left Review*, **168**, 24–64.

Gordon, M. (1964) *Assimilation in American Life* (New York, Oxford University Press).

Gordon, R. and Williams, P. (1998) 'Strengthening Co-operation Against Transnational Crime', *Survival*, **40** (3), 66–88.

Gough, I. (1996) 'Social Welfare and Competitiveness', *New Political Economy*, **1** (2), 209–32.

Gray, J. (1998) *False Dawn* (London, Granta).

Green, A. (1997) *Education, Globalization and the Nation State* (Basingstoke, Macmillan).

Green, A. (1999) 'Education and Globalization in Europe and East Asia', *Journal of Education Policy*, **14** (1), 55–71.

Green, R.H. (1995) 'Reflections on Attainable Trajectories: Reforming Global Economic Institutions', in J.M. Griesgraber and B.G. Gunter (eds) *Promoting Development* (London, Pluto).

Greene, O. (1997) 'Environmental Issues', in J. Baylis and S. Smith (eds) *The Globalization of World Politics* (Oxford, Oxford University Press).

Greenwood, A.M. (1999) 'Gender issues in labour statistics', *International Labour Review*, **138** (3), 273–86.

Guillen, A.M. and Alvarez, S. (2001) 'Globalization and the Southern Welfare States' in R. Sykes, B. Palier and P.M. Prior (eds) *Globalization and European Welfare States* (Basingstoke, Palgrave).

Haddad, L., Ruel, M.T. and Garrett, J.L. (1999) 'Are Urban Poverty and Undernutrition Growing?', *World Development*, **27** (11), 1891–1904.

Ham, C. and Honigsbaum, F. (1998) 'Priority Setting and Rationing Health Services', in R.B. Saltman, J. Figueras, C. Sakellandes (eds) *Critical Challenges for Health Care Reforms in Europe* (Oxford, Oxford University Press).

Hammar, T. (1995) 'Development and immobility: why have not many more migrants left the south?', in R.van der Erf and L. Heering (eds) (1995) *Causes of International Migration* (Luxembourg, Office of the European Communities).

Harding, J. (2000) *The Uninvited Refugees at the Rich Man's Gate* (London, Profile Books).

Harvey, D. (1989) *The Condition of Postmodernity* (Oxford, Blackwell).

Held, D. and McGrew, A. (1994) 'Globalization and the Liberal Democratic State', in Y. Sakamoto (ed.) *Global Transformation: Challenges to the State System* (Tokyo, United Nations University Press).

Held, D., McGrew, A., Goldblatt, D. and Perraton, J. (1999) *Global Transformations: Politics, Economics and Culture* (Cambridge, Polity Press).

Higgott, R.A. (1999) 'Economics, Politics and (International) Political Economy: the Need for a Balanced Diet in an Era of Globalization', *New Political Economy*, **4** (1), 23–36.

Hirst, P. (1994) 'The Global Economy: Myths and Realities', *International Affairs*, **73** (3), 409–25.

Hirst, P. and Thompson, G. (1996) *Globalization in Question* (Cambridge, Polity Press).

Hirst, P. and Thompson, G. (1999) *Globalization in Question* 2nd edn (Cambridge, Polity Press).

HMSO (1942) *Social Insurance and Allied Services* (Cmd 6404, London).

HMSO (1993) *Containing the Cost of Social Security – the International Context* (London, HMSO).

Hollifield, J.F. (2000) 'The Politics of International Migration', in C.B. Brettell and J.F. Hollifield (eds) *Migration Theory* (London, Routledge).

Holton, R.J. (1998) *Globalization and the Nation State* (Basingstoke, Macmillan).

Home Office (1995) *The Settlement of Refugees in Britain* (London, Home Office).

Hood, C. (1998) *The Art of the State* (Oxford, Clarendon Press).

Hoogvelt, A. (2000) *Globalization and the Postcolonial World* 2nd edn (Basingstoke, Macmillan).

Horton, S. (1999) 'Marginalization Revisited: Women's Market Work and Pay, and Economic Development', *World Development*, **27** (3), 571–82.

Hoselitz, B. (1960) *Sociological Aspects of Economic Growth* (New York, Free Press).

Hurrell, A. and Kingsbury, B. (1992) 'The International Politics of the Environment' in A. Hurrell and B. Kingsbury (eds) *The International Politics of the Environment* (Oxford, Clarendon).

Hurrell, A. and Woods, N. (eds) (1999) *Inequality, Globalization and World Politics* (Oxford, Oxford University Press).

Iganski, P. and Jacobs, S. (1997) 'Racism, Immigration and Migrant Labour', in T. Spybey (ed.) *Britain in Europe* (London, Routledge).

ILO (1998) *World Development Report, 1998/99* (Geneva, ILO).

ILO (2000) *World Labour Report* (Geneva, ILO).

Jacobs, A. (1998) 'Seeing Difference: Market Health Reform in Europe', *Journal of Health Politics, Policy and Law*, **23** (1), 1–33.

Jacobson, J.L. (1993) 'Women's Health' in M. Koblinsky, J. Timyan and J. Gay (eds) *The Health of Women: A Global Perspective* (Boulder, CO, Westwood Press).

Jellena, A. (2000) 'Trends in basic education', in J. Randel, T. German and D. Ewing (eds) *The Reality of Aid 2000* (London, Earthscan).

Jenkins, R. (1966) Address given on 23 May 1966 to a meeting of the Voluntary Liaison Committees in London, quoted in E.J.B. Rose *et al.* (1969) *Colour and Citizenship* (Oxford, Oxford University Press).

Joekes, S. (1985) 'Working for Lipstick?', in H. Afshar and B. Agarwal (eds) *Women, Poverty and Ideology in Asia* (Cambridge, Cambridge University Press).

Johnson, C. and Soderholm, P. (1996) 'IGO and NGO Relations and HIV /AIDS: Innovation and Stalemate', in T.G. Weiss and L. Gordenker (eds) *NGOs, the UN and Global Governance* (London, Lynne Rienner).

Jolly, R. (2000) 'Global Inequality, Human Rights and the Challenge for the 21st Century', in OECD, *The Creative Society of the 21st Century* (Paris, OECD).

Jones, T. (1998) 'Economic Globalisation and the Environment: An Overview of the Linkages', in OECD, *Globalisation and the Environment* (Paris, OECD).

Kapstein, E.B. (1996a) 'Governing Global Finance' in B. Roberts (ed.) *New Forces in the World Economy* (Cambridge, MA, MIT Press).

Kapstein, E.B. (1996b) 'Workers and the World Economy', *Foreign Affairs*, **75** (3), 16–37.

Kapstein, E.B. (1999) 'Distributive Justice as an International Public Good', in I. Kaul, I. Grunberg and M.A. Stern (eds) *Global Public Goods* (New York, Oxford University Press).

Kasente, D. (2000) 'Gender and Social Security in Africa', *International Social Security Review*, **53** (3), 27–43.

Kaul, I. and Langmore, J. (1999) 'Potential Uses of the Revenue from a Tobin tax', in M. Haq, I. Kaul and I. Grunberg (eds) *The Tobin Tax* (New York, Oxford University Press).

Kaul, I., Grunberg, I. and Stern, M.A. (1999) 'Introduction', in I. Kaul, I. Grunberg and M.A. Stern (eds) *Global Public Goods* (New York, Oxford University Press).

Kaya, I. (2000) 'Modernity and Veiled Women', *European Journal of Social Theory*, 3 (2), 195–214.

Kelly, M.J. (1998) *Primary Education in a Heavily-Indebted Poor Country: the case of Zambia in the 1990s*, a report for Oxfam and Unicef.

Kennedy, P. (1994) *Preparing for the Twenty First Century* (London, Fontana).

Keohane, R.O. (1998) 'International Institutions: Can Interdependence Work?', *Foreign Policy*, 110, 82–96.

Kerr, C., Dunlop, J., Harbison, F. and Myers, C. (1973) *Industrialism and Industrial Man* (Harmondsworth, Penguin).

Kiely, R. (1998) 'Transnational companies, global capital and the Third World', in R. Kiely and P. Marfleet (eds) *Globalisation and the Third World* (London, Routledge).

Klasen, S. (1994) '"Missing Women" Reconsidered', *World Development*, 22 (7), 1061–71.

Klein, R. (1997) 'Learning from Others: Shall the Last Be First?', *Journal of Health Politics, Policy and Law*, 22 (5), 1267–78.

Kotkin, J. (1992) *Tribes: How Race, Religion and Identity Determine Success in the New Global Economy* (New York, Random House).

Krueger, A.O. (1998) *The WTO as an International Organisation* (Chicago, University of Chicago Press).

Krugman, P. (1995) 'Growing World Trade: Causes and Consequences', *Brookings Papers on Economic Activity*, pp. 327–77.

Kudrle, R.T. (2000) 'Does globalization sap the fiscal power of the state?', in A. Prakash and J.A. Hart (eds) *Coping with Globalization* (London, Routledge).

Kvist, J. (1999) 'Welfare Reform in the Nordic Countries in the 1990s: Using Fuzzy Set Theory to Assess Conformity to Ideal Types', *Journal of European Social Policy*, 9 (3), 231–52.

Larkin, M. (1998) 'Global Aspects of Health and Health Policy in Third World Countries', in R. Kiely and P. Marfleet (eds) *Globalisation and the Third World* (London, Routledge).

Lawrence, R.Z. (1996) 'Resist the Binge', *Foreign Affairs*, 75 (3), 170–73.

Lawson, R. (1996) 'Germany: Maintaining the Middle Way', in V. George and P. Taylor-Gooby (eds) *European Welfare Policy: Squaring the Welfare Circle* (Basingstoke, Macmillan).

Lee, E. (1996) 'Globalization and Employment: Is Anxiety Justified?', *International Labour Review*, 135 (5), 485–97.

Lee, E. (1997) 'Globalization and Labour Standards: A Review of the Issues', *International Labour Review*, 136 (2), 173–88.

Lee, K. and Zui, A. (1996) 'A Global Political Economy Approach to AIDS: Ideology, Interests and Implications', *New Political Economy*, 1 (3), 355–73.

Leibfried, S. and Pierson, P. (1994) 'The Prospects for Social Europe', in A. de Swaan (ed.) *Social Policy beyond Borders* (Amsterdam, Amsterdam University Press).

Leibfried, S. and Pierson, P. (1995) 'Semi Sovereign Welfare States: Social Policy in a Multi-tiered Europe', in S. Leibfried and P. Pierson (eds) *European Social Policy* (Washington, Brookings Institute).

Levin, B. (1998) 'An Epidemic of Education Policy: (what) can we learn from each other?', *Comparative Education*, 34 (2), 131–41.

Loescher, G. (1992) *Refugee Movements and International Security* (London, International Institute for Strategic Studies).

Mac an Ghaill, M. (1999) *Contemporary Racisms and Ethnicities* (Buckingham, Open University Press).

Martin, H.P. and Schumans, H. (1997) *The Global Trap* (London, Zed).

Martin, L.P. (1997) 'The Impacts of Immigration on Receiving Countries', in E.M. Ucarer and D.J. Puchala (eds) *Immigration and Western Societies* (London, Pinter).

Martin, R. (1998) 'Central and Eastern Europe and the International Economy: The Limits of Globalisation', *Europe-Asia Studies*, 50 (1), 7–26.

McCarthy, J.D. (1997) 'The Globalization of Social Movement Theory', in J. Smith, C. Chatfield, R. Pagnucco (eds) *Transnational Social Movements and Social Rights* (New York, Syracuse University Press).

Mehra, R. and Gammage, S. (1999) 'Trends, Countertrends, and Gaps in Women's Employment', *World Development*, 27 (3), 533–50.

Meiksins Wood, E. (1997) 'Labor, The State and Class Struggle', *Monthly Review*, 49 (3) 1–17.

Michalski, W., Miller, R. and Stevens, B. (1997) 'Economic Flexibility and Social Cohesion in the 21st Century: an Overview of the Issues and Key Points of the Discussion', in OECD, *Social Cohesion and the Globalising Economy* (Paris, OECD).

Michie, J. (1999) 'Introduction', in J. Michie and J. Grieve Smith (eds) *Global Instability* (London, Routledge).

Milner, H.V. and Keohane, R.O. (1996) 'Internationalization and Domestic Politics: a Conclusion', in R.O. Keohane and H.V. Milner (eds) *Internationalization and Domestic Politics* (Cambridge, Cambridge University Press).

Mingione, E. (ed.) (1996) *Urban Poverty and the Underclass* (Oxford, Blackwell).

Mishra, R. (1998) 'Beyond the Nation State: Social Policy in an Age of Globalization', *Social Policy and Administration*, **32** (5), 481–500.

Mishra, R. (1999) *Globalization and the Welfare State* (Cheltenham, Edward Elgar).

Mittelman, J.H. and Johnston, R. (1999) 'The Globalization of Organised Crime, the Courtesan State, and the Corruption of Civil Society', *Global Governance*, **5** (1), 103–26.

Moran, M. (1999) *Governing the Health Care State* (Manchester, Manchester University Press).

Moran, M. and Wood, B. (1996) 'The Globalization of Health Care Policy', in P. Gummett (ed.) *Globalization and Public Policy* (Cheltenham, Edward Elgar).

Mossialos, M. (1998) 'Regulating Expenditure on Medicines in EU Countries', in R.B. Saltman, J. Figueras and C. Sakellandes (eds) *Critical Challenges for Health Care Reforms in Europe* (Oxford, Oxford University Press).

Mwengo, T.S.M. (2000) 'Africa: aid, debt and development', in J. Randel, T. German and D. Ewing (eds) *The Reality of Aid, 2000* (London, Earthscan).

Navarro, V. (1998) 'Neoliberalism, 'Globalization', Unemployment, Inequalities and the Welfare State', *International Journal of Health Services*, **28** (4), 607–82.

O'Brien, R., Goetz, A.M., Scholte, J.A. and Williams, M. (2000) *Contesting Global Governance* (Cambridge, Cambridge University Press).

OECD (1994) *Reform of Health Care Systems: A Review of 17 OECD Countries* (Paris, OECD).

OECD (1995a) *OECD Jobs Study: Taxation, Employment and Unemployment* (Paris, OECD).

OECD (1995b) *Governance in Transition* (Paris, OECD).

OECD (1997a) *Towards A New Global Age* (Paris, OECD).

OECD (1997b) *Making Work Pay: Taxation, Benefits, Employment and Unemployment* (Paris, OECD).

OECD (1997c) *Implementing the OECD Jobs Strategy* (Paris, OECD).

OECD (1998) *Harmful Tax Competition: An Emerging Global Issue* (Paris, OECD).

OECD (1999a) *A Caring World: the New Social Policy Agenda* (Paris, OECD).

OECD (1999b) *The Future of the Global Economy* (Paris, OECD).

Office for National Statistics (1996) *Social Focus on Ethnic Minorities* (London, HMSO).

Office of Multicultural Affairs (1989) *National Agenda for a Multicultural Australia* (Canberra, Government Publishing House).

Ohmae, K. (1990) *The Borderless World* (London, Collins).

Ohmae, K. (1993) The rise of the region-state, *Foreign Affairs*, **72** (3), 78–87.

Ohmae, K. (1996) *The End of the Nation State*, (New York, Free Press).

Owens, J. (1993) 'Globalisation: the Implications for Tax Policies', *Fiscal Studies*, **14** (3), 21–44.

Oxford University Press (1998) *Our Global Neighbourhood* (Oxford, Oxford University Press).

Pahl, J. (1989) *Money and Marriage* (Basingstoke, Macmillan).

Park, R.E. and Burgess, E.W. (1921) *Introduction to the Science of Sociology* (Chicago, Chicago University Press).

Paterson, M. (1999) 'Globalisation, Ecology and Resistance', *New Political Economy*, **4** (1), 129–45.

Patten, C. (1998) *East and West* (Basingstoke, Macmillan).

Perrons, D. and Gonas, L. (1998) 'Perspectives on Gender Inequality in European Employment', *European Urban and Regional Studies*, **5** (1), 5–12.

Peterson, E.R. (1996) 'Surrendering to Markets', in B. Roberts (ed.) *New Forces in the World Economy* (Cambridge, MA, MIT Press).

Petrella, R. (1996) 'Globalization and Internationalization', in R. Boyer and D. Drache (eds) *States Against Markets* (London, Routledge).

Pettman, J. (1997) 'Gender Issues', in J. Bayliss and S. Smith (eds) *The Globalization of World Politics* (Oxford, Oxford University Press).

Pierson, P. (1998a) 'Irresistible Forces, Immovable Objects: post industrial welfare states confront permanent austerity', *Journal of European Public Policy*, **5** (4), 539–60.

Pierson, P. (1998b) 'Contemporary Challenges to Welfare State Development', *Political Studies*, **XLVII**, 777–94.

Pieterse, J.N. (2000) 'Globalization and human integration: we are all migrants', *Futures*, **32**, 385–98.

Plantenga, J. and Hansen, J. (1999) 'Assessing equal opportunities in the European Union', *International Labour Review*, **138** (4), 351–79.

Polanyi, K. (1957) *The Great Transformation* (New York, Beacon).

Radice, H. (2000) 'Responses to Globalisation: A Critique of Progressive Nationalism', *New Political Economy*, **5** (1), 5–19.

Ramprakash, D. (1994) 'Poverty in the Countries of the European Union', *Journal of European Social Policy*, **4** (2), 117–28.

Ratcliffe, P. (1999) 'Housing inequality and "race": some critical reflections on the concept of "social exclusion"', *Ethnic and Racial Studies*, **22** (1), 1–22.

Redclift, M. and Sage, C. (1999) 'Resources, Environmental Degradation, and Inequality', in A. Hurrell and N. Woods (eds) *Inequality, Globalization and World Politics* (Oxford, Oxford University Press).

Reich, R.B. (1991) *The Work of Nations: Preparing Ourselves for 21st-Century Capitalism* (London, Simon & Schuster).

Rhodes, M. (1997) 'The Welfare State: Internal Challenges, External Constraints', in M. Rhodes, P. Heywood and V. Wright (eds) *Developments in West European Politics* (Basingstoke, Macmillan).

Rhodes, M. (1998) 'Globalisation, Labour Markets and Welfare States: A Future of Competitive Corporatism?', in M. Rhodes and Y. Meny (eds) *The Future of European Welfare: A New Social Contract* (Basingstoke, Macmillan).

Rhodes, M. and Apeldoorn, B. van (1998) 'Capital Unbound: The Transformation of European Corporate Governance', *Journal of European Public Policy*, **5** (3), 406–27.

Rieger, E. and Leibfried, S. (1998) 'Welfare State Limits to Globalization', *Politics and Society*, **26** (3), 363–90.

Roberts, S. and Bolderson, H. (1999) 'Inside Out: Migrants' Disentitlement to Social Security Benefits', in J. Clasen (ed.) *Comparative Social Policy* (Oxford, Blackwell).

Robertson, R. (1992) *Globalization: Social Theory and Global Culture* (London, Sage).

Robinson, W. (1996) 'Globalisation: nine theses on our epoch', *Race and Class*, **38** (2), 13–33.

Robinson, W. (1999) 'Latin America and global capitalism', *Race and Class*, **40** (2/3), 111–32.

Rodrik, D. (1997) *Has Globalization Gone too Far?* (Washington, DC, Institute for International Economics).

Rose, E.J.B. *et al.* (1969) *Colour and Citizenship* (Oxford, Oxford University Press).

Rosenau, J. (1990) *Turbulence in World Politics* (Princeton, NJ, Princeton University Press).

Rostow, W. (1962) *The Stages of Economic Growth* (Cambridge, Cambridge University Press).

Ruggie, J.G. (1994) 'Trade, Protectionism and the Future of Welfare Capitalism', *Journal of International Affairs*, **48** (1), 1–11.

Ruspins, E. (1998) 'Women and Poverty Dynamics', *Journal of European Social Policy*, **8** (4), 291–316.

Sassen, S. (1998) 'The de facto Transnationalizing of Immigration Policy', in C. Joppke (ed.) *Challenge to the Nation-State* (Oxford, Oxford University Press).

Sassen, S. (2000) 'Regulating Immigration in a Global Age: A New Policy Landscape', *Annals of the American Academy of Political and Social Sciences*, **570** (July), 65–78.

Scharpf, F.W. (2000) 'The Viability of Advanced Welfare States in the International Economy: Vulnerabilities and Options', *Journal of European Public Policy*, **70** (2), 190–228.

Scholte, J.A. (1996) 'Beyond the Buzzword: Towards a Critical Theory of Globalisation' in E. Kofman and G. Youngs *Globalization: Theory and Practice*, (London, Pinter).

Scholte, J.A. (1997) 'The Globalization of World Politics', in J. Baylis and S. Smith (eds) *The Globalization of World Politics* (Oxford, Oxford University Press).

Scholte, J.A. (1997a) 'Global Capitalism and the State', *International Affairs*, **73** (3), 427–52.

Scholte, J.A. (1997b) 'Global Trade and Finance', in J. Baylis and S. Smith (eds) *The Globalization of World Politics* (Oxford, Oxford University Press).

Scholte, J.A. (2000) *Globalization: a critical introduction* (Basingstoke, Macmillan).

Schuck, P.H. (1998) 'The Re-Evaluation of American Citizenship', in C. Joppke (ed.) *Challenge to the Nation-State* (Oxford, Oxford University Press).

Schulze, G.G. and Ursprung, H.W. (1999) 'Globalization of the Economy and the Nation State', *The World Economy*, **22** (3), 295–352.

Schuster, L. (2000) 'A Comparative Analysis of the Asylum Policy of Seven European Governments', *Journal of Refugee Studies*, **13** (1), 118–32.

Seifert, W. (1996) 'Occupational and Social Integration of Immigrant Groups in Germany', *New Community*, **22** (3), 417–36.

Sen, A. (1999) *Development as Freedom* (Oxford, Oxford University Press).

Shaw, M. (1994) *Global Social and International Relations* (Cambridge, Polity Press).

Shelley, L.I. (1995) 'Transnational Organised Crime: An Imminent Threat to the Nation State?', *Journal of International Affairs*, **48** (2), 463–89.

Sivanandan, A. (1998/99) 'Globalism and the Left', *Race and Class*, **40** (2/3), 5–20.

Sklair, L. (1991) *Sociology of the Global System* (Baltimore, John Hopkins University Press).

Sklair, L. (1995) *Sociology of the Global System*, 2nd edn (Baltimore, John Hopkins University Press).

Smyke, P. (1991) *Women and Health* (London, Zed Books).

Soderholm, P. (1999) 'Aids and Multilateral Governance', in M.G. Schechter (ed.) *Innovation in Multilateralism* (Basingstoke, Macmillan).

Soros, G. (1998) *The Crisis of Global Capitalism: Open Society Endangered* (London, Little, Brown).

Soysal, Y.N. (1994) *Limits of Citizenship* (Chicago, Chicago University Press).

Soysal, Y.N. (2000) 'Citizenship and Identity: living in diasporas in post-war Europe', *Ethnic and Racial Studies*, **23** (1), 1–16.

Speth, J.G. (1999) 'The Plight of the Poor', *Foreign Affairs*, **78** (3), 13–18.

Spybey, T. (1996) *Globalization and World Society* (Cambridge, Polity Press).

Standing, G. (1999a) *Global Labour Flexibility* (Basingstoke, Macmillan).

Standing, G. (1999b) 'Global Feminization Through Flexible Labor: A Theme Revisited', *World Development*, **27** (3), 583–602.

Stationery Office (2000) *Eliminating World Poverty: Making Globalization Work for the Poor* (London, Cm 5006, Stationery Office).

Steele, J. (2000) 'Fortress Europe Confronts the Unthinkable', *The Guardian*, 30 October.

Stewart, F. and Berry, A. (1999) 'Globalization, Liberalization, and Inequality', in A. Hurrell and N. Woods (eds) *Inequality, Globalization and World Politics* (Oxford, Oxford University Press).

Strange, S. (1995) 'The Limits of Politics', *Government and Opposition*, **30** (3), 292–312.

Strange, S. (1996) *The Retreat of the State: The Diffusion of Power in the World Economy* (Cambridge, Cambridge University Press).

Streeck, W. (1996) 'Public Power Beyond the Nation State', in R. Boyer and D. Drache (eds) *States Against Markets* (London, Routledge).

Streeck, W. (1997) 'German Capitalism: Does it Exist? Can it Survive?, *New Political Economy*, **2** (2), 237–56.

Sutcliffe, B. (1998) 'Freedom to Move in the Age of Globalization', in D. Baker, G. Epstein and R. Pollin (eds) *Globalization and Progressive Economic Policy* (Cambridge, Cambridge University Press).

Swank, D. (1998) 'Funding the Welfare State: Globalization and the Taxation of Business in Advanced Market Economies', *Political Studies*, **XLVI**, 671–92.

Sweezy, P.M. (1997) 'More or (Less) on Globalization', *Monthly Review*, **49** (4), 1–5.

Tabb, W.K. (1997) 'Globalization is an Issue, the Power of Capital is The Issue', *Monthly Review*, **49** (2), 20–31.

Tang, C., Wong, D., Cheung, F. and Lee, A. (2000) 'Exploring How Chinese Define Violence', *Women's Studies International Forum*, **23** (2), 197–209.

Taylor-Gooby, P. (1996) 'The Future of Health Care in Six European Countries: the Views of Policy Elites', *International Journal of Health Services*, **26** (2), 203–19.

Therborn, G. (1999) 'The Unemployment Iceberg: What is Beneath, Behind and Ahead?, *International Journal of Health Services*, **29** (3), 545–63.

Todaro, M.P. (2000) *Economic Development*, 7th edn (Harlow, Pearson Education).

Togeby, L. (1998) 'Prejudice and tolerance in a period of increasing ethnic diversity and growing unemployment: Denmark since 1970', *Ethnic and Racial Studies*, **21** (1), 1137–55.

Turshen, M. (1995) 'African Women and Health Issues', in M.J. Hay and S. Strichter (eds) *African Women South of the Sahara* (Harlow, Longman).

Tzannatos, Z. (1999) 'Women and Labor Market Changes in the Global Economy: Growth Helps, Inequalities Hurt and Public Policy Matters', *World Development*, **27** (3), 551–69.

United Nations Development Programme (UNDP) (1995) *Human Development Report 1995* (New York, Oxford University Press).

United Nations Development Programme (UNDP) (1997) *Human Development Report 1997* (New York, Oxford University Press).

United Nations Development Programme (UNDP) (1999) *Human Development Report 1999* (New York, Oxford University Press).

UNICEF (1999) *After the Fall: the human impact of ten years of transition* (Florence, UNICEF).

United Nations Organization (1998) *Demographic Yearbook 1996* (New York, UNO).

United Nations Organization (1999) *World Economic and Social Survey 1999* (New York, UNO).

United States Census Bureau (1999) *Statistical Abstract of the United States: 1999* (Washington, DC, USCB).

Vogel, D. (1998) 'The Globalization of Pharmaceutical Regulation', *Governance*, **11** (1), 1–27.

Wade, R. (1996) 'Globalization and its Limits: Reports of the Death of the National Economy are Greatly Exaggerated', in S. Berger and R. Dore (eds) *National Diversity and Global Capitalism* (Ithaca, NY, Cornell University Press).

Wagner, P. (1996) *Environmental Activism and World Civic Politics* (New York, State University of New York).

Waters, M. (1995) *Globalization* (London, Routledge).

Watson, M. (1999) 'Rethinking Capital Mobility, Re-regulating Capital markets', *New Political Economy*, **4** (1), 55–75.

Weiner, M. (1995) *The Global Migration Crisis* (New York, Harper Collins).

Weiss, L. (1998) *The Myth of the Powerless State* (Cambridge, Polity Press).

White House (1998) *Economic Report to the President* (Washington, DC).

White House (1999) *Economic Report to the President* (Washington, DC).

WHO (1997) *1997 Tobacco or Health: Global Status Report* (Geneva, WHO).

Wickham-Jones, M. (1997) 'Social Democracy and Structural Dependency: the British Case. A note on Hay', *Politics and Society*, **25** (2), 257–65.

Wilkin, P. (1996) 'New myths for the South: globalisation and the conflict between private power and freedom', *Third World Quarterly*, **17** (2), 227–38.

Wilkinson, R. and Hughes, S. (2000) 'Labour Standards and Global Governance: Examining the Dimensions of International Engagement', *Global Governance*, **6**, 259–79.

Wilks, S. (1996) 'Class Compromise and the International Economy: the Rise and Fall of Swedish Social Democracy', *Capital and Class*, **58**, 89–111.

Willetts, P. (1997) 'Transnational Actors and International Organizations in Global Politics' in J. Bayliss and S. Smith (eds) *The Globalization of World Politics*, (Oxford, Oxford University Press).

Willetts, P. (2000) 'From "Consultative Arrangements" to "Partnership" – the Changing Status of NGOs in Diplomacy at the UN', *Global Governance*, **6**, 191–212.

Williams, P. (1999) 'Emerging Issues: Transnational Crime and its Control', in G. Newman (ed.) *Global Report on Crime and Justice* (New York, Oxford University Press).

Wood, A. (1994) 'How Trade Hurts Unskilled Workers', *Journal of Economic Perspectives*, **9** (3), 57–80.

Wood, A. (1995) *North-South Trade, Employment and Inequality* (Oxford, Clarendon Press).

World Bank (1980) *World Development Report 1980* (New York, Oxford University Press).

World Bank (1990) *World Development Report 1990* (New York, Oxford University Press).

World Bank (1994) *World Development Report 1994: Averting the Old Age Crisis* (Washington, DC, World Bank).

World Bank (1995) *World Development Report 1995*, (New York, Oxford University Press).

World Bank (1997) *World Development Report 1997: the State in a Changing World* (New York, Oxford University Press).

World Bank (1999) *World Development Report 1999/2000* (New York, Oxford University Press).

World Bank (2000) *World Development Report 2000/2001: Attacking Poverty* (New York, Oxford University Press).

Wriston, W. (1988/89) 'Technology and Society', *Foreign Affairs*, **67**, 63–75.

Yeates, N. (1999) 'Social Politics and Policy in an Era of Globalization: Critical Reflections', *Social Policy and Administration*, **33** (4), 372–93.

Yeates, N. (2001) *Globalization and Social Policy* (London, Sage).

Yin, R. (1998) 'Forestry and the Environment in China: the Current Situation and the Strategic Choices', *World Development*, **26** (12), 2153–67.

Zarsky, L. (1997) 'Stuck in the Mud: Nation States, Globalisation and Environment', in OECD *Globalisation and Environment, Paris OECD*.

Name Index

Subject Index